# Warships of the World

Antony Preston

# WARSHIPS OF THE WORLD

JANE'S
LONDON · NEW YORK · SYDNEY

First published in the United Kingdom in 1980 by
Jane's Publishing Company Limited
Paulton House, 8 Shepherdess Walk
London N1 7LW

ISBN 0 7106 0020 8

Published in the United States of America in 1980 by
Jane's Publishing Incorporated
730 Fifth Avenue
New York
N.Y. 10019

ISBN 0 531 03704 5



Design: Geoffrey Wadsley

Printed in Great Britain by
Netherwood Dalton & Co. Ltd., Huddersfield

# Contents

# Introduction

Looking at the steady flow of new warships being built in every major maritime country, it is hard to believe that 20 years ago the need for surface warships of any sort was in question. After 1945 it was argued that the atom bomb had rendered the warship obsolete; then it was the bomber, and then the nuclear submarine became the bogey. Yet the surface warship is still here, bigger and more powerful than ever before.

What has happened is that ship technology has kept pace with the development of aircraft and air-launched weapons, thanks to the computer's ability to handle information rapidly. The stand-off missile no longer looms so large as a major threat, and even the sea-skimmer can be handled by computer-controlled gunfire. The ship may not be able to keep pace with the nuclear submarine, but the ship-launched helicopter has no difficulty in outpacing the target. As always, an overwhelming threat produces a countermeasure, and nothing has so short a life as the "ultimate weapon".

What has changed beyond recognition is the relative importance of shipboard weapons, and this has had the biggest effect on the size and shape of warships. Long-range guided-weapon systems, backed up by light-calibre guns for close-in or last-ditch actions, are vital for the defence of ships against air attacks, and these all need a means of tracking and plotting targets. The threat to a ship materialises so quickly that a computer-aided action information or data-handling system must be used to select the appropriate weapons. Above water an attacker must rely on radar or infra-red detection, and these sensors are vulnerable to countermeasures. The best known of these is jamming, but that is only one of what are known as electronic countermeasures (ECM). This in turn leads to electronic counter-counter-measures (ECCM), fitted to missiles and aircraft to enable them to get through jamming. To enable the defending ship to detect and classify the equipment it is up against, there are electronic support measures (ESM). In the Second World War radar turned night into day, but in a future naval battle the victory may well go to the ship which leaves all her sensors turned off.

For underwater actions there are passive and active homing torpedoes capable of responding to acoustic and magnetic influences. Sonar is more limited in its applications than radar, simply because water is an unpredictable medium for transmitting sound. The colossal power of a nuclear submarine is offset by the fact that she is partially blind when submerged, and for that reason the surface warship has not been driven from the seven seas. Moreover, the high speeds possible on nuclear power are of more use when disengaging *after* an attack, since high-speed running creates a readily audible "signature" which the surface warship's sonar can pick up at great range. The submarine's most devastating tactic is, as ever, to keep silent.

The change in the priority of weaponry and the way in which it is used has a direct bearing on the appearance of the ship. Gone are the dozens of gun barrels which used to bristle, and in their place are single guns, insignificant missile launchers, and lots of fire control and radars. One joke going the rounds a few years ago had it that there would soon be ships with infallible fire control but no guns.

Many people, used to the ships of even 20 years ago, think that Western warships are short of fighting power, particularly when they see photographs of Soviet vessels armed with plenty of guns, missiles and torpedo tubes. But it is easily forgotten just how potent a modern warship is, even if it does lack the visual reassurance of the 15in guns and lofty bridgework of a battleship, the size of an aircraft carrier or the slim purposefulness of a destroyer. A surface-to-surface or surface-to-air missile is some hundreds of times more likely to hit first time than a 15in shell of 40 years ago. More important, yesterday's guns would stand no chance at all against modern aircraft. An expensive lesson learned by the Royal Navy long before anyone else was that one anti-aircraft gun and two fire-control sets were better than two guns and one fire-control set; two sets could at least cover different arcs, whereas two

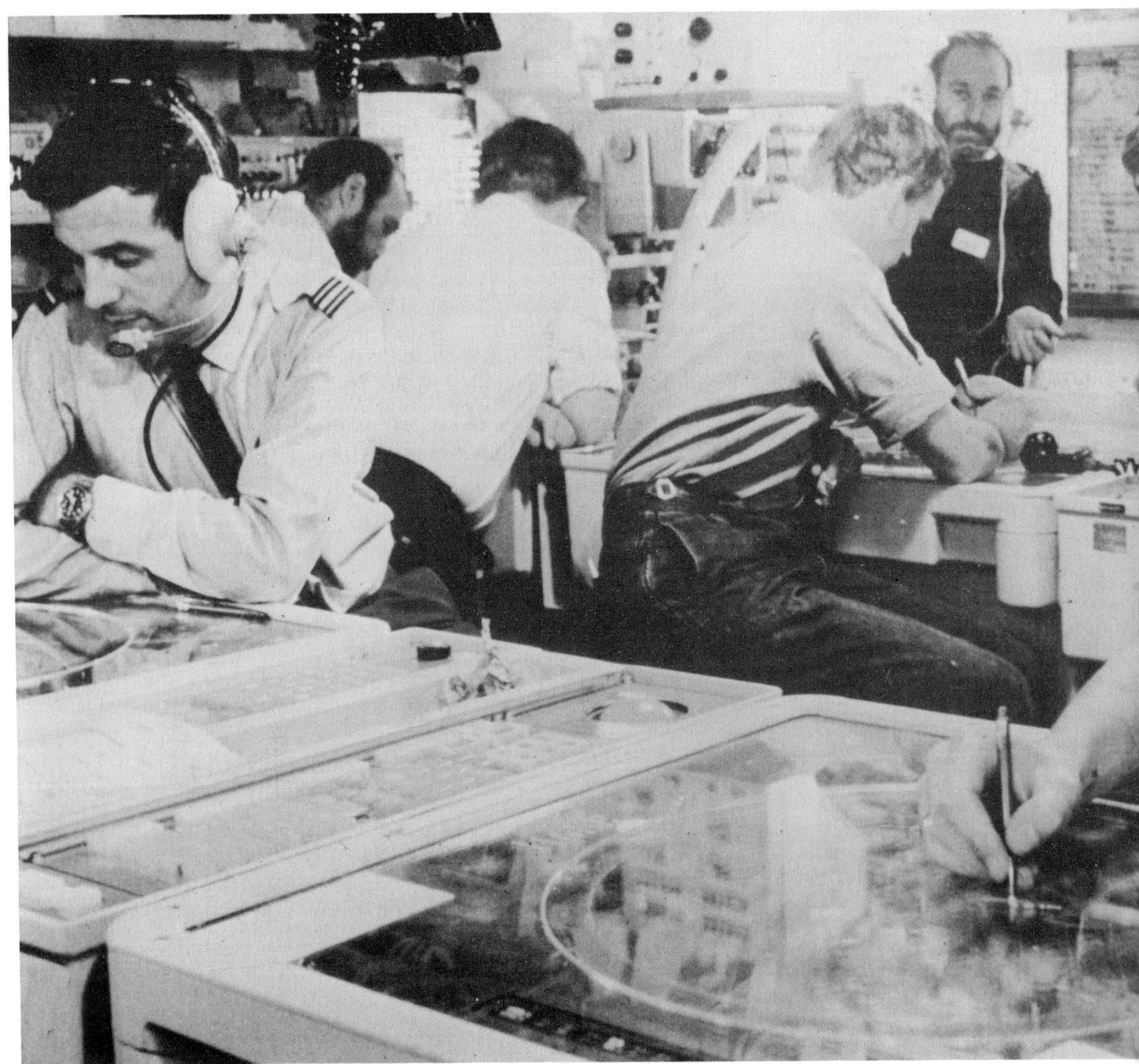

The heart of a modern warship is its operations room, where the raw data from signals, communications and sensors are correlated, plotted and displayed electronically. This enables the captain and principal warfare officer (PWO) to respond to a threat and to use the ship's weaponry to maximum effect.

guns linked to one fire control could only hit one target at a time. Weapons without fire control are a waste of valuable space and money; they contribute nothing to defending the ship because they will not hit anything.

If we accept that back-up to the weapons – in the form of fire control, action information organisation (AIO) and communications – is essential, then it is interesting to compare how some well armed British wartime and post-war ships compare with their modern counterparts. One method of comparing fighting power fairly, given the impossibility of making a genuine comparison between weapons of 1945 and those of today, is to add up the area of internal deck space allotted to each element of fighting power:

| | Modified *Black Swan* frigate (1942) | *Daring*-class destroyer (1952) | *Leander*-class frigate (1962) | *Sheffield*-class DDG (1975) |
|---|---|---|---|---|
| Aviation | 0% | 0% | 1.98% | 2.33% |
| Armament | 9.93% | 7.85% | 8.16% | 5.64% |
| Sonar | 0.93% | 0.75% | 2.69% | 1.12% |
| Radar and fire control | 1.47% | 2.46% | 0.71% | 2.88% |
| Operations room, AIO | 0% | 1.26% | 2.34% | 2.61% |
| Communications | 1.31% | 1.38% | 3.71% | 2.63% |
| Total area devoted to armament | 13.6% | 13.7% | 19.3% | 17.2% |

A breakdown by internal volume produces very similar ratios, but even this simple comparison takes no account of the vastly increased effectiveness of modern weapons. The 4in guns of the Modified *Black Swan* cannot be compared with the Sea Dart area-defence missile armament of HMS *Sheffield*, for example.

The next question is, how do the Russians manage to arm their ships so heavily? The first answer to this is that all too often like is not compared with like. Moreover, first estimates of Soviet ships' capabilities are often heavily exaggerated, with the result that they appear to be much faster than they really are; the same applies to their weaponry, and there have been many red faces in the past few years when long-range missiles suddenly become short-range missiles, or when they turn out to have a completely different role.

The Soviet Navy is a sea-denial force, intended to force Western naval formations to disperse from key areas or keep their distance from the coast of the USSR. Western navies, particularly those of Nato and the United States, have to be able to exercise sea control if they are to reinforce any area that they choose and to preserve the shipping on which their trade and economic

HMS *Norfolk* fires her first Exocet surface-to-surface missile in 1974. Fitting such missiles to existing ships is comparatively simple because of their lightness and lack of recoil. Apart from the rewiring and provision of "black boxes" between decks, this conversion required only the removal of "B" turret.

survival depend. This classic role is what used to be called "blue water" sea power, which rests on the assumption that the oceans remain under your side's control. The French in the 18th century and the Germans in the 20th both sought to interfere with their enemy's sea control without being capable of exercising it themselves. Known as *guerre de course* by the French or commerce raiding by the Germans, it was deadly if unchecked.

Ships designed for sea denial have since time immemorial tended to be well armed; they run the risk of counter-attack by a concentration of enemy forces and must be able to survive as long as possible if they are to be effective. The Japanese took this doctrine to its ultimate conclusion by trying to make each class of ship the fighting equal of any contemporary, and in many ways the modern Russians seem to have tried to emulate them. Thus a Kresta II-class cruiser has no fewer than five major weapon systems: a long-range anti-submarine missile system, two surface-to-air missile systems, and two twin AA gun mountings. There are also close-range guns, ASW rocket launchers, two sets of torpedo tubes, and an anti-submarine helicopter.

Now Western navies know from experience that such weapons and their back-up occupy large amounts of between-decks space, and need power supplies and men to run them. To pack all these items into a hull without making adequate provision for their efficient use may, paradoxically, have two welcome effects: it will impress the political heads of the Soviet armed forces and it will provide ships which have a powerful political impact

wherever they are seen in peacetime. In other words, the Soviet Navy is designed to act as a political or propaganda weapon, a fact which has been repeatedly stated by its commander-in-chief, Admiral Gorshkov.

Genuine comparisons of warships are always hard to make, and without access to information on the staff requirements which led up to a design one must resort largely to guesswork. However, comparison of ships of genuinely similar size shows that the Russians do not have quite as much edge as some commentators would have us believe. The Krivak class, for example, can be compared with the British *Sheffield* class. The Soviet ship has four long-range SS-N-14 ASW missiles forward, two close-range SA-N-4 SAM systems for air defence, 76mm guns and torpedo tubes. The British ship's main armament is the dual-purpose Sea Dart long-range SAM/SSM, while close-range defence is provided by a Seacat SAM system. She also carries a Lynx ASW/attack helicopter in a hangar (thereby at least doubling its effectiveness), a 4.5in gun for shore bombardment and soft targets, and ASW torpedo tubes. With the Sea Skua anti-ship missile on the Lynx the *Sheffield* will have five weapon systems on board, two of them capable of flexible use in more than one role.

There is another point of divergence between the Soviet and Western ship-design philosophies. Today a hull life of 30 years is normal, given effective underwater painting, cathodic protection and good maintenance. The effective life of an advanced weapon system, on the other hand, is about 7-10 years. In current Western designs such as the American *Spruance* and the British *Broadsword* classes room has been left for growth, which means that weaponry can be updated once or even twice in the ship's lifetime. But a mid-life refit in the first class of Soviet missile cruisers, the Kyndas, for example, will be a nightmare. Every square foot of deck space has been filled with weapons, and the ship will either have to be gutted or left as a wasting asset, unfit to face a modern opponent in battle.

Changes in propulsion machinery have had as revolutionary an impact on warships as anything else. Nuclear propulsion is still too expensive to be justified for small warships, and apart from submarines and one or two Soviet icebreakers the only nuclear-powered warships are the big carriers and carrier-escort cruisers of the US Navy. The main effects of nuclear propulsion on hull design lie in the volume needed to accommodate the reactor and its shielding, and the absence of funnels, which allows radars to be more advantageously placed.

For smaller warships the gas turbine has become accepted as the most promising powerplant, although the diesel still has its adherents. The advantages of gas-turbine drive are lightness, ease of replacement and quietness; against these must be set a short life and heavy fuel consumption. When gas turbines were first used in warships it was hoped that their compactness would release much-needed internal volume for weapons and fighting equipment. But their very ease of removal has meant bigger machinery spaces, with vast ventilating trunks to provide air. Just when naval architects were turning to the combined mast/funnel or "mack" (from the US mast/stack) to provide more deck space, the gas turbine appeared, bringing with it the need for bigger funnels than before.

For anti-submarine work the gas turbine produces much less radiated noise than diesels, but navies without a primary ASW mission favour a combination of gas turbines for high speeds and diesels for cruising. Another reason why gas turbines and diesels are displacing steam turbines is the

19

manning problem. Steam means dirty conditions and it is harder than ever to recruit stokers; gas turbines and diesels can be run with very small engine-room complements. For smaller navies with a rapid turnover of semi-skilled conscripts, the simplicity of diesels is also appealing. Whereas a major repair to steam plant means six months in dock, diesels or gas turbines can be replaced, and in the latest ships the turbine can be lifted out and replaced within 24 hours.

There is insufficient space to describe the range and capability of all modern warships, but the selection which follows is designed to give an idea of the most numerous, the most representative and some of the more interesting older warships in the world's navies. Every navy is different, with different requirements giving rise to a profusion of ship designs. It is this variety which makes the study of warships so rewarding and so intriguing for the uninitiated.

Antony Preston
December 1979

---

*Note on ships' tonnages*

The different tonnages quoted for warships can be confusing, and so a short explanation is necessary. Warships differ from merchantmen in that their size is measured in weight (long tons or metric tonnes), whereas merchantmen are measured in terms of capacity (1 gross ton = 100 cubic feet of enclosed space). Thus a 90,000-ton deadweight tanker cannot be compared with a 90,000-ton aircraft carrier.

Originally (i.e. from the 1870s) the tonnage quoted for a warship was "normal" displacement: the weight of water displaced by the fully armed hull, plus an allowance for coal, crew and stores. This allowance was nominal and usually assumed that bunkers and storerooms were only half-full (it varied from navy to navy). The maximum allowance of ammunition, stores and the full war complement was known as "full load" displacement.

Things might have remained in that simple state but for the Washington Disarmament Conference of 1922. One of its major achievements was the definition of a new "standard" displacement, including full ammunition, stores and complement but excluding fuel and reserve feed water for the boilers. This was heavier than normal displacement but significantly less than full load; HMS *Hood*, for example, displaced 41,200 tons normal, 42,100 tons standard and 45,200 tons full load.

Although standard displacement was to all intents abolished when the naval limitation treaties lapsed in 1939, the term "standard displacement" is still used, even when meaningless for ships which are not steam-powered. In fact it now approximates to the old normal displacement in describing the ship in peacetime, without her war complement and with about half her stores and fuel expended. The term "standard" is made even less meaningful by the fact that many modern warships have compensating fuel tanks which automatically take in seawater as ballast. It is however convenient for describing the ship when in a seagoing condition but not fully loaded.

*Abbreviations in data tables*

AA: anti-aircraft; A/S: anti-submarine; ASM: anti-submarine/anti-ship missile; bhp: brake horsepower; CODOG: combined diesel or gas turbine; COGOG: combined gas turbine or gas turbine; COSAG: combined steam and gas turbine; DP: dual-purpose; fd: flight deck; oa: overall; PO: petty officer; pp: peak-to-peak; SAM: surface-to-air missile; shp: shaft horsepower; SLBM: submarine-launched ballistic missile; SSM: surface-to-surface missile; wl: waterline

---

Contrasting styles in radar arrays. Left to right: an American guided missile destroyer, a German destroyer and a Canadian helicopter-carrying destroyer. Note also how their freeboards differ, from the very weatherly Canadian DDH, designed for the North Atlantic, down to the low-freeboard German ship, designed for the Baltic Approaches.

# Photograph Credits

Aérospatiale: pages 10, 34 (upper), 210 (middle); Armada Republica Argentina: pages 38 (upper), 65; Dr Giorgio Arra: page 119; Marius Bar: pages 107, 125; Bath Iron Works Corporation: pages 158, 159; Blohm & Voss: page 151; Boeing Marine Corporation: pages 125, 199; Canadian Forces: page 176; Chilean Navy: pages 118–119; CNR: pages 182, 183, 210 (bottom); Creusot-Loire: page 170; David Brown Gear Industries: pages 28, 161; *Defence*/Ferranti: page 8; DTCN: page 30; ECPA: pages, 31, 32, 33, 34 (lower), 56, 58, 78, 172, 173, 206; Empresa Nacional Bazán: page 190; Engins Matra: page 211 (middle); Federal German Navy: pages 66, 115, 180; Finnish Navy: page 213 (bottom left); Aldo Fraccaroli: pages 93, 94, 124, 138, 139, 142; General Dynamics: page 41, 209 (bottom); General Dynamics Pomona Division: pages 116, 117, 214 (top); Goodyear Aerospace Corporation: page 217 (bottom); Ambrose Greenway: pages 135, 155; C. Heijkoop: page 187; Italcantieri: pages 35, 36, 60; Italian Navy: pages 92, 95, 214 (bottom); Japan Maritime Self-Defence Force: page 185; Kockums: pages 62, 63; Koninklijke Marine: page 137; Litton Industries: pages 113, 217 (top); Marinha do Brasil: pages 38 (lower), 46, 55, 88; MEL: page 218 (bottom); Ministry of Defence: pages 48, 50, 51, 52, 54, 80, 81, 82, 84 (upper), 100, 102, 105, 126, 127, 128, 129, 130, 168, 196, 208 (middle), 209 (top and middle), 212 (middle), 213 (top); Ministry of Defence (Navy): pages 13, 26, 27; Ministry of Defence (Navy)/RNAS Yeovilton: page 29; Musées de la Marine: page 106; Naval Photograph Club: page 218 (middle); Navpic: page 156; Novosti: pages 49, 195, 210 (top); Oerlikon-Bührle: page 213 (middle and bottom right); PEAB: page 208 (bottom); Giovanni Peditto: page 84; Norman Polmar: page 197; via Antony Preston: page 181; Eberhard Rossler: page 67; Royal Australian Navy: page 164; Royal Norwegian Navy: page 200; Royal Swedish Navy: pages 148, 202; *Ships of the World*: pages 143, 144, 145; Sistel: pages 211 (bottom); South African Navy: pages 59, 198; Spanish Navy: page 155; Tass: pages 23, 24, 25, 83, 85, 108, 109; C. & S. Taylor: pages 37, 74, 76, 77, 98, 104, 115, 120, 134, 136, 140, 141, 150, 162, 166, 167 (upper and lower), 188, 189, 211 (top), 215 (middle), 216 (top); Thomson-CSF: pages 122, 216 (bottom); US Navy: pages 17, 18, 22, 43, 44, 47, 49 (upper), 69, 71, 72, 112, 212 (top), 215 (bottom); Vosper Thornycroft: pages 146, 147, 204, 205, 208 (top), 212 (bottom), 214 (middle), 215 (top), 218 (top); Anthony J. Watts Collection: page 131.

The following photographs were supplied by courtesy of the *Jane's Fighting Ships*/Imperial War Museum Collection: *Forrestal* (page 19), *Bon Homme Richard* (page 20), *Albany* (page 73), *Coronel Bolognesi* (page 86), *Almirante Grau* (page 90), *Truxtun* (page 96), *Skory*-class destroyer (page 132), Riga-class escort (page 174), Mirka-class escort (page 175), *Peder Skram* (page 178), *Flora* (page 184).

The following photographs were supplied by courtesy of *Maritime Defence*: *Guam* (page 22), *Ohio* (page 41), Foxtrot-class submarine (page 50), *Long Beach* (page 72), *Antrim* (page 102), *Boyky* (page 130), *Mohawk* (page 168), *Ayase* (page 185), *Pegasus* (page 193), *Jim Fouche* (page 198), *Rapp* (page 200), *Spica* (page 202).

# Aircraft Carriers and Helicopter Carriers

The aircraft carrier evolved remarkably quickly, little more than a decade after the first powered flight in 1901. The first man to fly an aircraft off a warship was Eugene B. Ely, who on 14 November 1910 flew a Curtiss pusher biplane off the forecastle of the light cruiser USS *Birmingham*. Ely also made the first landing on a ship when two months later he touched down on the armoured cruiser USS *Pennsylvania*.

In 1913 the British and French broke new ground by using the first aircraft-carrying ships, the light cruiser *Hermes* and the torpedo depot ship *Foudre* respectively. Both ships took part in the fleet manoeuvres that year and proved that aircraft could carry out valuable reconnaissance. But even after such a promising start the contribution made by naval aircraft in the early years of the First World War was not significant. The reasons were the fragility of the machines themselves and the lack of a reliable radio set. The Royal Navy paid a great deal of attention to the problem of getting aircraft to sea with the Fleet, but the solitary seaplane which got airborne at the Battle of Jutland failed to achieve anything. Only in 1917 did things begin to improve, when the large cruiser *Furious* was taken over for conversion into the first ship capable of operating landplanes.

Wheeled aircraft, unimpeded by heavy, drag-producing floats, offered high speed and rate of climb. Their light airframes also made it possible to fly them off very short platforms, and soon Sopwith Pup fighters were taking off from platforms in light cruisers and on top of battleships' gun turrets. Their quarry was the Zeppelin long-range reconnaissance airship, and they proved a most efficient counter to the "snoopers" which had hitherto given away many ship movements. Experiments with torpedo-dropping dated back to 1915, when a Short 184 from a seaplane carrier torpedoed a Turkish transport in the Aegean. In October 1916 a requirement for a landplane capable of dropping an 18in torpedo was drawn up. This resulted in the Sopwith Cuckoo, which, but for the Armistice in November 1918, would have been used in a big attack on the German Fleet.

Serious development of the aircraft carrier began after the First World War, when the brake put on battleship construction left suitable large hulls available in the United States, Japan, Great Britain and France. The two decades between the wars saw a number of ideas tested, and by 1939 the basic details of fleet carriers had been settled. The Americans and Japanese had the best naval air forces, with modern aircraft and large carriers, while the British had given control of their naval aircraft to the Royal Air Force and carrier development had lagged behind as a result. This difference meant that the three navies followed separate development paths. The Americans and Japanese plumped for unarmoured carriers, relying on large aircraft complements to protect the ship and using defensive anti-aircraft gunnery as a last resort. The British, with very poor aircraft, decided to armour their carriers and rely on defensive gunfire and the armoured box hangar to safeguard the aircraft.

Neither of these philosophies worked out quite like that in practice. The American and Japanese carriers proved inferior to the British in their ability to withstand battle damage, as much because of the Admiralty's stringent fire regulations as of the armoured hangar itself. The British, however, would have been infinitely better off with a larger complement of good aircraft, and the box hangar ultimately proved a blind alley in carrier design. The most effective carriers of the Second World War were without any doubt the US Navy's 27,000-ton *Essex* class, which must be contenders for the title of the most cost-effective major warships ever built.

The success of the American fast carrier task forces is legendary. With battleships as escorts they wrought havoc across the Pacific and showed that they could take on and defeat a land-based air force, something which air power extremists had denied strenuously for years. What the carriers showed was the versatility of carrier-borne aircraft; they could reconnoitre, strafe ground positions, provide fighter cover during amphibious landings and sink enemy capital ships.

The Korean and Vietnam wars showed that carrier aircraft were ideal for supporting ground troops in limited or "brushfire" wars, and this role remains the prime task of the big US Navy carriers. In the late 1940s the obsession with the nuclear deterrent led to the provision of twin-engined nuclear bombers aboard US carriers to act as a seaborne complement to the Air Force's land-based bombers. But this proved to be an expensive luxury, and the designation of the USN's big carriers changed from CVA (attack carrier) to CV (multi-purpose carrier) in 1975.

When the jet fighter appeared on the scene at the end of the Second World War it was feared that its high landing speed would make operations from carriers impossible, but the technical problems were soon overcome. Naval interceptors first saw action in Korea, and today very few propeller-driven aircraft survive in carriers.

The next step was to improve deck-landing techniques. After experiments with a flexible rubber deck the British came up with the angled deck, which allowed an aircraft to land clear of the forward aircraft park. This saved a large number of crashes into the barrier, which had killed many pilots and written off even more aircraft; it also permitted the pilot to make a "touch-and-go" landing if his tail-hook failed to catch an arrester wire. Another factor in deck landing was the "batsman," who manually signalled information to the pilot on his approach angle and line-up; this was automated by means of the mirror landing sight, which gave the pilot the same information in the form of light signals. A third invention, the steam catapult, solved the problem of the growing weight of naval aircraft; it enabled the heaviest aircraft to be catapulted off the flight deck, even if the ship was not moving. The cumulative effect of these three British inventions was to allow carriers to operate much faster and heavier aircraft and to improve the handling of aircraft on the flight deck.

The next step was the introduction of nuclear power, in the giant American carrier *Enterprise*. Apart from the luxury of continuous high speed, nuclear power conferred a number of specific benefits: the dangerous turbulence and loss of visibility caused by funnel smoke is avoided, and the effectively unlimited steam supply permits constant use of as many as four catapults simultaneously.

The big drawback to the nuclear carrier is her cost, both in money and manpower. The *Enterprise* cost over $450 million in 1961, and in 1976 the cost of the *Nimitz* was estimated to have risen to $1,881 million. Even then Congress vetoed the F-14 Tomcat fighter for the air group of the new carrier, and she went to sea with the cheaper but much less effective F-4 Phantom embarked. In a further attempt to keep the cost within "reasonable" limits, the *Nimitz* class are not being given the bow-mounted SQS-23 sonar fitted to earlier CVs. But manning costs are the real problem, and the *Nimitz* carries 142 officers and 2,989 enlisted men just to run the ship, and a further 304 officers and 2,323 enlisted men in her air group.

With the first of the post-war carriers, the *Franklin D. Roosevelt*, already scrapped and the *Forrestal* commissioned a quarter of a century ago, the problem of replacing the giant CVs is under consideration. But political opposition to the rising cost of the *Nimitz* class makes it almost impossible for the US Navy to hope for any more of this type. The Royal Navy had a similar decision thrust upon it as long ago as 1966, when its replacement carriers were axed. The RN's last big carrier, HMS *Ark Royal*, paid off at the end of 1978, and before too long the French *Aéronavale* will have a similar painful decision to make about the *Foch* and *Clemenceau*.

The US Navy has already grappled with the problem once, when the Sea Control Ship was projected. This was a "utility" carrier capable of operating helicopters and V/Stol aircraft, and designed purely to defend underway replenishment groups, amphibious operations and convoys. The lead ship was estimated to cost only $172 million, and the request for the first ship was made in Fiscal Year 1974. Cost overruns on nuclear submarines and big surface ships ate up the money, however, and after some hesitation the idea was dropped.

The British also took up the idea, with the decision to build a ship capable of operating the new Sea Harrier single-seat V/Stol strike aircraft and anti-submarine helicopters. Although the political aftermath of the cancellation of the big fleet carriers in 1966 prevented any immediate decision to buy Sea Harriers for the new ship, she was in fact a V/Stol aircraft carrier, complete with angled deck and starboard island superstructure. For political reasons she continued to be known as a "through-deck cruiser," then a "command cruiser" and finally an "ASW cruiser". But as memories of 1966 fade, the forbidden term "aircraft carrier" is creeping in again. However, the problem of cost is still there, and the price tag on HMS *Invincible* is about £250 million.

The Russians have followed the same path, with the second of a class of three hybrid cruiser-carriers in service by the beginning of 1979. The *Kiev* class has heavy armament forward, an island and an angled deck, but although a single flight of Yak-36 Forger V/Stol aircraft has been seen on the flight deck, the main air component is made up of anti-submarine helicopters. Although much has been made of the Russians getting into the carrier business, the *Kiev* is intended for sea control and is not a fleet carrier. She is a logical outcome of the Soviet Navy's desire to build a first-class fleet with a balance of various types of warship and, even more important, she marks the growing awareness of the threat from nuclear submarines.

For the Americans the choice is not an easy one: between big fleet carriers on the one hand and V/Stol carriers on the other. The simple fact is that V/Stol aircraft have not developed enough to take the place of the big interceptors and bombers carried aboard the CVs. Current V/Stol aircraft are good for the strike mission but are too slow and too heavy on fuel to take over the roles so superbly performed by conventional carrier aircraft. In other words, a switch to V/Stol would rob the US Navy of an enormous part of its offensive capability, with nothing in return. The danger is that the politicians are clutching at straws, trying to picture the Sea Harrier or the new AV-8B as a cheap substitute for the Corsairs, Phantoms, Intruders and other carrier aircraft. The very phase "jump jet" indicates how easily the Press has become confused about the capability of V/Stol aircraft; in fact vertical take-off, using enormous quantities of fuel, is the least useful function of such aircraft. To increase the take-off weight (and hence useful load) of a Sea Harrier it is necessary to provide at least a short runway if not a catapult; once the fuel and weapon load are expended the aircraft can land vertically with as much ease as a helicopter.

Once again science has come to the aid of naval aviation at a crucial moment. The Ski-jump ramp, invented by a British naval officer, allows the aircraft to make a very short take-off, giving the Sea Harrier vital wing lift at the moment of take-off and enabling the pilot to make a quicker transition from pure jet lift. The Ski-jump also provides a greater margin of safety by reversing the ballistic path followed by an aircraft as it takes off over the end of a normal flight deck.

Even if the V/Stol aircraft had not made such rapid progress, the growing importance of helicopters at sea, both as submarine-hunters and as weapon-deliverers, would ensure the survival of the flat-topped ship. Despite claims 20 years ago that the missile had rendered the manned aircraft redundant, the human brain still has the edge over any electronic computing device when in command of an aircraft of any sort. This remains true for the foreseeable future and so aircraft of all types will continue to operate with and against ships.

# *Nimitz* class

| Name | Number | Laid down | Launched | Completed | Builder |
|---|---|---|---|---|---|
| ***Nimitz*** | CVN-68 | 22 Jun 1968 | 13 May 1972 | 3 May 1975 | Newport News SB & DD Co |
| ***Dwight D. Eisenhower*** | CVN-69 | 14 Aug 1970 | 11 Oct 1975 | 18 Oct 1977 | Newport News SB & DD Co |
| ***Carl Vinson*** | CVN-70 | 11 Oct 1976 | Mar 1979 | 1981 | Newport News SB & DD Co |
| unnamed | CVN-71 | 1980 | – | – | – |

**Displacement** 81,600 tons (standard), 91,400 tons (full load), 93,400 tons (combat load)
**Dimensions** 317m (wl), 332m (oa) × 40.8m × 11.3m (1,040ft (wl), 1,092ft (oa) × 134ft × 37ft)
**Propulsion** 4 shafts, geared steam turbines, 2 pressurised water-cooled A4W nuclear reactors; 260,000 shp = 30+ knots
**Protection** Armoured flight decks and anti-torpedo protection
**Aircraft** Approx 100, depending on type
**Armament** 3 × 8-cell Sea Sparrow Basic Point Defence Missile Systems (BPDMS)
**Complement** 3,131 officers and enlisted men + 2,627 air group

The first of three new nuclear-powered aircraft carriers was ordered for the US Navy in Fiscal Year 1967. The other two followed in FY 1970 and 1974 respectively, after an acrimonious debate about their cost. Delays and soaring inflation sent the cost from $1,881 million for the *Nimitz* in 1976 to an estimated $2,000 million each for the *Eisenhower* and *Vinson*. At the end of 1979 a long awaited decision was made to build a fourth ship.

In many ways this class resembles the *Enterprise* (CVN-65), despite being built nearly ten years later, with the same length, a foot more beam and greater draught. The most obvious outward difference is the island, which is smaller and more like that of the conventionally powered *Kitty Hawk* class. The enormous strides made in nuclear propulsion mean that the new ships need only two nuclear reactors to develop nearly the same power as the eight-reactor *Enterprise*.

While under construction the first two ships were reclassified from attack aircraft carriers (CVAN) to multi-mission

The nuclear-powered USS *Nimitz* with her escort, the cruiser *California*, cruising in formation as part of Task Force 60. The unlimited endurance of the nuclear carrier created the need for a new generation of nuclear-powered escorts armed with guided weapons.

carriers (CVN) and equipped to operate anti-submarine aircraft. In practice this meant the addition of an anti-submarine control centre and facilities for handling A/S aircraft and helicopters. They are not fitted with sonar, however.

The growing trend towards reliance on aircraft for defence is evident in the *Nimitz* class. Whereas the *Kitty Hawk* class has twin Terrier missile launchers, the *Nimitz* class relies on three Sea Sparrow short-range missile systems.

The angled deck and deck-edge lifts combine to give an immense area for flying operations in the *Nimitz* class. The angled deck leaves the forward part of the flight deck clear for launching aircraft, though they can also be launched simultaneously off the angled deck when necessary.

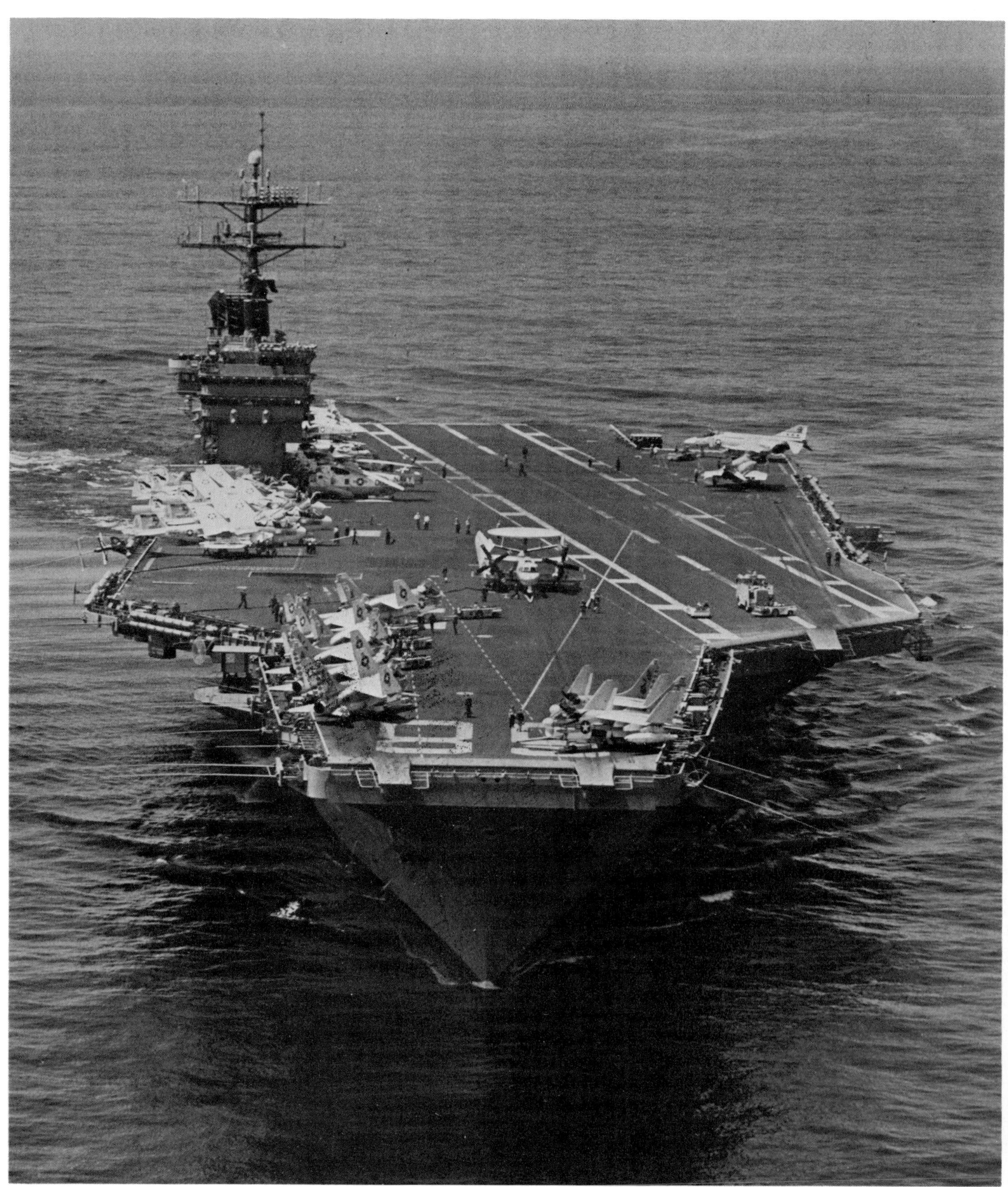

## *Forrestal* class

| Name | Number | Laid down | Launched | Completed | Builder |
|---|---|---|---|---|---|
| ***Forrestal*** | CV-59 | 14 Jul 1952 | 11 Dec 1954 | 1 Oct 1955 | Newport News SB & DD Co |
| ***Saratoga*** | CV-60 | 16 Dec 1952 | 8 Oct 1955 | 14 Apr 1956 | New York Naval Shipyard |
| ***Ranger*** | CV-61 | 2 Aug 1954 | 29 Sep 1956 | 10 Aug 1957 | Newport News SB & DD Co |
| ***Independence*** | CV-62 | 1 Jul 1955 | 6 Jun 1958 | 10 Jan 1959 | New York Naval Shipyard |

**Displacement** 60,000 tons (standard), 78,000 tons (full load)
**Dimensions** 301.8m (wl), 316.7-319m (oa) × 38.5m × 11.3m (990ft (wl), 1,039-1,046.5ft (oa) × 129.5ft × 37ft)
**Propulsion** 4 shafts, geared steam turbines, 8 boilers; 260,000-280,000 shp = 33 knots
**Protection** Armoured flight deck and anti-torpedo protection
**Aircraft** 85
**Armament** 2 × 8-cell Sea Sparrow BPDMS missile systems (in *Forrestal*, *Independence* and *Saratoga*)
4 × 5in/54-cal Mk 42 DP guns (4 × 1) in *Ranger*
**Complement** 145 officers, 2,645 enlisted men + 2,150 air group

In 1948-49 the debate between the US Air Force and the Navy over the respective merits of heavy bombers and fleet carriers reached a head. The US Navy laid down a large carrier in April 1949, to be named *United States* (CVA-58), but Congress changed its mind and the ship was cancelled. The brilliant performance of US and British carrier aircraft in the Korean War a year later helped the Navy to reverse the decision, and in Fiscal Year 1952 another carrier was ordered. This time there was no hesitation, and three more were laid down at yearly intervals.

The design of the *Forrestal* class, the first post-Second World War carriers built anywhere in the world, drew heavily on the cancelled CVA-58, and their main purpose was to provide a mobile platform for nuclear bombers. They incorporated all of the wartime improvements, such as deck-edge lifts, as well as post-war features like the angled deck (added during construction of *Forrestal*), steam catapult and mirror landing sight. Their original classification was Large Aircraft Carrier (CVB), but this was altered to Attack Carrier (CVA) in 1952, and in 1973-75 they changed to CV to indicate a combined attack and ASW role.

The original armament of eight 5in guns has been progressively reduced, and *Ranger* is the only one with any left. She has four guns whereas her sisters have two Sea Sparrow missile systems.

Four more of an improved design, known as the *Kitty Hawk* class (CV-63, 64, 66 and 67), were built in 1956-68. Ways of extending the hull life of these big but nonetheless valuable ships to 40-45 years are now being studied. *Forrestal* is due to begin her two-year Service Life Extension Programme (SLEP) in 1981.

The older *Forrestal* and her sisters are similar to the nuclear carriers in layout. The 5in guns originally fitted have been removed, and a Sea Sparrow close-range missile launcher can be seen on the former starboard gun sponson. The starboard lifts are lowered to hangar level.

# *Hancock* class

| Name | Number | Laid down | Launched | Completed | Builder |
|---|---|---|---|---|---|
| ***Hornet*** | CVS-12 | 3 Aug 1942 | 29 Aug 1943 | 29 Nov 1943 | Newport News SB & DD Co |
| ***Lexington*** | AVT-6 | 15 Jul 1941 | 26 Sept 1942 | 17 Feb 1943 | Bethlehem Steel Co, Quincy |
| ***Bennington*** | CVS-20 | 15 Dec 1942 | 29 Apr 1944 | 26 Nov 1944 | New York Navy Yard |
| ***Intrepid*** | CVS-11 | 1 Dec 1941 | 26 Apr 1943 | 16 Aug 1943 | Newport News SB & DD Co |
| ***Bon Homme Richard*** | CVA-31 | 1 Feb 1943 | 26 Feb 1944 | 6 Aug 1944 | New York Navy Yard |
| ***Oriskany*** | CV-34 | 1 May 1944 | 13 Oct 1945 | 25 Sep 1950 | New York Navy Yard |
| ***Shangri-La*** | CVS-38 | 15 Jan 1943 | 24 Feb 1944 | 15 Sep 1944 | Norfolk Navy Yard |

**Displacement** Approx 33,000 tons (standard), 40,000-44,700 tons (full load)
**Dimensions** (CVS-12 and 20) 249.9m (wl), 271.3m (oa) × 31m × 9.4m (820ft (wl), 890ft (oa) × 102ft × 31ft) (CVS-11 etc) 249.9m (wl), 271.3-272.6m (oa) × 30.8-32.5m × 9.4m (820ft (wl), 890-894.5ft (oa) × 103-106.5ft × 31ft)
**Propulsion** 4 shafts, geared steam turbines, 8 boilers; 150,000 shp = 30 knots

**Protection** Armoured hangar deck and side belt
**Aircraft** 45
**Armament** 4 × 5-in/38-cal DP guns (2 in *Oriskany*, none in *Lexington*)
**Complement** 75-115 officers, 1,365-1,500 enlisted men + 800 air group

Only seven of the famous *Essex*-class carriers of Second World War fame are left; only the *Lexington* remains in service, as a training carrier. The rest are not destined to see further service, and all have been decommissioned. The *Oriskany*'s completion was delayed until 1950 to allow the incorporation of new features which allowed her to operate jet aircraft, and these improvements were subsequently extended to others of the class.

The *Essex* class was originally divided into two types, and in all 17 of both groups have been scrapped, including the *Hancock*. None has been transferred to other navies, although in 1966 the *Shangri-La* was earmarked for temporary loan to the Royal Navy.

The armament of the ships varies, but none is fitted with guided missiles. The aircraft which can be carried vary from S-2 Trackers, E-1 Tracers and SH-3 Sea King helicopters in the ASW carriers to front-line attack aircraft in the *Bon Homme Richard*. During her last commission the *Lexington* carried no air group.

The *Bon Homme Richard* seems small by comparison with the *Forrestal* class but modernisation extended her useful life by another 15 years. She can carry strike aircraft as a CVA, while her sisters can operate ASW aircraft.

## *Iwo Jima* class

| Name | Number | Laid down | Launched | Completed | Builder |
|---|---|---|---|---|---|
| ***Iwo Jima*** | LPH-2 | 2 Apr 1959 | 17 Sep 1960 | 26 Aug 1961 | Puget Sound Naval Shipyard |
| ***Okinawa*** | LPH-3 | 1 Apr 1960 | 14 Aug 1961 | 14 Apr 1962 | Philadelphia Naval Shipyard |
| ***Guadalcanal*** | LPH-7 | 1 Sep 1961 | 16 Mar 1963 | 20 Jul 1963 | Philadelphia Naval Shipyard |
| ***Guam*** | LPH-9 | 15 Nov 1962 | 22 Aug 1964 | 16 Jan 1965 | Philadelphia Naval Shipyard |
| ***Tripoli*** | LPH-10 | 15 Jun 1964 | 31 Jul 1965 | 6 Aug 1966 | Ingalls SB Corporation, Pascagoula |
| ***New Orleans*** | LPH-11 | 1 Mar 1966 | 3 Feb 1968 | 16 Nov 1968 | Philadelphia Naval Shipyard |
| ***Inchon*** | LPH-12 | 8 Apr 1968 | 24 May 1969 | 20 Jun 1970 | Ingalls SB Corporation, Pascagoula |

**Displacement** 17,000 tons (light), 18,300 tons (full load)
**Dimensions** 180m (oa) 25.6m × 7.9m (592ft (oa) × 84ft × 26ft)
**Propulsion** 1 shaft, geared turbine, 2 boilers; 22,000 shp = 20 knots
**Protection** Nil
**Aircraft** 28-32 helicopters
**Armament** 4 × 3in/50-cal AA guns, 2 Sea Sparrow BPDMS missile systems
**Complement** 48 officers, 480 enlisted men + 2,090 marines

In FY 1958 Congress authorised the construction of the first of seven Amphibious Assault Ships (LPH). These light helicopter carriers can accommodate a Marine Corps battalion landing team and its artillery, vehicles and equipment, and as such were the first warships in the world designed to operate helicopters. They resemble Second World War escort carriers in having hulls built to mercantile standards, but they have many of the refinements of fixed-wing carriers, such as deck-edge lifts, proper island superstructure and an enclosed bow.

A combination of four heavy, 20-24 medium and four observation helicopters can be carried, and seven can be operated simultaneously on the flight deck. Late in 1971 the *Guam* was modified to allow her to operate V/Stol AV-8 Harriers and in January 1972 she began operations as the "Interim Sea Control Ship" while discussions continued about the building of new ships for this role. Although the ship officially reverted to her amphibious role in 1974 she continues to operate Harriers.

Although four Mk 33 twin 3in gun mountings were originally mounted, the two at the after end of the flight deck have been replaced by Sea Sparrow missile systems. The odd sequence of hull numbers is accounted for by the fact that five older carriers also served as LPHs for a limited time. These have since been scrapped.

The LPH-2 design resembles an aircraft carrier but is in fact an assault ship operating helicopters. The *Guam* has however operated AV-8 Harrier V/Stol aircraft for ground support since 1972. One of the twin 3in gun mountings is at the starboard end of the flight deck.

# *Kiev* class

| Name | Number | Laid down | Launched | Completed | Builder |
|---|---|---|---|---|---|
| ***Kiev*** | — | Sep 1970 | Dec 1972 | May 1975 | Nikolaiev |
| ***Minsk*** | — | Dec 1972 | May 1975 | Feb 1978 | Nikolaiev |
| ***Kharkov*** | — | Oct 1975 | Dec 1978 | 1980? | Nikolaiev |

**Displacement** About 32,000 tons (light), about 38,000 tons (full load)
**Dimensions** 274.0m (oa) × 48.0m (max), 41.2m × ?m (898.7ft (oa) × 157.4ft (max), 135ft × ?ft)
**Propulsion** 4 shafts, geared steam turbines; 160,000 shp (approx) = 30 knots (approx)
**Protection** Unknown
**Aircraft** Estimated 20-25, including Hormone-A helicopters and Yak-36 Forger V/Stol aircraft
**Armament** 4 twin SS-N-12, 2 twin SA-N-3, 2 SA-N-4, 1 SUW-N-1 missile launchers, 2 twin 76mm guns, 4 "Gatlings", 2 × 12-barrel MBU 2500A A/S rocket launchers, 10 × 533mm torpedo tubes
**Complement** ?

The arrival of the *Kiev* in the Bosphorus on 18 July 1976 caused great consternation in Western naval circles. The demise of Western naval supremacy was predicted, and even the ship's designation, "Large Anti-Submarine Cruiser", was questioned on the grounds that it was merely a subterfuge to avoid the provisions of the Montreux Convention, which apparently barred aircraft carriers from using the Dardanelles.

The facts are that the *Kiev* and her sister *Minsk* represent a radical departure from previous Soviet philosophy. She is in fact a hybrid vessel, combining the characteristics of a helicopter and V/Stol aircraft carrier with the heavy armament of a cruiser. But the poor performance of the small number of Yak-36 Forger V/Stol strike aircraft seen so far means that she is not a fleet carrier in the same class as the US Navy's CVs, which are capable of operating aircraft of the highest performance. The logical deduction must therefore be that her Hormone-A anti-submarine helicopters and her SS-N-14 missiles, backed up by SS-N-12 surface-to-surface missiles,

The first Soviet-published view of the *Kiev*, showing three Yak-36 Forger strike aircraft spotted on the flight deck. Even with V/Stol aircraft and helicopters the angled deck makes movement of aircraft easier and balances the weight of the big island superstructure.

90

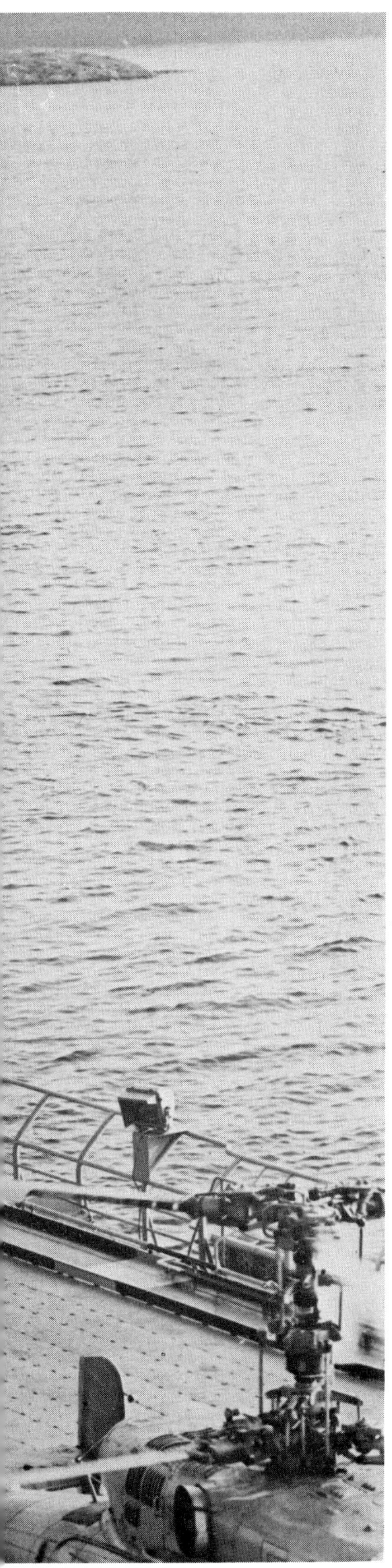

▲ *Kiev*'s sister *Minsk*, second of the class, at sea in February 1979. She differs little from *Kiev* apart from the deck markings and the recognition letter "M" painted on the deck aft. The very wide transom stern and the fore-and-aft passageway outboard of the island can be seen clearly.

◀ Two of *Kiev*'s Hormone-A anti-submarine helicopters, one hovering over the flight deck and the other spotted on a landing circle. The heat-resistant tiling on the deck was mistaken by some observers for wooden planking, but this view shows clearly what it is.

form the main armament. In current terminology her role is that of "sea control" and she is therefore an enlarged version of the British *Invincible* class, her additional tonnage providing for a heavy surface armament.

There are several mysteries about this class. Two sets of figures have been estimated from photographs, the first postulating an overall length of 934ft (284.8m) and a maximum beam of 170ft (51.8m), and the second coming down to 898.7ft (274m) and 157.4ft (48m) respectively. She was at first assumed to be powered by gas turbines, giving a speed of more than 30 knots. This would have required some 150,000 hp and massive internal volume, to say nothing of the resulting problems with air intakes and ventilation. The squat single funnel suggests steam propulsion with four turbines, however, and the speed may be more modest than first thought. The complement of the air group may also be smaller than most sources think, and many observers believe that the Forger flight seen on board *Kiev* may have been embarked purely for evaluation; *Minsk* has however been seen with eight Hormone-As and Forgers.

The second of the class, *Minsk*, was spotted south of Crete at the end of February 1979, and the third ship, *Kharkov*, is likely to be at sea towards the end of 1980. *Kharkov* was reported to be called *Komsomolets* for a time, but city names seem to be the pattern. It is doubtful whether any more units will follow these three. *Kiev* took five years to build, her sister has taken at least as long and *Kharkov* is no faster. Furthermore, the Forgers are such a snug fit on the after lift that we must assume that the ships could not operate any development of this type. The aviation world is not impressed by the Yak-36, and it certainly does not deserve promotion to the rank of fighter/interceptor. If anything, it is a strike/support aircraft and a relatively inefficient one at that.

Apart from suppression of the 533mm torpedo tubes in the hull, *Minsk* appears to differ from *Kiev* only in her flight-deck markings.

# *Moskva* class

| Name | Number | Laid down | Launched | Completed | Builder |
|---|---|---|---|---|---|
| ***Leningrad*** | 853 | 1964 | 1966 | 1968 | Nikolaiev |
| ***Moskva*** | 847 | 1963 | 1965 | Jul 1967 | Nikolaiev |

The dual cruiser-carrier appearance of the *Moskva* class is well shown in this aerial view. The two twin-arm launchers are for the SA-N-1 Goblet anti-aircraft missiles, and the starboard 57mm twin gun mounting is level with the funnel. Two Ka-25 Hormone A/S helicopters are on the centreline.

**Displacement** 14,500 tons (standard), 18,000 tons (full load)
**Dimensions** 196.6m (oa) × 35m × 7.6m (644.8ft (oa) × 115ft × 25ft)
**Propulsion** 2 shafts, geared steam turbines, 4 boilers; 100,000 shp = 30 knots
**Protection** Unknown
**Aircraft** 18 Ka-25 Hormone-A helicopters
**Armament** 2 twin SA-N-3, 1 twin SUW-N-1 missile launchers, 2 twin 57mm guns, 2 × 12-barrel MBU 2500A A/S rocket launchers, 10 × 21in (533mm) torpedo tubes (2 ×5), no longer in *Moskva*
**Complement** Approx 800 officers + men

By the early 1960s the Soviet Union's leaders had clearly realised that the country's air defences were capable of dealing with bombers launched from Western aircraft carriers. This fact, coupled with growing American disenchantment with the concept of naval strategic bombing and the increasing threat from nuclear submarines, resulted in a new emphasis on anti-submarine warfare.

The first important evidence of this switch was the appearance of the first Russian helicopter carrier, the *Moskva*, in 1968. Equipped with Ka-25 Hormone-A helicopters, she and her sister, the *Leningrad*, still managed to find room for a heavy defensive armament. Both ships are intended to cruise in distant waters, providing anti-submarine cover for striking forces, as well as hunting enemy submarines in the approaches to Soviet waters.

It is difficult to do more than guess at Soviet shipbuilding policy, but reports from American sources indicate that the two ships were originally intended to be followed by others, and this would conform with previous Soviet practice. If so, the rumoured design fault, which resulted in a "set" by the bows of as much as two feet, could be the reason why the class ran to only two examples. On the other hand, there could be general dissatisfaction with the design. Certainly in other countries' carriers the turbulence from a "cliff face" at the forward end of the flight deck has proved a severe handicap, even with helicopters. It is possible that the *Kiev* was substituted as a more capable design, but suffered subsequent delays.

Like the *Kiev* class, the *Moskva*s are rated as anti-submarine cruisers, which underlines their ocean role. But they are only armed for self-defence and area defence, and are not equipped for surface attack apart from the heavy torpedo armament, which is probably dedicated to ASW in any case.

The *Moskva* lost her torpedo tubes at the last refit, a possible reflection on their diminishing usefulness. Estimates of the helicopter complement are high, and some observers question the figure of 18 on grounds of internal space available. The speed is also slightly suspect: the heavier *Invincible*, with 112,000 hp, is rated at only 28 knots, while the Russians get a higher speed on less power.

In 1974 *Leningrad* carried two Mi-8 Hip helicopters for minesweeping in the Suez Canal. The fact they could not fit on the lifts suggests that the Ka-25 may have been designed specially for the *Moskva* class, which are fitted with slots and guide rails positioned to fit the Hormone's wheels.

# *Invincible* class

| Name | Number | Laid down | Launched | Completed | Builder |
|---|---|---|---|---|---|
| ***Invincible*** | R 05 | 20 Jul 1973 | 3 May 1977 | Mar 1979 | Vickers, Barrow |
| ***Illustrious*** | — | 7 Oct 1976 | 1 Dec 1978 | 1980 | Swan Hunter, Wallsend |
| ***Ark Royal*** (ex-***Indomitable***) | — | 14 Dec 1978 | 1981 | 1983 | Swan Hunter, Wallsend |

**Displacement** 16,000 tons (standard), 19,500 (full load)
**Dimensions** 167.8m (flight deck), 206.6m (oa) × 31.9m × ?7.3m (550ft (fd), 677ft (oa) × 104.6ft × ?24ft)
**Propulsion** 2 shafts, geared gas turbines (4 Olympus); 112,000 shp = 28 knots
**Protection** Nil
**Aircraft** 15, comprising 10 Sea Kings and 5 Sea Harriers
**Armament** 1 twin Sea Dart SAM launcher
**Complement** 31 officers, 869 men + ? aircrew

The growing cost of maintaining fixed-wing aircraft carriers forced the Royal Navy to abandon its plans to build new attack carriers (CVAs) in the 1960s. The government of the day instituted a traumatic defence review in 1966 which

HMS *Invincible* on contractors' sea trials in 1979, showing the broad flight deck, the Ski-jump ramp forward and the two massive funnels. An unusual feature is the open forecastle, which replaces the "hurricane" or enclosed bow of earlier carriers. She has the same missiles as the *Sheffield*-class DDGs.

*Invincible* leaves Barrow in charge of tugs on her maiden voyage. She is riding high out of the water, without stores, aircraft or a full complement, and her lofty superstructure is apparent. Unarmoured and spacious internally, she is relatively large for her displacement.

cancelled plans to build an unnamed carrier designated CVA 01 and envisaged an end of naval fixed-wing flying by 1972.

But a growing realisation that the Royal Air Force lacked the manpower or the aircraft to provide effective screening of ships at sea, and the demonstration of the inflexibility of such an arrangement (yet again, despite the bitter experience of the Second World War), forced the government and the RAF to concede the point. Furthermore, the threat to Nato and Western shipping from long-range bombers, long-range missiles and submarines focused attention on the lack of powerful anti-submarine forces and strike power. To remedy this an earlier project, designated CCH 1, was resurrected; this was a helicopter-cruiser not unlike the French *Jeanne d'Arc* and intended to provide area defence and limited surface attack by means of Sea Dart missiles, and task-force anti-submarine cover with Sea King helicopters.

The new ship was designed to operate at "fleet speed," 28 knots continuous, and although the political climate was particularly hostile to any attempt to revive fixed-wing aviation, it was courageously decided to design in the ability to operate V/Stol aircraft. This would be the as yet unbuilt Sea Harrier, a much improved version of the RAF Harrier capable of shooting down Soviet reconnaissance bombers and helicopters before they could pass targeting information back to a missile-cruiser, and of dealing with fast strike craft. This capability, combined with the anti-submarine cover provided by the Sea King helicopters, would confer "sea control" – not the same as the striking power of Phantom interceptors and Buccaneer bombers, but much better than attempting to operate in the Eastern Atlantic with nothing but shore-based air support.

The troubled political background accounts for the ludicrous nomenclature applied to the class. First of all *Invincible* was a "through-deck" cruiser to disguise the flight deck, then a command cruiser, and only now is she rated as an aircraft carrier. But HMS *Invincible* finally emerged for her contractors' sea trials on 26 March 1979, a major addition to the Royal Navy's strength and a timely replacement for the *Ark Royal*. The keel of a second ship was laid in 1976, and the third (named *Ark Royal* in honour of the old fleet carrier) was ordered at the end of 1978.

The massive air intakes demanded by gas turbines necessitate two big funnels, the first time such excrescences have been seen in a carrier since the old *Eagle* in 1924. The ship is very capacious internally, with great emphasis on accessibility and ease of removal. The four Olympus gas turbines have their own hoists to allow them to be removed, and two spare gas-generators are carried on board. While *Invincible* was under construction the revolutionary Ski-jump was tested and accepted, and so she was fitted with a 7° ramp on the port side of the flight deck. *Illustrious* will have a similar ramp, but *Ark Royal* will have a different arrangement to allow a greater ramp angle; in the existing ships a steeper ramp would mask the Sea Dart missile launcher.

In addition to her aircraft and her area-defence capability the *Invincible* will provide valuable command-and-control facilities for a task force, something the RN will lack more and more as the County-class DLGs and the *Tiger*-class cruisers disappear.

# PA 75

| Name | Number | Laid down | Launched | Completed | Builder |
|---|---|---|---|---|---|
| PA 75 | – | 1981? | – | – | DCAN, Brest |

**Displacement** 16,400 tons (for trials), 18,400 tons (full load)
**Dimensions** 202m (flight deck), 208m (oa) × 26.4m × ?m (662.6ft (fd), 682.2ft (oa) × 86.6ft × ?ft)
**Propulsion** 2 shafts, geared steam turbines, one CAS 230 nuclear reactor; 2 AGO diesels for auxiliary propulsion; 65,000 shp = 28 knots
**Protection** Nil
**Aircraft** 25 Lynx or 10 Super Frelon + 15 Puma helicopters
**Troops** 1,000 to 1,500 in temporary accommodation
**Armament** 2 Crotale 8-cell surface-to-air missile systems, 2 × 100mm DP guns
**Complement** 840 officers and men + 50 amphibious warfare staff + 1,500 troops (in emergency)

In 1974 the French Navy revealed that it is designing a nuclear-powered helicopter carrier. Known for the time being simply as the PA 75 project, it is comparable to the American *Iwo Jima* class in size but is designed primarily for anti-submarine operations. The decision to choose nuclear propulsion makes the *Marine Nationale* the second navy to build a nuclear-propelled surface warship, and it remains to be seen if the running costs of nuclear propulsion in a relatively small hull can compete with those of conventional powerplants.

The CAS 230 reactor, rated at 230 megawatts, is being designed under the supervision of l'Etablissement des Constructions et Armes Navales (ECAN) at Indret. The reactor and its associated systems will supply steam to two turbines, and there will be two diesels for emergency running. Enough fuel will be carried for 3,000 miles' endurance on diesels, plus 1,250 tons for the replenishment of escorts. Conventionally powered destroyers would otherwise have difficulty in keeping at sea with PA 75, throwing away most of the tactical freedom conferred by nuclear propulsion.

Construction has not yet started, which means that the original completion date, 1981, will not now be achieved. The delay has also resulted in several changes in design, and the ship will almost certainly differ from the published sketch design.

Offical sketch of the PA 75 projected nuclear helicopter carrier. Note the two starboard side lifts and the eight-cell Crotale missile launchers above the island and right aft. Apart from the lack of a funnel, her appearance is conventional, even down to the enclosed bow.

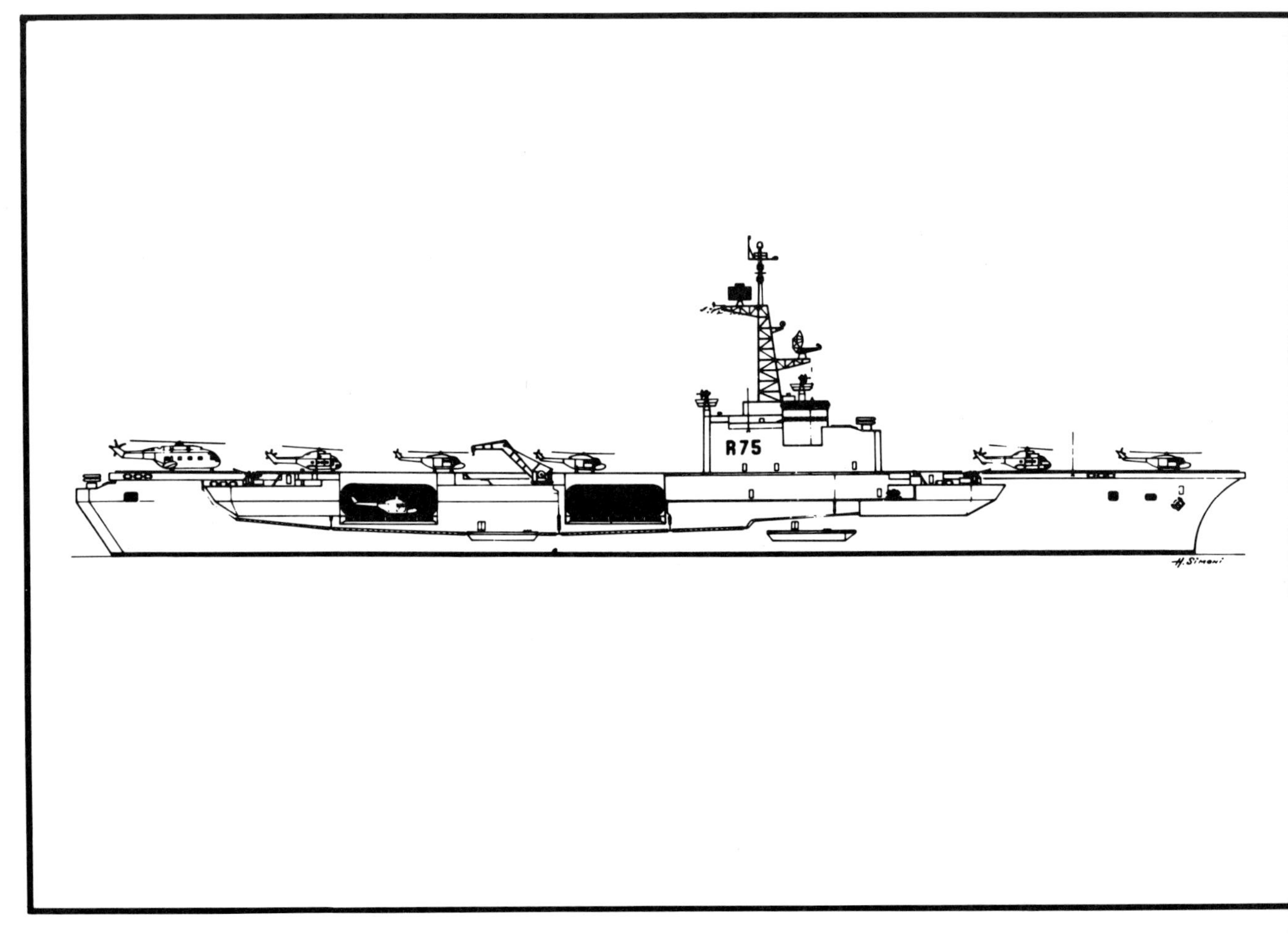

## *Clemenceau* class

| Name | Number | Laid down | Launched | Completed | Builder |
|---|---|---|---|---|---|
| ***Clemenceau*** | R 98 | Nov 1955 | 21 Dec 1957 | 22 Nov 1961 | DCAN, Brest |
| ***Foch*** | R 99 | Feb 1957 | 28 Jul 1960 | 15 Jul 1963 | Chantiers de l'Atlantique |

**Displacement** 27,307 tons (normal), 32,780 tons (full load)
**Dimensions** 238m (pp), 265m (oa) × 31.7m (over bulges) × 8.6m (normal) (780.8ft (pp), 869.4ft (oa) × 104.1ft (over bulges) × 28.2ft (normal))
**Propulsion** 2 shafts, geared steam turbines, 6 boilers; 126,000 shp = 32 knots
**Protection** Armoured flight deck and internal bulkheads
**Aircraft** 40 maximum
**Armament** 8 × 100mm DP guns
**Complement** 65 officers, 1,163 men

Although aircraft carriers were laid down for the *Marine Nationale* before the Second World War, the first to be completed were two medium-sized ships authorised in 1953 and 1955 respectively. They were conventional in design and leaned heavily on British and American experience. In the past 15 years both ships have been extensively modernised, with angled flight decks,

The *Clemenceau* and her sister *Foch* incorporate many features of American and British carriers, including two steam catapults, angled deck and a starboard deck-edge lift abaft the island. The single 100mm guns are in four quadrant positions forward and aft.

mirror landing sights and steam catapults to enable them to operate modern aircraft.

The aircraft carried include three flights: one of Etendard IVs, one of F-8 Crusaders and one of Breguet Alizés. Both ships are currently refitting to allow them to operate the new Super Etendard, a faster and heavier version of the standard attack aircraft.

The two carriers are now halfway through their effective lives, and will not need further reconstruction to match the current generation of aircraft. If the *Aéronavale* adopts V/Stol aircraft, as is believed to have been considered, they may well finish their careers as "Harrier carriers" instead of being expensively rebuilt.

The deck recognition letters of the two ships are "F" for *Foch* and "U" for *Clemenceau*. The pennant numbers are R 99 and R 98 respectively.

*Foch* refuels the frigate *Suffren* under way. It is common practice for carriers, with their large fuel capacity, to replenish their escorts if an oiler is not handy. A carrier usually has to replenish her own liquid and dry stores once every three days.

# Jeanne d'Arc

| Name | Number | Laid down | Launched | Completed | Builder |
|---|---|---|---|---|---|
| ***Jeanne d'Arc*** | R 97 | 7 Jul 1960 | 30 Sep 1961 | 1 Jul 1963 | DCAN, Brest |

**Displacement** 10,000 tons (standard), 12,265 tons (full load)
**Dimensions** 172m (pp), 182m (oa) × 24m × 7.3m (564.2ft (pp), 597.1ft (oa) × 78.7ft × 24ft)
**Propulsion** 2 shafts, geared steam turbines, 4 boilers; 40,000 shp = 26½ knots
**Protection** Nil
**Aircraft** 4/8 large helicopters
**Armament** 6 Exocet surface-to-surface missile cells, 4 × 100mm DP guns
**Complement** 30 officers, 587 men + 192 cadets

Under the 1957 Estimates the French Navy ordered an unusual vessel, a combined training ship and helicopter carrier. She was intended to replace the old *Jeanne d'Arc*, herself a hybrid cruiser/training ship, and she was given the interim name of *La Résolue*. She commissioned under that name in mid-1963 and did not assume her correct name until the old *Jeanne d'Arc* was decommissioned and stricken the following year.

Experience has shown that the centreline position of the funnel was not ideal, causing turbulence over the flight deck. In any case the original funnel was too short, and it had to be made much taller. The position of the lift is unusual in being right aft at the end of the deck.

The ship carries 192 officer cadets in peacetime, as well as operating four large Super Frelon anti-submarine helicopters. In wartime she would carry twice that number, and could be rapidly converted to accommodate 700 troops. *Jeanne d'Arc* is a handsome and effective compromise between a training ship, carrier and cruiser, and could even operate V/Stol aircraft if needed.

In 1975 six Exocet missile cells were added and it is intended to fit a Crotale short-range missile system.

The attractive lines of the *Jeanne d'Arc* were enhanced when her funnel was heightened. In peacetime she carries officer cadets and only four Super Frélon helicopters; in wartime she could carry eight helicopters and 700 troops in more spartan conditions.

► The addition of six Exocet surface-to-surface missiles in 1975 enhanced the *Jeanne d'Arc*'s cruiser qualities, though not at the expense of her other roles. Note the comprehensive radar array, rivalling that in *Foch* or *Clemenceau*. A Crotale SAM system is to be added.

▼ A contrast in big ships, with the *Colbert* steaming alongside the *Jeanne d'Arc*. The helicopter carrier has fuller lines because of the need to provide internal volume for aircraft and troops, while in designing the cruiser it was necessary to restrict the extent of the superstructure to avoid excess topweight.

## *Giuseppe Garibaldi*

**Displacement** 12,000 tons (standard), 13,250 tons (full load)
**Dimensions** 180.2m (oa) × 30.4m (max) × 6.7m (max) (590ft (oa) × 98ft × 22ft)
**Propulsion** 2 shafts, COGOG gas turbines; 80,000 shp = 29½ knots
**Aircraft** 12 Sea King helicopters (provisional)
**Armament** 4 Teseo (Otomat Mk 2) SSMs, 2 Albatros 8-cell SAM launchers, 6 × 40mm L/70 guns (3 × 2), 2 SCLAR chaff dispensers, 6 × 324mm (12.75in) Mk 32 A/S torpedo tubes (2 × 3)
**Complement** 105 officers, 324 POs, 396 ratings

The need to replace the *Andrea Doria*-class missile cruisers led the Italian Navy to design a proper helicopter carrier, its first flat-topped vessel since the abortive scheme to convert two liners to aircraft carriers in the Second World War, and indeed the first carrier ever to be built from the keel up in Italy.

At the time of writing (1979) the ship has just been laid down and already the sketch design and details published some two years ago have changed drastically. She is to have four Fiat-General Electric LM-2500 gas turbines in an installation similar to that of the US Navy's *Spruance*-class destroyers. The armament is heavy, with close-range defence provided by two Nato Sea Sparrow or Aspide missile systems, four Otomat surface-to-surface missiles, and three twin Breda Compact 40mm L/70 gun mountings; anti-submarine torpedoes are also carried.

The present aircraft complement is restricted to 16 Sea King helicopters, but as Italy has signed a declaration of intent with France and Great Britain these may be replaced by the new WG.34 Sea King Replacement. An alternative stowage scheme for 10 Sea Harriers and 2 Sea Kings has been released, but the Italian Navy states that it has no intention of buying the aircraft, which remains an option for overseas customers.

Curiously, the sketch design reveals a "wasp-waisted" hangar plan similar to that of the British *Invincible*, and there may have been some consultation with British Aerospace and the Ministry of Defence on features necessary to make the ship compatible with the Sea Harrier.

It is possible that this ship could emulate the cruiser *Garibaldi*, which at the turn of the century was sold before completion to an overseas customer, since Australia has shown great interest in her as a replacement for the *Melbourne*. Otherwise, she is unlikely to enter service before 1985, and any sister ships built will take even longer. Italy's parlous financial condition makes her something of an extravagance, and she could ultimately be cancelled.

The current sketch design for the *Giuseppe Garibaldi* shows a forward Ski-jump similar to the 7° ramp in HMS *Invincible*, and a singularly graceless island/funnel combination. The positioning of the lifts on the starboard side is intended to ease congestion during flying operations and in the hangar.

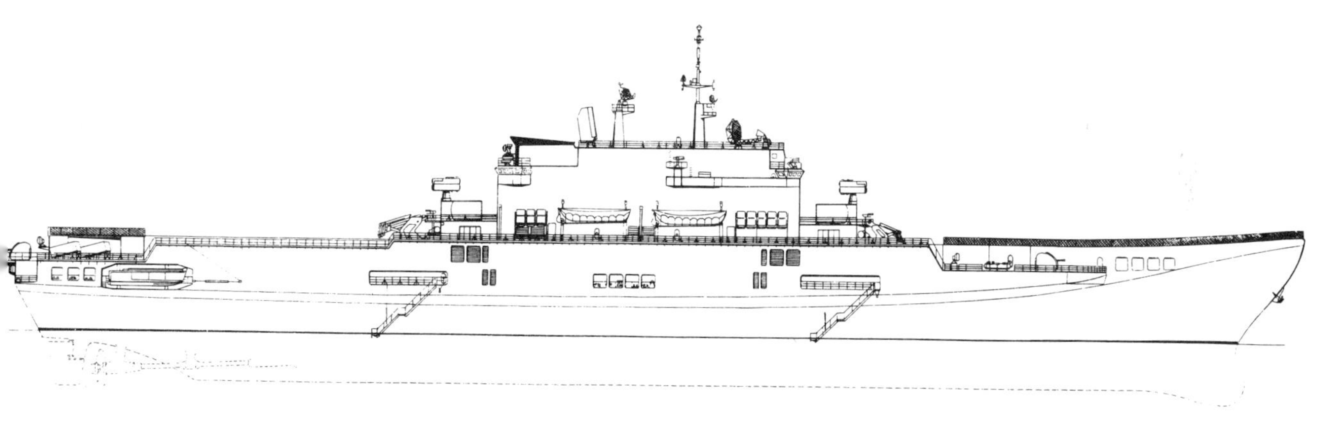

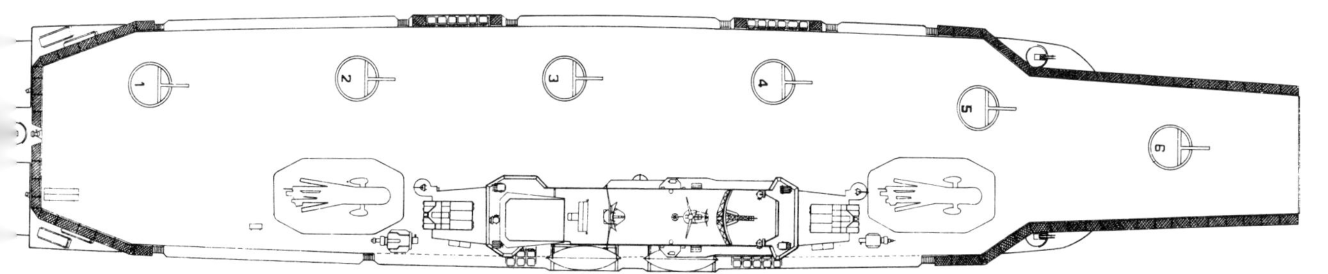

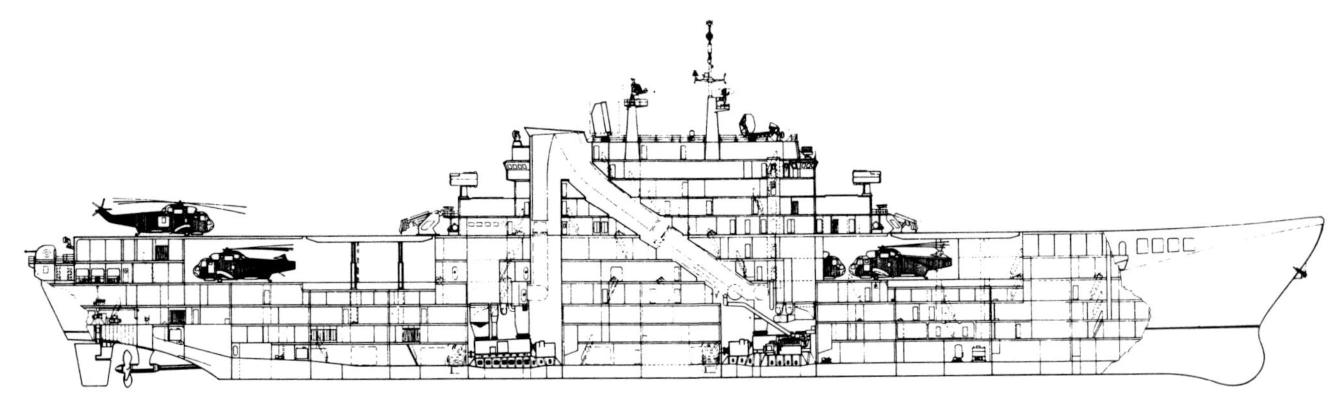

**HANGAR: helicopters (SH3D) version**

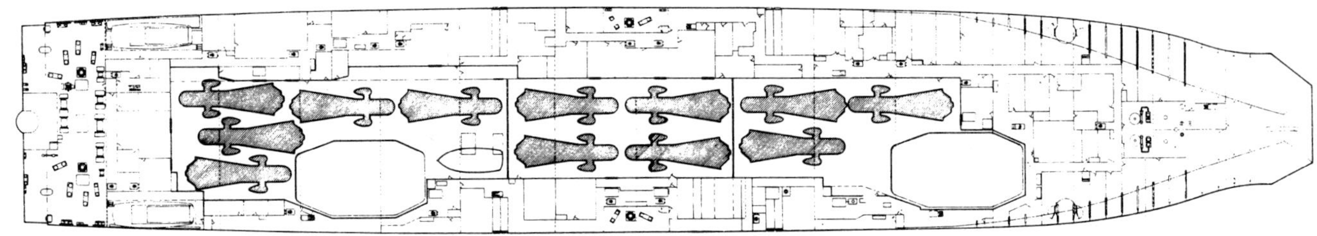

**HANGAR: V/STOL (Sea Harriers) version**

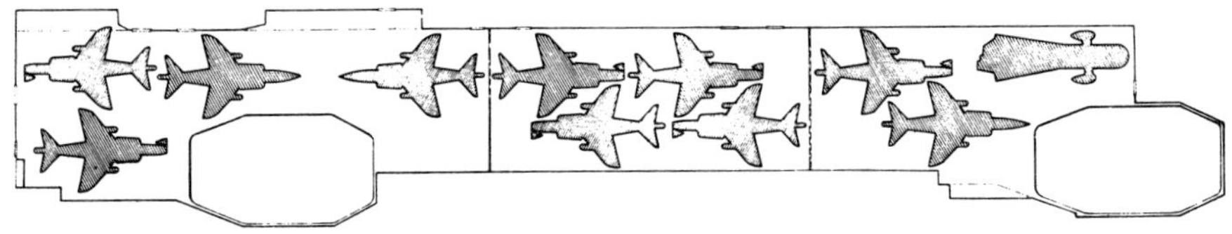

# ex-*Colossus* and *Majestic* classes

**Displacement** 18,000-19,500 tons (original full load), 15,700-16,000 tons (standard), 19,500-20,000 tons (full load)
**Dimensions** 192m (pp), 211.8m (oa) × 24.4m × 7.5m (630ft (pp), 695ft (oa) × 80ft × 24,5ft (average))
**Propulsion** 2 shafts, geared steam turbines, 4 × 3-drum boilers; 40,000 shp = 24½ knots (when new)
**Protection** Nil
**Aircraft** *Vienticinco de Mayo*
21, including S-2A Trackers, A-4Q Skyhawks and S-61B Sea Kings in varying numbers
*Melbourne*
24, including 6 S-2A Trackers, 8 A-4Q Skyhawks and 10 Mk 50 Sea Kings
*Minas Gerais*
20, including 7 S-2A Trackers and 4 Sea Kings
*Vikrant*
22, including 18 Seahawks and 4 Alizés

The internal layout of the *Giuseppe Garibaldi* shows even more unusual features. The Sea King A/S helicopters make heavy demands on hangar space, already limited by the starboard trunking for the separate gas turbine compartments. The final design might well revert to twin uptakes.

**Armament** *Vienticinco de Mayo*
9 × 40mm Bofors AA guns (9 × 1)
*Melbourne*
12 × 40mm Bofors AA guns (4 ×2, 4 × 1)
*Minas Gerais*
10 × 40mm Bofors AA guns (2 × 4, 1 × 2)
*Vikrant*
15 × 40mm Bofors AA guns (4 × 2, 7 × 1)
**Complement** Varies from 1,035 to 1,500. HMAS *Melbourne* embarks 75 officers, 995 ratings + 347 air group

The 16 light fleet carriers ordered by the Royal Navy in 1942-43 have proved to be some of the most long-lived carriers of all. Originally intended as stopgaps or utility carriers, all but one had successful careers as front-line carriers.

Today only five are left, four of which are serving in those smaller navies that cannot afford large and expensive fleet carriers. They are almost at the end of their effective lives and will probably all be scrapped by the end of the decade. Those already scrapped include: French *Arromanches* (ex-HMS *Colossus*); British *Perseus*, *Glory*, *Pioneer*, *Ocean*, *Theseus* and *Leviathan*; Argentinian *Independencia* (ex-HMS *Warrior*); Australian *Sydney* (ex-HMS *Terrible*); and Canadian *Bonaventure* (ex-HMS *Powerful*) and *Magnificent* (on loan from Royal Navy).

The Argentine's *Vienticinco de Mayo* is the most sophisticated of the four serving as carriers, having been fully modernised by the Royal Netherlands Navy and since then given the latest electronic aids. The Brazilian *Minas Gerais* was also reconstructed in a Dutch shipyard after being purchased, but looks very different. The Indian *Vikrant* and Australian *Melbourne* were bought from the Royal Navy while still incomplete and were finished to a revised design; both have since been overhauled and refitted. The exception is the fifth ship, HMS *Triumph*, which was converted into a heavy repair ship between 1958 and 1965, with her hangar fitted out as workshops and deckhouses on the flight deck. She is now cocooned at Chatham and would only be recommissioned in an emergency.

▼ The long, sleek hull of HMAS *Melbourne* does little to betray her age, though she was in fact commissioned 25 years ago. The original light fleet carrier design was simple and relatively unsophisticated but proved eminently capable of being adapted to accommodate new aircraft and equipment.

▲ The Argentinian *Vienticinco de Mayo* was commissioned as HMS *Venerable* as long ago as 1945. Transferred soon afterwards to the Royal Netherlands Navy as the *Karel Doorman*, she was modernised and totally rebuilt in 1955–58. She was finally sold to Argentina a decade later.

◀ The Brazilian *Minas Gerais* served in both the RN and Australian Navy as the *Vengeance* before being bought by Brazil in 1956. Although also reconstructed in the Netherlands, she was not completely transformed like her Argentinian sister apart from receiving a new funnel and lattice mast.

# Submarines

Odd as it may sound, the submarine has a pedigree more authentic than those of most modern warships. With none of the changes of definition suffered by the cruiser and the frigate and none of the modernity of the destroyer, it can trace an unbroken line of development from 1776. In that year Sergeant Ezra Lee of the American rebel army piloted the *Turtle* on a mission to destroy the British flagship, HMS *Eagle*, in the Hudson River.

The *Turtle* did not harm her intended victim but the fact that she got underneath and escaped unharmed distinguishes her as the only successful submarine for another century. Later submarines were attended by a series of disasters, both technical and financial, and it was not until 1888 that French inventor Gustave Zédé's little electrically driven *Gymnote* proved that submarines were a workable proposition.

Progress was slow, even after the introduction of the electric motor. In 1900 the French *Narval* showed that a light steam engine, despite its obvious drawbacks, would extend the radius of a submarine on the surface. In the same year the American *Holland* introduced the gasoline engine, which brought with it a new hazard, explosive vapour inside the boat. Four years later the French took up a German invention, the Diesel motor, and installed it in the *Aigrette*. This marked the beginning of the rise of the submarine, for diesel oil was much less volatile than gasoline, allowing design to advance with relative safety. Although the French continued to use steam for surface propulsion, the diesel rapidly became standard elsewhere. By 1914 all the major navies had built up impressive fleets of submarines, with Great Britain in the lead, followed by France, the United States and Germany.

The British put their submarines to the most ingenious use, paralysing the iron ore trade in the Baltic and disrupting Turkish communications in the Sea of Marmara, while the Germans found their U-Boats ideal for attacking the vast Allied merchant fleet. Millions of tons of shipping were sunk and – because the British were slow to perceive the nature of the threat and to take timely counter-measures such as building replacement tonnage and saving damaged ships – the U-Boat came near to offsetting the vast Allied preponderance in surface ships. But the introduction of convoy and measures to economise on the use of shipping frustrated the U-Boats, and within a year they began to suffer crippling casualties themselves.

On the German side, the war against commerce led them to concentrate on building the standard "Mittel-U" pre-war type with the minimum of alterations. But the ease with which solitary merchant ships could be sunk by gunfire led to an increase in the size and number of deck guns. In addition, the desire to operate on the far side of the Atlantic necessitated much larger fuel tanks, and this combination of requirements for greater range and heavier armament led to the giant "U-Cruisers" with 15cm (5.9in) guns. Although they made a great impression on the Allies they proved a blind alley; experienced commanders much preferred the handy "Mittel-U" and the wartime UB III types because they were smaller targets and more manoeuvrable. In fact the biggest lesson learned was that the number of torpedoes had much more bearing on the time a U-Boat could spend at sea than the size of her fuel tanks.

When the U-Boats gave up the struggle in November 1918 there was an unseemly scramble by the Allies to acquire U-Boats for themselves, and many German ideas found their way into British, French, US, Japanese and Italian submarines. Everybody but the British, who had their own submariners' experience to guide them, was fascinated by the big cruiser-submarine, and for some years these boats dominated the scene. The British built one giant submarine, the *X.1*, but she proved such a liability that she was scrapped prematurely. Instead the Royal Navy concentrated on developing the successful "L" class into overseas patrol submarines. The first classes were not successful because their external fuel tanks leaked oil and their diesels were none too reliable, but these faults were eliminated. It is interesting to note that Second World War U-Boats were slower to dive than the standard "S" boat designed in the early 1930s. The main reason for this was the fact that British submarines were expected to operate without air cover, and so the design emphasised quick diving as the only defence against air attack.

The Americans grew disillusioned with giant submarines and settled down to develop a reliable boat for long-range operations in the Pacific. The design of their boats stressed habitability and endurance, with good handling on the surface. The Japanese remained infatuated with the idea of cruiser-submarines, and built a series of very big boats with heavy armament. Following the lead given by the American and British experiments with submarine-launched floatplanes in the 1920s, they decided that cruiser-submarines needed aircraft to scout for them, and included a hangar and catapult in many designs.

The Germans were officially forbidden to build or design U-Boats, but as early as 1922 steps were taken to set up a "front" organisation in Holland with German Navy funds. This bureau designed submarines for Finland, Spain and Turkey among others, and secretly tested future prototypes against the day when Germany could shake off the shackles of the Versailles Treaty. When Hitler came to power he gave his approval to secret stockpiling of material, so that production of U-Boats could begin almost overnight when he denounced the Versailles Treaty in 1934.

But despite such chicanery it was not easy to accelerate production, and by the outbreak of war only 58 U-Boats had been commissioned. Even this small number made their mark, however, and by 1941 the British were locked in the Battle of the Atlantic, desperately seeking ways to protect convoys against the ever-growing numbers of U-Boats. It rapidly became a war of technology, with the scientists playing as important a part as the weapon designers. In practice the British (and later the Americans) made better use of their scientists than the German U-Boat command. The crisis came in March 1943, when the U-Boats were at their peak and the best Allied escort forces had been withdrawn to cover the landings in North Africa. But within a short space of four or five weeks the pendulum swung the other way and the U-Boats took such a mauling that Admiral Dönitz had to withdraw them temporarily from the battle.

Only superior technology could now win against the growing strength of the Allies. Dönitz pinned his faith on two ideas: the Electro U-Boat with increased battery capacity and a streamlined hull, and the Walther peroxide turbine, which promised an enormous increase in speed. While the Electro or Type XXI U-Boat still needed a *schnorchel* air mast to recharge her batteries, the Walther U-Boat was designed to be independent of outside oxygen and could become the first true submarine.

As things turned out, the Germans tried to cover too many bets. They continued to build conventional Type VIIC U-Boats, entrusted the complex Type XXIs to inexperienced labour and spent vast sums of money and precious time making the dangerous Walther turbine work. Germany might have made a comeback in 1944 had production been switched fully to the Type XXI, but only three of them were ready by May 1945.

In the Pacific the Japanese neglected the most rudimentary precautions against submarine attack on shipping. The Americans waged the only fully successful submarine campaign in history, bringing Japanese seaborne commerce to near-standstill and sinking merchantmen and warships with comparative ease. In contrast, the Japanese submarines scored a few successes against major warships but signally failed to interrupt the vital flow of munitions and men across the Pacific. They were then frittered away carrying food to outlying Army garrisons

The Type XXI U-Boat and the Walther turbine may have come too late to affect the outcome of the war but their influence was immense. As in 1918, the victors descended on the German shipyards to pillage as much information on the new U-Boat technology as they could carry away. The Russians, British and Americans all acquired U-Boats and subjected them to trials. Several high-test peroxide Type XVII boats fell into Soviet hands, and the RN and USN each got one. They proved as big a danger to their crews as any foe, however, and although the British and Russians persisted with the idea into the early 1950s the cost and risks proved too high.

The alternative was nuclear propulsion, and the United States was able to exploit its virtual monopoly of nuclear knowhow. Under the aegis of Admiral Hyman Rickover the enormous technical problems of producing a small enough nuclear reactor were tackled energetically, so that the keel of the world's first nuclear-powered submarine could be laid in 1952. The USS *Nautilus* commissioned in September 1954 and got under way for the first time on 17 January 1955. In principle the *Nautilus* was propelled in the same way as the submarines of 50 years earlier, in that the reactor was used with a heat-exchanger to create steam which drove two turbines.

Here at last was the true submarine, capable of travelling for long distances under water, independent of outside oxygen for her propulsion and limited only by the endurance of her crew. There was nothing else revolutionary about the *Nautilus* – her hull form was a combination of ideas from the Type XXI and the latest *Tang* class – but she was the precursor of great things.

One of the most important features of the Type XXI had been the streamlined hull, without the deck guns, conning-tower platforms and other fixtures of wartime submarines. While the nuclear programme and the faltering attempts to make the Walther turbine work were proceeding, the major navies set about building boats based on the Type XXI and adapting German ideas to their wartime boats, which still existed in large numbers. The Americans took the lead with their Greater Underwater Propulsive Power (GUPPY) programme from 1949, streamlining fleet submarines and inserting a new battery section to give them double the electrical capacity. To distinguish these diesel-electric submarines from the nuclear boats they have been divided into "conventional boats" or "submersibles," and "true submarines" – a distinction used originally by the French at the turn of the century.

The next big step forward was to redesign the hull shape. The Type XXI and the post-war submersibles were a great improvement but they still owed a lot to the notion that submarines had to spend a lot of time on the surface. While the *Nautilus* was still in construction the US Navy built the unarmed submarine *Albacore* to serve as a hydrodynamic test vehicle. She had a "teardrop" hull, with one propeller shaft, a nearly circular section and a very slim "sail" or "fin" instead of a conning tower. This resulted in mediocre handling on the surface but outstanding manoeuvrability underwater. Ironically, the idea of a single shaft with contra-rotating propellers had been introduced in the British "R" class in 1918, and they too had a circular hull form for high underwater speed.

The *Albacore* ideas were such a success that they were incorporated into the *Skipjack* class of nuclear submarines, and this has proved the standard for all subsequent submarines and submersibles.

The *Nautilus* and her successors proved most valuable as hunters of other submarines, being able to catch them and to use their sonars at depths impossible for surface ships. The big advantage of a fast submarine is that she is unaffected by surface weather conditions, though against this is the fact that high speed also produces noise. Stealth is still a submarine's greatest asset, and speed is most useful when getting clear of the scene or shadowing a task force at a distance. For this reason much research has gone into quieter hull forms, and propellers have been redesigned to cut down the "singing" caused by cavitation.

In 1956 the Soviet Navy caused great alarm by introducing a new class of submersibles capable of firing an intermediate-range ballistic missile. These Zulu V boats had to surface to fire three missiles housed in the fin and they were followed four years later by the nuclear-powered Hotel class. In response to this threat to their cities the Americans accelerated development of a terrifying new weapon, the underwater-launched Polaris IRBM.

Five *Skipjack*-class boats were modified during construction to carry 16 Polaris tubes abaft the fin, and the first commissioned at the end of 1959. They were followed by 36 more of the *Lafayette* and *Ethan Allen* classes. Today, twenty years on, Polaris has given way to Poseidon, and the first Trident missile-firing submarines, the *Ohio* class, are completing. The system is still almost impossible to knock out, if only because the oceans are so vast that Soviet ASW forces could never hope to find all the ballistic missile submarines (SSBNs) simultaneously to prevent them from firing their missiles. Even an elderly missile like the Polaris A-3 has a thermonuclear warhead with more destructive power than all the bombs dropped in the Second World War. To maintain the balance of terror the Soviet Navy has produced its own Yankee and Delta-class SSBNs.

The latest development in underwater weaponry is the missile which is fired from a torpedo tube and then leaves the water. In its earliest form this was the Subroc, which equipped US submarines from 1965. It rises out of the water to follow a ballistic trajectory and then re-enters the water to act as a depth charge. Now available is a submarine-launched version of the Harpoon anti-ship missile, capable of flying 60 miles and then homing on surface targets. The Tomahawk cruise missile, with much longer range, would be used for strategic attacks on cities and other land targets. The Russians have also developed a submarine-launched cruise missile, the SS-N-7, for use in their Charlie and Papa-class nuclear attack submarines; it can be fired at surface ships from a range of 25 miles.

The nuclear submarine is the most potent warship of all and the leading navies of the world are devoting all their energies to finding new counter-measures. Vast sums of money have been expended on hydrography, sonar research and bathythermography, to say nothing of new weapons. Though for the moment the submarine has the upper hand, this advantage may not last forever.

## *Ohio* class

**Displacement** 16,600 tons (surface), 18,700 tons (submerged)
**Dimensions** 170.7m (oa) × 12.8m × 10.8m (560ft (oa) × 42ft × 35.5ft)
**Propulsion** 1 shaft, geared steam turbines, 1 pressurised water-cooled General Electric S8G nuclear reactor; ? shp = ? knots
**Armament** 24 Trident 1 SLBM launch tubes, 4 × 21in (533mm) torpedo tubes
**Complement** 16 officers, 177 enlisted men

*Ohio* (SSBN-726), *Michigan* (SSBN-727) and 11 more building (728-735 + 4), ordered or projected from 1975, all to be built by General Dynamics (Electric Boat Division).

Despite rumours of Russian "underwater battleships" the *Ohio* class are the largest underwater craft known to have been built and are more than double the size of the preceding *Lafayette* class. They have been designed to launch the Trident missile, to match the SS-N-8 deployed in Soviet Delta-class SSBNs. Their principal advantage is the fact that the longer range of the Trident I (4,000 miles) permits it to be fired from anywhere in the world, rather than from waters likely to be dominated by Soviet ASW forces. In effect, Trident enhances the US nuclear deterrent by making possible an enormous increase in the area of the world's oceans available to the *Ohio* class.

In other respects the *Ohio*s are no more than improved *Lafayette*s, with 24 launch tubes instead of 16 and improved habitability by virtue of the greater size. The building method is radically different, however, with the hull being assembled on a special jig and then moved sideways. Improvements in the design of nuclear reactors give the S8G an estimated core life of nine years, which reduces running costs.

There are no fewer than five decks, with batteries and accommodation forward of the missile compartment. Like the latest attack submarines, the *Ohio*s have four torpedo tubes angled out abreast of the conning tower, leaving the bow compartment clear for a spherical sonar dome. Another feature is a pair of auxiliary rudders on the after diving planes, presumably to offset the additional keel effect of the long hull.

This night-time view of the Trident submarine *Ohio* on the building slip gives little idea of her immense size. The main purpose in providing the class with 50 per cent more missiles is to replace the 41 Polaris and Poseidon SSBNs with fewer hulls and to save skilled manpower.

# *Lafayette* class

Three classes of Polaris submarines were built for the US Navy: the five *George Washingtons* hurriedly adapted from a hunter-killer design to get the system to sea, five from-the-keel-up *Ethan Allens* adapted from the *Permit* design, and 31 *Lafayettes*, an enlarged and improved version for quantity production.

Strictly speaking, the class is divided into the *Lafayettes* (SSBN-616 to 636), and the *Benjamin Franklins* (SSBN-640 onwards) with quieter machinery. The first eight boats were armed with the A-2 Polaris, while the later boats received the A-3 version. Under conversion plan SCB-353 the class was refitted to operate the C-3 Poseidon, starting with SSBN-627 in February 1969 and ending with SSBN-626 in September 1977. Ten boats of the class began receiving the C-4 version, starting in 1979, and conversion of *Francis Scott Key* to serve as test submarine for the Trident I missile began recently. The Poseidon conversion involved provision of larger launch tubes and a new Mk 88 fire control system; there is no external change.

The *Daniel Webster* differs from her sisters in having bow-mounted diving planes on a specially faired cutwater, instead of carrying them on the sail.

One of the older SSBNs, the *Von Steuben*, entering Charleston, South Carolina. She completed a conversion from the Polaris A-3 missile to the Poseidon C-3 in 1970; this involved no external change. The planes on the "sail" make for faster diving and greater manoeuvrability.

**Displacement** 7,250 tons (surface), 8,250 tons (submerged)
**Dimensions** 129.5m (oa) × 10.1m × 9.6m (425ft (oa) × 33ft × 31.5ft)
**Propulsion** 1 shaft, geared steam turbines, 1 pressurised water-cooled Westinghouse S5W nuclear reactor; 15,000 shp = approx 20 knots (surface), approx 30 knots (submerged)
**Armament** 16 Poseidon C-3 SLBM launch tubes, 4 × 21in (533mm) torpedo tubes
**Complement** 20 officers, 148 enlisted men

31 *Lafayettes* built 1961-67 by General Dynamics (Electric Boat); Mare Island Navy Yard; Portsmouth Navy Yard; Newport News SB & DD Co.

| Name | Number |
|---|---|
| ***Lafayette*** | SSBN-616 |
| ***Alexander Hamilton*** | SSBN-617 |
| ***Andrew Jackson*** | SSBN-619 |
| ***John Adams*** | SSBN-620 |
| ***James Monroe*** | SSBN-622 |
| ***Nathan Hale*** | SSBN-623 |
| ***Woodrow Wilson*** | SSBN-624 |
| ***Henry Clay*** | SSBN-625 |
| ***Daniel Webster*** | SSBN-626 |
| ***James Madison*** | SSBN-627 |
| ***Tecumseh*** | SSBN-628 |
| ***Daniel Boone*** | SSBN-629 |
| ***John C. Calhoun*** | SSBN-630 |
| ***Ulysses S. Grant*** | SSBN-631 |
| ***Von Steuben*** | SSBN-632 |
| ***Casimir Pulaski*** | SSBN-633 |
| ***Stonewall Jackson*** | SSBN-634 |
| ***Sam Rayburn*** | SSBN-635 |
| ***Nathanael Greene*** | SSBN-636 |
| ***Benjamin Franklin*** | SSBN-640 |
| ***Simon Bolivar*** | SSBN-641 |
| ***Kamehameha*** | SSBN-642 |
| ***George Bancroft*** | SSBN-643 |
| ***Lewis and Clark*** | SSBN-644 |
| ***James K. Polk*** | SSBN-645 |
| ***George C. Marshall*** | SSBN-654 |
| ***Henry L. Stimson*** | SSBN-655 |
| ***George Washington Carver*** | SSBN-656 |
| ***Francis Scott Key*** | SSBN-657 |
| ***Mariano G. Vallejo*** | SSBN-658 |
| ***Will Rogers*** | SSBN-659 |

# *Los Angeles* class

| Name | Number |
|---|---|
| ***Los Angeles*** | SSN-688 |
| ***Baton Rouge*** | SSN-689 |
| ***Philadelphia*** | SSN-690 |
| ***Memphis*** | SSN-691 |
| ***Omaha*** | SSN-692 |
| ***Cincinnati*** | SSN-693 |
| ***Groton*** | SSN-694 |
| ***Birmingham*** | SSN-695 |
| ***New York City*** | SSN-696 |
| ***Indianapolis*** | SSN-697 |
| ***Bremerton*** | SSN-698 |
| ***Jacksonville*** | SSN-699 |
| ***Dallas*** | SSN-700 |
| ***La Jolla*** | SSN-701 |
| ***Phoenix*** | SSN-702 |
| ***Boston*** | SSN-703 |
| ***Baltimore*** | SSN-704 |
| ***San Francisco*** | SSN-711 |
| ***Atlanta*** | SSN-712 |
| ***Houston*** | SSN-713 |
| SSN-705-710, 712-719 | |
| + 6 authorised for FY 1979-82 | |

**Displacement** 6,000 tons (surface), 6,900 tons (submerged)
**Dimensions** 109.7m (oa) × 10.1m × 9.85m (360ft (oa) × 33ft × 32.3ft)
**Propulsions** 1 shaft, geared steam turbines, 1 pressurised water-cooled General Electric S6G nuclear reactor; ? shp = over 30 knots (submerged)
**Armament** 4 × 21in (533mm) torpedo tubes
**Complement** 12 officers, 115 enlisted men

Built from 1972 onwards by Newport News SB & DD Co and General Dynamics (Electric Boat) Co. 31 built, building or authorised, and a further 8 proposed.

The latest American nuclear hunter-killers, the *Los Angeles* are designed to counter the latest Russian types such as the Victors. They are the USN's standard hunter-killers and will continue to be built for some years.

The main difference between these boats and the preceding *Sturgeon* class is the 50 per cent increase in size, which permits more powerful and quieter machinery as well as a bigger sonar set. They will also be equipped with Sub-Harpoon and Tomahawk subsurface-to-surface missiles in due course.

The configuration is very similar to those of previous classes, with diving planes on the sail and torpedo tubes firing from abreast of the control room.

The former give greater manoeuvrability while the latter makes for a more efficient use of the bow sonar.

This class was the subject of an acrimonious squabble between the US Navy and General Dynamics, which culminated in GD's Electric Boat Division stopping work on its contracts. The cause was complex, a combination of design modifications, strikes in the yard and various delays, and phenomenal cost overruns were the result. The dispute has been settled but the whole class is well behind schedule, with the *Los Angeles* taking as long as five years to complete.

In recognition of the growing status of the nuclear submarine Congress named these boats after cities, departing from the tradition of giving fish names to attack submarines.

The sleek 360ft length of the USS *Baton Rouge* (SSN-689) slices through a calm sea. The "teardrop" hull of the modern nuclear boat is very wet on the surface and dangerous for crewmen, but comes into its own when running submerged. The big single rudder is positioned ahead of the propeller.

## Guppy types

| Name | Number | Type |
|---|---|---|
| ***Santa Fé*** (Argentina) (ex-***Catfish***) | S 21 | Guppy II |
| ***Santiago del Estero*** (ex-***Chivo***) | S 22 | Guppy IA |
| ***Goiaz*** (Brazil) (ex-***Trumpetfish***) | S 15 | Guppy III |
| ***Amazonas*** (ex-***Greenfish***) | S 16 | Guppy III |
| ***Guanabara*** (ex-***Dogfish***) | S 10 | Guppy II |
| ***Rio Grande do Sul*** (ex-***Grampus***) | S 11 | Guppy II |
| ***Bahia*** (ex-***Sea Leopard***) | S 12 | Guppy II |
| ***Rio de Janeiro*** (ex-***Odax***) | S 13 | Guppy II |
| ***Ceara*** (ex-***Amberjack***) | S 14 | Guppy II |
| ***Katsonis*** (Greece) (ex-***Remora***) | S 115 | Guppy III |
| ***Papanikolis*** (ex-***Hardhead***) | S 114 | Guppy III |
| ***Primo Longobardo*** (Italy) (ex-***Volador***) | S 501 | Guppy III |
| ***Gianfranco Gazzana Priaroggia*** (ex-***Pickerel***) | S 502 | Guppy III |
| ***La Pedrera*** (Peru) (ex-***Sea Poacher***) | S 49 | Guppy IA |
| ***Pacocha*** (ex-***Atule***) | S 50 | Guppy IA |
| ***Isaac Peral*** (Spain) (ex-***Ronquil***) | S 32 | Guppy IIA |
| ***Cosme Garcia*** (ex-***Bang***) | S 34 | Guppy IIA |
| ex-***Jallao*** | S 35 | Guppy IIA |
| ***Çanakkale*** (Turkey) (ex-***Cobbler***) | S 341 | Guppy III |
| ***Ikinci Inonü*** (ex-***Corporal***) | S 333 | Guppy III |
| ***Burak Reis*** (ex-***Seafox***) | S 335 | Guppy IIA |
| ***Murat Reis*** (ex-***Razorback***) | S 336 | Guppy IIA |
| ***Oruc Reis*** (ex-***Pomfret***) | S 337 | Guppy IIA |
| ***Uluç Ali Reis*** (ex-***Thornback***) | S 338 | Guppy IIA |
| ***Çerbe*** (ex-***Trutta***) | S 340 | Guppy IIA |
| ***Preveze*** (ex-***Entemedor***) | S 345 | Guppy IIA |
| ***Birinci Inonü*** (ex-***Threadfin***) | S 346 | Guppy IIA |
| ***Tiburon*** (Venezuela) (ex-***Cubera***) | S 21 | Guppy IIA |
| ***Picuda*** (ex-***Grenadier***) | S 22 | Guppy IIA |

**Displacement** Guppy II 1,870 tons (surface), 2,440 tons (submerged), Guppy III 1,975 tons (surface), 2,450 tons (submerged), Guppy IA 1,830 tons (surface), 2,440 tons (submerged), Guppy IIA 1,848 tons (surface), 2,440 tons (submerged)
**Dimensions** Guppy III 99.4m (oa) × 8.2m × 5.2m (326.5ft (oa) × 27ft × 17ft), Guppy IA, II, IIA 93.8m (oa) (307ft)
**Propulsion** 2 shafts, diesel-electric drive; Guppy I 4,160 shp = 17.2 knots (surface), 14.5 knots (submerged), Guppy IA 4,610 shp = 17.3 knots (surface), 15 knots (submerged),

Guppy II 4,610 shp = 18 knots (surface), 16 knots (submerged), Guppy IIA 3,430 shp = 17 knots (surface), 14.1 knots (submerged)
**Armament** 10 × 21in (533mm) torpedo tubes
**Complement** 8 officers, 74 enlisted men (78 in Guppy III)

*Balao* and *Tench* classes built 1942-49.
10 modified to Guppy IA in 1951.
24 modified to Guppy II in 1948-50.
16 modified to Guppy IIA in 1952-54.
9 modified from Guppy II to Guppy III in 1960-62. Spanish *Narciso Manturiol* (Guppy IIA) deleted 1977 after mechanical failure.

Following trials with two captured German Type XXI boats in 1945 the US Navy decided to modify a large number of its latest fleet submarines to increase their underwater speed. Known as Project Guppy (Greater Underwater Propulsive Power), the programme involved an increase in battery storage capacity, and streamlining by removal of guns and obstructions.

The main item in the programme was a new type of 126-cell battery, about two-thirds the weight of the old *Sargo*-type battery but delivering twice the power. In 1947 it was estimated that a Guppy-type battery would provide current for 4,520 shp, against 2,688 shp for the old type at maximum or half-hour rate; at the six-hour rate it would be about 50 per cent more powerful, and 40 per cent better at maximum endurance.

The first two Guppies were *Pomodon* and *Odax*, but as they had no snorkel they were quickly superseded by ten Guppy II conversions, which differed in having a bigger sail to incorporate a second periscope and a snorkel mast. In all 22 Guppy IIs were authorised, while the original Guppy Is were modified to the same standard. However, the cost of the Guppy battery and uncertainty about the future role of these submarines led to the Guppy IA, with a streamlined hull, an old-type *Sargo* battery and a

streamlined sail and snorkel. The IAs are not to be confused with the "Fleet Snorkel" conversion, which did not have the streamlined hull.

The Guppy IIA had the *Sargo* battery and a much improved sonar outfit comprising the passive AN/BQR-2, the active BQS-2 and a precision passive tracking sonar, the GQR-3. All these conversions (including the Fleet Snorkel boats) were given the Mk 106 underwater fire-control system, which permitted the use of electrically set homing torpedoes.

The Fleet Rehabilitation and Modernisation (FRAM) programme initiated in 1958 allowed for the rebuilding and modernisation of nine Guppy IIs into Guppy IIIs. The conversion included the addition of a 10ft hull section to allow a plotting room and a longer sail. Weaponry was updated to include the Mk 45 Astor nuclear torpedo, and the BQG-4 passive fire-control sonar, known as PUFFS (Passive Underwater Fire Control Feasibility Study). This meant that for the first time a submarine could triangulate sources of underwater noise without having to execute special manoeuvres.

Although now superseded in the US Navy by nuclear submarines, the Guppies continue to serve in minor navies overseas and will be valuable for ASW training and coastal defence for some years.

▲ The USS *Darter* and the similar *Tang* class commissioned in the 1950s and their features were incorporated into the Guppy III FRAM conversion. *Darter* is seen here in 1960 taking part in an ASW exercise with surface ships, helicopters and aircraft.

◀ The Brazilian *Rio Grande do Sul* was the USS *Grampus*, a Guppy III transferred in 1972. The Guppy I and II conversions improved the underwater performance of wartime fleet boats, while the Guppy III conversion was a further "stretch" of the Guppy II to extend the life of the hull.

## Delta class

**Delta I**

**Displacement** 8,350 tons (surface), 9,300 tons (submerged)
**Dimensions** 135m (oa) × 12.0m × 9m (442.8ft (oa) × 39.4ft × 29.5ft)
**Propulsion** 2 shafts, geared steam turbines, nuclear reactors; 40,000 shp = approx 25-30 knots (submerged)
**Armament** 12 SS-N-8 SLBM launch tubes, 6 × 21in (533mm) torpedo tubes
**Complement** Approx 120 officers and men

19 built 1972–77 at Severodvinsk.

**Delta II and III**

**Displacement** 9,350 tons (surface), 11,000 tons (submerged)
**Dimensions** 152.7m (oa) × 12m × 9m (500ft (oa) × 39.4ft × 29.5ft)
**Propulsion** Probably as Delta I
**Armament** Probably as Delta I (Delta III reported to have 16 tubes for SS-N-18)
**Complement** 132

At the end of 1972 it was announced that a new class of Soviet SSBNs had been identified, code-named the Delta class. Successors to the Yankee class, they are reported to have a new missile, the SS-N-8, with more than twice the range of the SS-N-6. The missile is clearly much bulkier than its predecessors, as each Delta has only 12 launch tubes instead of the previous 16.

After a total of 15 had been built a modified version, the Delta II, appeared at the end of 1973. The hull is slightly longer but otherwise similar, and the latest production figure is five boats built and three building. A Delta III armed with SS-N-18 missiles has been reported.

The Soviet Delta-class nuclear submarines have twelve vertical launch tubes for SS-N-8 ballistic missiles. The casing abaft the fin accommodates the upper part of the missiles, as in Western SSBNs. The twin "track" on the casing is for safety lines for crewmen working on deck.

## Charlie class

**Displacement** 3,900 tons (surface), 4,700 tons (submerged) (Charlie I)
**Dimensions** 94m (oa) × 10.0m × 7.5m (304.8ft (oa) × 32.8ft × 24.6ft)
**Propulsion** 3 shafts, geared steam turbines, 2 nuclear reactors; approx 25,000-30,000 shp = 20 knots (surface), 30 knots (submerged)
**Armament** (Charlie I) 8 × SS-N-7 missiles, 6 × 21in (533mm) torpedo tubes; (Charlie II) 8 × SS-N-7 missiles, 8 × 21in torpedo tubes; ? SS-N-15 tube-launched A/S missiles
**Complement** 100 officers and men

12 delivered from Gorky from 1968 onwards, followed by 3 Charlie IIs.

First seen in 1968, this class of nuclear hunter-killer submarines caused a wave of panic which has only just begun to subside. What alarmed Western observers was the sight of eight ports in the bow casing covering vertical tubes for the missile designated SS-N-7. This is claimed to be a 25-mile-range cruise-type missile, capable of being fired underwater and "popping up" into the atmosphere before entering its cruise phase. This was obviously a major addition to the Soviet armoury, not so much because of the range of the missile but because of its effectiveness in the event of a Charlie slipping inside the ASW screen of a carrier task group, for example. Having reduced the warning time in this way, a Charlie-class captain could use the SS-N-7's rather modest range to advantage against big surface targets, and it has been assumed that the missile is an anti-carrier weapon.

A total of 12 Charlies were built at Gorky from about 1964 to 1971, and in 1973 an enlarged Charlie II class of three units was reported. At about the same time a larger type of similar configuration, the Papa class, was reported. It is not clear how successful the original Charlie design has been, but all three variants have been seen far afield, from the Arctic to the Pacific Ocean.

The Charlie class introduced a new dimension into undersea warfare with their underwater-launched SS-N-7 missiles, housed forward of the fin under eight hatches. In other ways the class resembles the contemporary Victors, which also entered service in 1967–68.

# November class

**Displacement** 4,200 tons (surface), 5,000 tons (submerged)
**Dimensions** 110.0m (oa) × 9.8m × 7.4m (360.9ft (oa) × 32.1ft × 24.3ft)
**Propulsion** 2 shafts, geared steam turbines, 1 nuclear reactor; 32,500 shp = 20 knots (surface), 28 knots (submerged)
**Armament** 6 × 21 in (533mm) torpedo tubes, 4 × 16in (406mm) torpedo tubes
**Complement** 88 officers and men

14 built between 1954 (?) and 1963 at Severodvinsk.

The first generation of Soviet nuclear submarines, the November class introduced the now-characteristic silhouette, with a long, low fin. To the experienced submariner's eye the large number of free-flooding holes in the casing betrayed the fact that they were noisy, and this has proved so in practice. They did however provide valuable experience for the Soviets and prepared the way for the next class, the Victors.

The Novembers have been deployed all over the world to gain experience in navigation and to test the capabilities of their nuclear plant. One sank after an accident about 70 miles south-west of Cornwall in the United Kingdom in April 1970; no further mishaps have been reported.

The Victor class superseded the Novembers, which they resemble in appearance; the Victors have fewer free-flooding holes in the casing to reduce noise. Soviet submarines have distinctive small fins with a pronounced rake to the after end, and many are fitted with ice guards.

## Foxtrot class

**Displacement** 2,100 tons (surface), 2,400 tons (submerged)
**Dimensions** 89m (oa) × 8.3m × 4.8m (292ft (oa) × 27.2ft × 15.7ft)
**Propulsion** 2 shafts, diesel-electric drive; 6,000 bhp = 18 knots (surface), 5,000 hp = 17 knots (submerged)
**Armament** 10 × 21in (533mm) torpedo tubes
**Complement** 70 officers and men

60+ built from 1958 onwards at Sudomekh and Leningrad. 8 supplied to India, 6 being built for Libya.

Although the Soviet Navy has devoted great efforts to building up a fleet of nuclear hunter-killers and SSBNs, it has also built conventional submersibles in large numbers. These are presumably used for coastal defence and for training, and they were also needed to replace the ageing Whiskey and Zulu types built in the 1950s.

As some 60 Foxtrots were built, all at the Sudomekh shipyard, Leningrad, they are frequently sighted by Western ships and aircraft. They are reputed to be successful, although the Indian Navy has had some problems with the type. They form the bulk of the Soviet force in the Mediterranean, to which they are better suited than the big nuclear boats.

Production ended with the delivery of the last boats in about 1968, and Foxtrots have since been transferred to India and Libya. The Indian Navy has eight: the *Kalvari*, *Kanderi*, *Karanj* and *Kursura* (S 121-4), and *Vela, Vaqir, Vagli* and *Vagsheer* (S 40-43). They were delivered between 1968 and 1975 but it is not clear which are additional construction and which are stock boats transferred from the active strength. Libya took delivery of the *Al Badr* in 1976, the *Al Ahad* in 1977 and the *Al Fateh* in 1978. Three more are on order; these are definitely new building.

In a departure from the usual Soviet practice, some names have been announced: *Pskovski Komsomolets*, *Jaroslavski Komsomolets* and *Vladimirski Komsomolets*. It is believed that a number will be transferred to friendly navies as replacements for Whiskey-class boats in the next few years, as the class has been superseded in Soviet Navy service by the later Bravo and Tango designs.

▼ A Foxtrot conventional diesel-electric submersible in rough weather. The light strips on the bow sonar dome and on the bow itself are probably coatings of noise-absorbent material, as fitted to some Western surface ships. The small protrusion on the fin contains the diesel exhaust.

## *Resolution* class

| Name | Number | Laid down | Launched | Completed | Builder |
|---|---|---|---|---|---|
| ***Renown*** | S 26 | 25 Jun 1964 | 25 Feb 1967 | 15 Nov 1968 | Cammell Laird, Birkenhead |
| ***Repulse*** | S 23 | 12 Mar 1965 | 4 Nov 1967 | 28 Sep 1968 | Vickers, Barrow |
| ***Resolution*** | S 22 | 26 Feb 1964 | 15 Sep 1966 | 2 Oct 1967 | Vickers, Barrow |
| ***Revenge*** | S 27 | 19 May 1965 | 15 Mar 1968 | 4 Dec 1969 | Cammell Laird, Birkenhead |

**Displacement** 7,500 tons (surface), 8,400 tons (submerged)
**Dimensions** 129.5m (oa) × 10.1m × 9.1m (425ft (oa) × 33ft × 30ft)
**Propulsion** 1 shaft, geared steam turbines, 1 pressurised water-cooled nuclear reactor; 15,000 shp = 20 knots (surface), 25 knots (submerged)
**Amament** 16 Polaris A-3 SLBM launch tubes, 6 × 21in (533mm) torpedo tubes
**Complement** 13 officers, 130 men

► The hunter and the hunted: a Sea King helicopter over the British Polaris submarine *Resolution*. Although generally similar to American SSBNs, the *Resolutions* have a British-designed hull, propulsion and systems. The A-3 Polaris missiles have a semi-MIRV (multiple independently targeted re-entry vehicle) triple warhead originally developed for the Blue Streak missile.

The British Government's determination to have an independent deterrent led to a decision in February 1963 to replace the RAF's V-bombers with five Polaris-armed submarines. Although later cut to four boats by a following government, the programme went ahead and the first boat commissioned in October 1967. The Polaris programme remains the only major UK defence project to be completed on time and within the cost limits, an achievement made all the more remarkable by the fact that the crews had to be trained at USN establishments in the United States.

In general configuration the *Resolution* boats resemble the American *Ethan Allen* class, but with bow planes and a slightly different bow form to accommodate a British sonar. As with the US Navy's Polaris boats, two crews are assigned to each *Resolution* to ensure maximum sea time, with Port and Starboard crews exchanging at the end of a three-month patrol. The decision to axe the fifth boat (reported to have been called *Ramillies*) has meant a severe strain on the crews, as the refit schedule is so tight; even with five boats it would have been a struggle to keep at least one on patrol at any given time.

Hanging over the class is the fact that the A-3 Polaris missile will not remain credible through the 1980s in the face of improved ABM defences and the intensified Russian ASW effort. Although a British order for the third-generation Trident SLBM remains a possibility, the class could thus reach the end of its effective life in about 1988. With it would go a deterrent whose independence rather than effectiveness was always conjectural. Certainly the RN would be better off with four nuclear hunter-killer submarines.

## *Swiftsure* class

| Name | Number | Laid down | Launched | Completed | Builder |
|---|---|---|---|---|---|
| ***Sovereign*** | S 108 | 17 Sep 1970 | 17 Feb 1973 | 11 Jul 1974 | Vickers, Barrow |
| ***Superb*** | S 109 | 16 Mar 1972 | 39 Nov 1974 | 13 Nov 1976 | Vickers, Barrow |
| ***Sceptre*** | S 110 | 25 Oct 1973 | 20 Nov 1976 | 14 Feb 1978 | Vickers, Barrow |
| ***Spartan*** | S 111 | 24 Apr 1976 | 7 Apr 1978 | Sep 1979 | Vickers, Barrow |
| ***Splendid*** (ex-***Severn***) | S 112 | 1 Nov 1977 | 5 Oct 1979 | 1981 | Vickers, Barrow |
| ***Swiftsure*** | S 126 | 15 Apr 1969 | 7 Sep 1971 | 17 Apr 1973 | Vickers, Barrow |

**Displacement** 4,200 tons (surface), 4,500 tons (submerged)
**Dimensions** 82.9m (oa) × 9.8m × 8.2m (272ft (oa) × 32.3ft × 27ft)
**Propulsion** 1 shaft, geared steam turbines, 1 pressurised water-cooled nuclear reactor; 15,000 shp = 30 knots (submerged)
**Armament** 5 × 21in (533mm) torpedo tubes
**Complement** 12 officers, 85 men

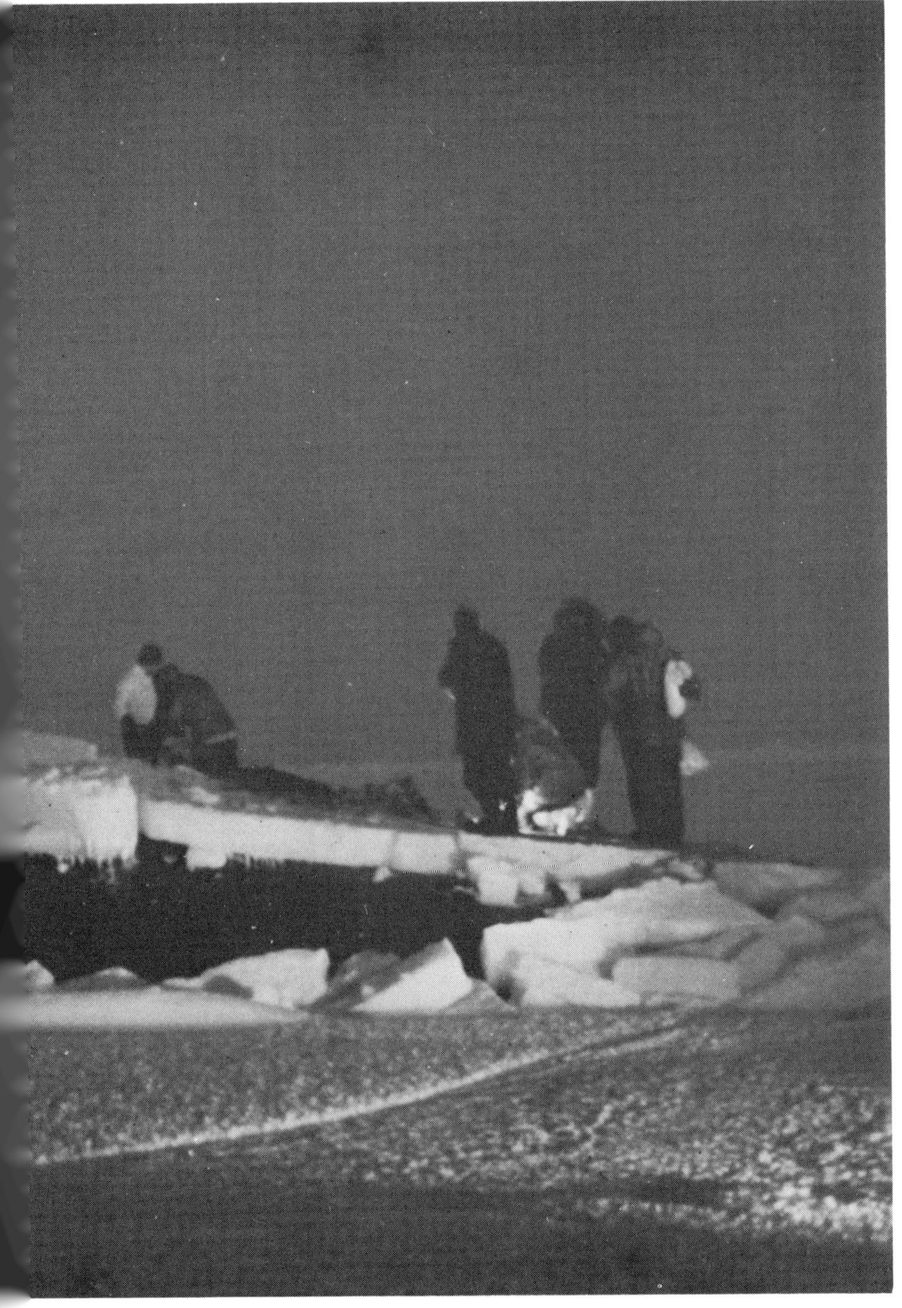

This class could be described as a compact edition of the first British nuclear hunter-killer class, the *Valiant*s, shorter but with a fuller hull form to give better handling underwater. Because of the different fore section there are only five torpedo tubes, but the diving depth is greater than before. Another improvement over the previous class is the provision of an auxiliary diesel for emergency use.

The *Swiftsure*s have proved successful in service and as each new boat comes forward she is being used to develop the RN's new concept of task groups operating with nuclear hunter-killers. The other role for these submarines and the older boats is the escort of Polaris boats in and out of harbour so that they cannot be harassed or shadowed by Soviet boats.

The class is to receive the Mk 24 Tigerfish torpedo, the Sub-Harpoon surface-to-surface missile and the new Type 2020 sonar. Construction will end with *Splendid*, which will be followed by the new *Trafalgar* class.

The hunter-killer HMS *Sovereign* on the surface at the North Pole. Ever since the epic voyage of the *Nautilus*, nuclear submarines have travelled beneath the polar ice cap, mainly because it would be a good place from which to launch ballistic missiles, through cracks in the ice.

## *Oberon* class

**Displacement** 2,030 tons (surface), 2,410 (submerged)
**Dimensions** 90m (oa) × 8.1m × 5.5m (295.2ft (oa) × 26.5ft × 18ft)
**Propulsion** 2 shafts, diesel-electric drive; 3,680 bhp = 12 knots (surface), 6,000 shp = 17 knots (submerged)
**Armament** 8 × 21in (533mm) torpedo tubes (6 bow, 2 stern)
**Complement** 6 officers, 62 men

13 built for Royal Navy from 1957 to 1967. 6 built for Australia, 3 for Brazil, 3 for Canada and 2 for Chile from 1962 to 1977.

Following the success of the *Porpoise* class, a repeat class embodying minor internal improvements became the best of its day. In all 27 *Oberon* boats have been built for five navies, and the class still has an enviable reputation for quietness. It is now outclassed by later designs, however, if only because the hull form reflects ideas of the 1950s and because so many changes have taken place in submarine technology in the intervening years.

The original RN programme was extended as various units were sold to overseas navies, and eventually ran to 13

boats. The armament of the various navies' *Oberon*s differs. For example, the RN boats will not get the Tigerfish torpedo and will continue to carry the Mk 23 and Mk 20 until the end of their lives; the Canadian boats are armed with the Mk 37-C anti-submarine homing torpedo and have no anti-ship role; the Australians are fitting the American Mk 48 to their boats.

This class embodied a number of new materials: there is glass-fibre laminate in the superstructure forward and abaft the fin, while *Orpheus* has an aluminium-alloy fin. The Brazilian *Tonelero* was badly damaged by a fire which originated in her cabling while fitting out at Barrow. She was given a new 60ft section amidships at Chatham in 1975 before being towed back to Vickers for completion. The accident led to the Chilean boats being recabled, but *Hyatt* suffered a minor explosion in January 1976, which further delayed her.

▲ The Brazilian *Humaita*, the first of three *Oberon*s ordered from British shipyards, was commissioned in 1973. She is armed with Mk 20 (Improved) torpedoes and the Vickers TIOS fire-control system, but otherwise differs little from the standard *Oberon* design.

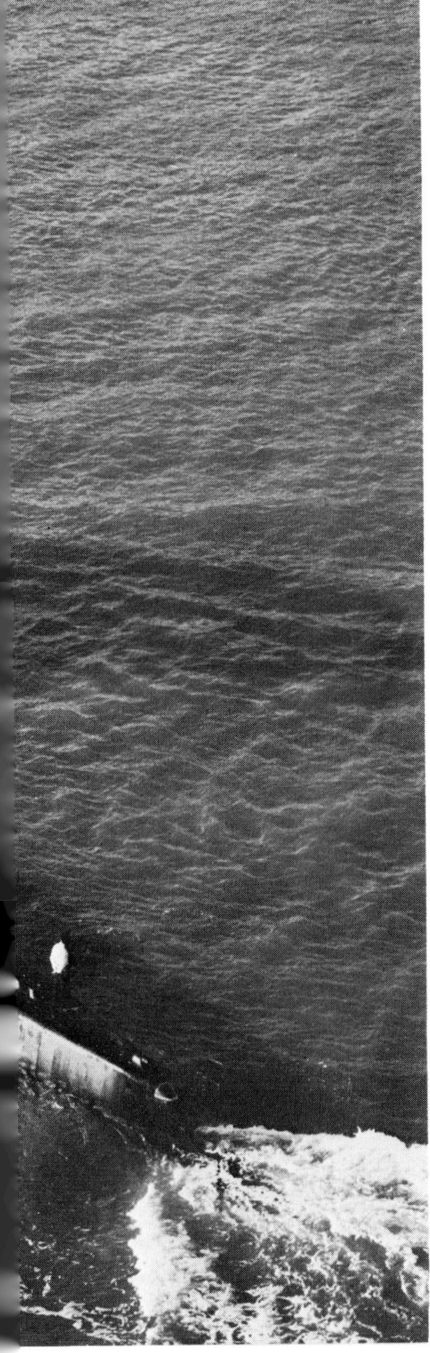

◀ HMS *Osiris* leaving her base at Fort Blockhouse, Gosport. Like the earlier *Porpoise* class, these highly successful submersibles incorporate not only the lessons of the Second World War but improvements from the German Type XXI boats. Their greatest virtue is their quietness.

| Name | Number | Builder |
|---|---|---|
| ***Oberon*** | S 09 | Chatham Dockyard |
| ***Odin*** | S 10 | Cammell Laird, Birkenhead |
| ***Orpheus*** | S 11 | Vickers, Barrow |
| ***Olympus*** | S 12 | Vickers, Barrow |
| ***Osiris*** | S 13 | Vickers, Barrow |
| ***Onslaught*** | S 14 | Chatham Dockyard |
| ***Otter*** | S 15 | Scotts, Greenock |
| ***Oracle*** | S 16 | Cammell Laird |
| ***Ocelot*** | S 17 | Chatham Dockyard |
| ***Otus*** | S 18 | Scotts |
| ***Opossum*** | S 19 | Cammell Laird |
| ***Opportune*** | S 20 | Scotts |
| ***Onyx*** | S 21 | Cammell Laird |
| ***Ojibwa*** (Canada) (ex-***Onyx***) | 72 | Chatham Dockyard |
| ***Onondaga*** | 73 | Chatham Dockyard |
| ***Okanagan*** | 74 | Chatham Dockyard |
| ***Oxley*** (Australia) | 57 | Scotts |
| ***Otway*** | 59 | Scotts |
| ***Onslow*** | 60 | Scotts |
| ***Orion*** | 61 | Scotts |
| ***Otama*** | 62 | Scotts |
| ***Ovens*** | 70 | Scotts |
| ***Humaita*** (Brazil) | S 20 | Vickers |
| ***Tonelero*** | S 21 | Vickers |
| ***Riachuelo*** | S 22 | Vickers |
| ***O'Brien*** (Chile) | 22 | Scotts |
| ***Hyatt*** (ex-***Condell***) | 23 | Scotts |

## *Le Redoutable* class

| Name | Number | Laid down | Launched | Completed | Builder |
|---|---|---|---|---|---|
| ***Le Foudroyant*** | S 610 | 12 Dec 1969 | 4 Dec 1971 | 6 June 1974 | Cherbourg Naval Dockyard |
| ***Le Redoutable*** | S 611 | 30 Mar 1964 | 29 Mar 1967 | 1 Dec 1971 | Cherbourg Naval Dockyard |
| ***Le Terrible*** | S 612 | 24 June 1967 | 12 Dec 1969 | 1 Jan 1973 | Cherbourg Naval Dockyard |
| ***L'Indomptable*** | S 613 | 4 Dec 1971 | 17 Aug 1974 | Dec 1976 | Cherbourg Naval Dockyard |
| ***Le Tonnant*** | S 614 | Oct 1974 | 17 Sep 1977 | May 1980 | Cherbourg Naval Dockyard |

**Displacement** 7,500 tons (surface), 9,000 tons (submerged)
**Dimensions** 128.7m (oa) × 10.6m × 10m (422.25ft (oa) × 34.8ft × 32.8ft)
**Propulsion** 1 shaft, steam turbo-electric drive, 1 pressurised water-cooled nuclear reactor; 15,000 shp = 20 knots (surface), 25 knots (submerged)
**Armament** 16 MSBS M-2 or M-20 SLBM launch tubes, 4 × 21in (533mm) torpedo tubes
**Complement** 15 officers, 120 men

For much the same reasons as the British, the French wanted to have an independent deterrent *(force de dissuasion)* in case at some time a nuclear attack on France was not immediately answered by an American counterstrike. As part of this policy it was announced that France would build her own SSBNs or *Sousmarins Nucléaires Lance Engins* (SNLE).

The first snag was that the United States, angered at France's hostility to itself and Nato, refused to sell the A-3 Polaris. This meant that France had to develop her own *Mer-Sol Balistique Stratégique* (MSBS) underwater-launched ballistic missiles. This resulted in the M-1, which was replaced in *Le Redoutable* by the M-2 version in 1976. The M-20 with a more powerful warhead is being fitted (*L'Indomptable* was the first to receive it), and the 3,000-mile-range M-4 is being tested.

The propulsion system differs from those of British and US nuclear boats, with twin turbines and turbo-alternators providing current for a single electric motor. The configuration is very similar to that of the Polaris boats, but with diving planes on the fin, as in US Navy nuclear boats, rather than bow planes.

Four boats were originally projected in 1967, but in 1972 a fifth was announced, followed by a sixth of improved and enlarged type two years later. There has been talk of acquiring the American Subroc missile, but it is an obsolescent system and the development of the SM.39 underwater version of Exocet or even the purchase of Sub-Harpoon appears more likely.

Although superficially like the American SSBNs, the *Redoutable* class are wholly French in design. As a result of a difference of opinion between General de Gaulle and the United States, France was forced to develop her own ballistic missile for her *Force de Dissuasion*.

## *Daphne* class

**Displacement** 869 tons (surface), 1,043 tons (submerged)
**Dimensions** 57.8m (oa) × 6.8m × 4.6m (189.6ft (oa) × 22.3ft × 15.1ft)
**Propulsion** 2 shafts, diesel-electric drive; 1,300 bhp = 13.5 knots (surface), 1,600 bhp = 16 knots (submerged)
**Armament** 12 × 21.7in (550mm) torpedo tubes
**Complement** 6 officers, 39 men

9 *Daphnes* built for French Navy 1958-70. 3 built for South Africa, 3 for Pakistan, 4 for Portugal and 4 (built in Spain) for Spain.

Although not as highly regarded as the British *Oberon* class, this French design runs it a close second in export sales, principally because the French Government shows no reluctance in selling to nations proscribed by other arms-producing nations in the West. Thus *Daphnes* have been sold to South Africa, Portugal and Spain, all countries to which the British could not sell for various reasons.

The *Daphne* class resembles the diesel-electric submersible of other navies in most respects but is noteworthy for a very heavy torpedo armament: in addition to eight bow tubes there are two internal stern tubes and two external tubes. However, the relatively small hull (100ft shorter and 4ft narrower than that of the 2,000-ton *Oberon*) precludes reloads.

The class has not been without its problems since the first boat commissioned in 1964. In January 1968 the *Minerve* was lost by accident in the Western Mediterranean, followed by the *Eurydice* in the same area in March 1970. In 1972 the *Sirène* sank at Lorient as a result of a faulty torpedo tube; she was raised 11 days later and subsequently returned to service. There have been unconfirmed rumours of another accident to a South African *Daphne*. The Pakistani *Hangor* is the only submarine to have fired a torpedo in anger in recent years, having sunk the Indian frigate *Kukri* in 1971. The *Cachalote* was bought from Portugal in December 1975 and renamed *Ghazi*. The French boats are being refitted with new sonars and the latest homing torpedoes.

A South African submarine of the *Daphne* type on the Synchrolift at Simonstown. The four after torpedo tubes can be seen, two angled out from the casing and two facing directly aft above the rudder. Submarines demand a higher level of maintenance than surface ships of equivalent tonnage.

The *Daphne* herself, showing the distinctive bulbous bow housing the DUUA-2 active sonar. A total of 26 have been built, making them the second most successful export submarine type of the 1960s. The Pakistani boats are the only Western designs known to have been used on active service since 1945.

| Name | Number | Builder |
|---|---|---|
| ***Daphne*** | S 641 | Dubigeon, Nantes |
| ***Diane*** | S 642 | Dubigeon |
| ***Doris*** | S 643 | Cherbourg Arsenal |
| ***Flore*** | S 645 | Cherbourg Arsenal |
| ***Galatée*** | S 646 | Cherbourg Arsenal |
| ***Junon*** | S 648 | Cherbourg Arsenal |
| ***Vénus*** | S 649 | Cherbourg Arsenal |
| ***Psyche*** | S 650 | Brest Arsenal |
| ***Sirène*** | S 651 | Brest Arsenal |
| ***Maria van Riebeeck*** (South Africa) | S 97 | Dubigeon |
| ***Emily Hobhouse*** | S 98 | Dubigeon |
| ***Johanna van der Merwe*** | S 99 | Dubigeon |
| ***Albacora*** (Portugal) | S 163 | Dubigeon |
| ***Barracuda*** | S 164 | Dubigeon |
| ***Delfin*** | S 166 | Dubigeon |
| ***Hangor*** (Pakistan) | S 131 | Brest Arsenal |
| ***Shushuk*** | S 133 | C.N. Ciotat, Le Trait |
| ***Mangro*** | S 133 | C.N. Ciotat, Le Trait |
| ***Ghazi*** (ex-***Cachalote***) | S 134 | Dubigeon |
| ***Delfin*** (Spain) | S 61 | Empresa Naçional Bazán, Cartagena |
| ***Tonina*** | S 62 | Empresa Naçional Bazán, Cartagena |
| ***Marsopa*** | S 63 | Empresa Naçional Bazán, Cartagena |
| ***Narval*** | S 64 | Empresa Naçional Bazán, Cartagena |

## *Nazario Sauro* class

| Name | Number | Laid down | Launched | Completed | Builder |
|---|---|---|---|---|---|
| ***Nazario Sauro*** | S 518 | 15 Jul 1974 | 9 Oct 1976 | April 1978 | Italcantieri, Monfalcone |
| ***Fecia di Cossato*** | S 519 | 15 Nov 1975 | 16 Nov 1977 | Oct 1978 | Italcantieri, Monfalcone |
| ***Leonardo da Vinci*** | S 520 | 1977 | 20 Oct 1979 | 1982 | Italcantieri, Monfalcone |
| ***Guglielmo Marconi*** | S 521 | 1977 | — | 1983 | Italcantieri, Monfalcone |

**Displacement** 1,456 tons (surface), 1,631 tons (submerged)
**Dimensions** 63.9m (oa) × 6.8m × 5.7m (210ft (oa) × 22.5ft × 18.9ft)
**Propulsion** 1 shaft, diesel-electric drive; 3,210 bhp = 11 knots (surface), 3,650 hp = 20 knots (submerged)
**Armament** 6 × 21in (533mm) torpedo tubes (bow, 12 torpedoes carried)
**Complement** 45 officers and men

After delays to allow recasting of the design, the first two of this class were ordered in 1967, cancelled in 1968 and reinstated in 1972. They are nearly three times the tonnage of the previous Italian submarine class and 60ft longer, a reflection of the growth in the volume of fire-control equipment and sonar since the mid-1960s.

The *Nazario Sauro* incorporates the latest ideas in submersible design, with a British-designed seven-bladed special bronze-alloy propeller for silent running, diving planes on the fin and high-capacity batteries. Although much of the equipment is of Italian design, the general features are based on the US Navy's *Barbel* class. The same HY 80 steel is used to permit an increased diving depth, and every piece of welding is X-rayed for flaws and hairline cracks.

A feature of the Whitehead Motofides A.184 torpedoes is that they can be fired either by the "swim-out" method or by piston ejection. Both methods avoid the weight of automatic compensating gear and do away with the tell-tale bubbles of compressed air.

The *Nazario Sauro*, first of a class of four, on preliminary trials. Although war experience suggests that small submarines are better for the Mediterranean, modern fire control, weaponry and associated systems have pushed tonnage to nearly three times that of the previous class.

# *Näcken* class

| Name | Number | Laid down | Launched | Completed | Builder |
|---|---|---|---|---|---|
| ***Näcken*** | Näk | Nov 1972 | 26 Apr 1978 | 1 Apr 1979 | Kockums, Malmö |
| ***Najad*** | Naj | Sep 1973 | 1979 | 1980 | Karlskrona |
| ***Neptun*** | Nep | Mar 1974 | 6 Dec 1978 | 1981 | Kockums, Malmö |

**Displacement** 1,303 tons (surface), 1,408 tons (submerged)
**Dimensions** 49.5m (oa) × 5.7m × 5.5m (162ft (oa) × 19ft × 18ft)
**Propulsion** 1 shaft, diesel-electric drive; 3,500 shp = 20 knots
**Armament** 4 × 21in (533mm) torpedo tubes (8 torpedoes carried)
**Complement** 19 officers and men

The newest class of Swedish submarines is a development of the successful *Sjöormen* design, with the same short, beamy hull and a unique X-form rudder arrangement. The main improvements are in automation and fire control, and the crew has been reduced from 23 to 19 as a result.

A closed-cycle Stirling engine was considered for this class but the project is still under development and so they were given conventional diesel-electric drive. The unusual arrangement of rudders and diving planes is claimed to give much greater manoeuvrability than the normal cruciform rudders. The torpedoes are the wire-guided Tp61 type, running on high-test peroxide.

A development of the *Näcken* (Type A14) is under development. Known as the A17, it may have the Stirling closed-cycle propulsion originally planned for the present class.

Construction of the class has been protracted. So far the *Näcken* is the only one completed. She made history by being lowered into the water by crane instead of being launched by the traditional method, and the others will be put afloat in the same manner.

Apart from some uniquely Swedish features, the *Näcken* class are typical of modern submersibles in layout, with accommodation forward and electric motors and diesel generators aft. The "teardrop" hull provides more depth, allowing even relatively small boats to have two decks and so making internal arrangements easier.

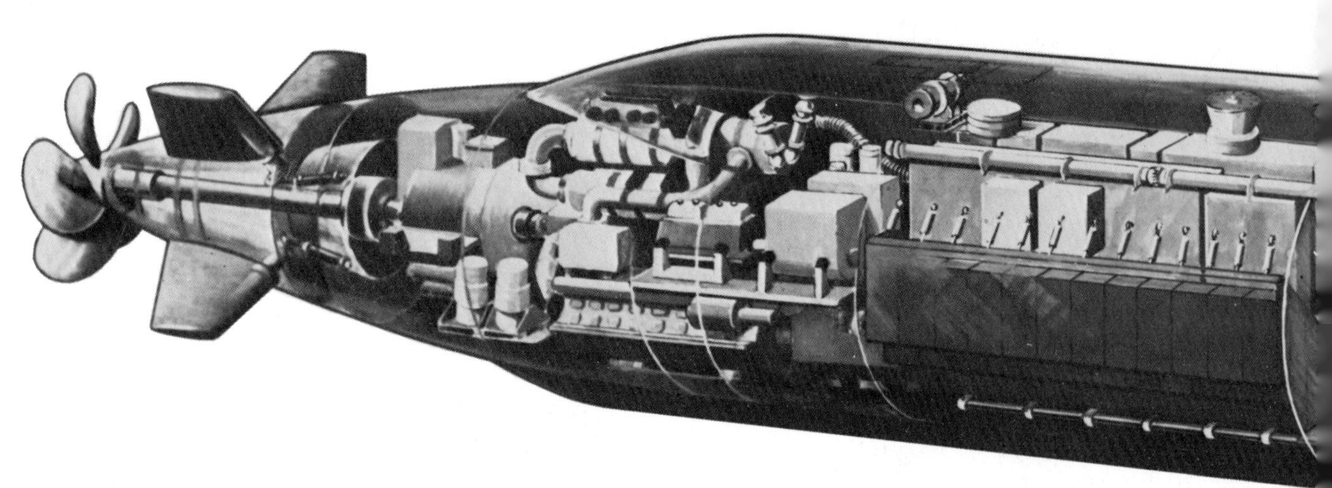

The *Näcken*, showing her stubby hull and X-form rudders, takes to the water in April 1978. The recognition letters "Näk" on the fin are typical of Swedish submarines, contrasting with the pennant numbers used in other navies. The hull form was first introduced by the class which preceded the *Näckens*.

# IKL Type 209

| Name | Number | Builder |
|---|---|---|
| ***Salta*** (Argentina) | S 31 | Howaldt, Kiel |
| ***San Luis*** | S 32 | Howaldt, Kiel |
| ***Pijao*** (Colombia) | SS 28 | Howaldt, Kiel |
| ***Tayrona*** | SS 29 | Howaldt, Kiel |
| ***Shyri*** (Ecuador) | S 11 | Howaldt, Kiel |
| ***Huancavilca*** | S 12 | Howaldt, Kiel |
| ***Glavkos*** (Greece) | S 110 | Howaldt, Kiel |
| ***Nereus*** | S 111 | Howaldt, Kiel |
| ***Triton*** | S 112 | Howaldt, Kiel |
| ***Proteus*** | S 113 | Howaldt, Kiel |
| ***Possidon*** | S 114 | Howaldt, Kiel |
| ***Amfitriti*** | S 115 | Howaldt, Kiel |
| ***Okeanos*** | ? | Howaldt, Kiel |
| ***Pontos*** | ? | Howaldt, Kiel |
| ***Cakra*** (Indonesia) | 401 | Howaldt, Kiel |
| ***Candrasa*** | 402 | Howaldt, Kiel |
| ***Islay*** (Peru) | S 45 | Howaldt, Kiel |
| ***Arica*** | S 46 | Howaldt, Kiel |
| unnamed | S 47 | Howaldt, Kiel |
| unnamed | S 48 | Howaldt, Kiel |
| unnamed | S 49 | Howaldt, Kiel |
| unnamed | S 50 | Howaldt, Kiel |
| ***Atilay*** (Turkey) | S 347 | Howaldt, Kiel |
| ***Saldiray*** | S 348 | Howaldt, Kiel |
| ***Batiray*** | S 349 | Howaldt, Kiel |
| ***Yildiray*** | S 350 | Golcük |
| unnamed | S 351 | Golcük |
| ***Sabalo*** (Venezuela) | S 31 | Howaldt, Kiel |
| ***Caribe*** | S 32 | Howaldt, Kiel |

**Displacement** 990 tons (surface), 1,350 tons (submerged)
**Dimensions** 177.1ft (oa) × 20.3ft × 18ft (54m (oa) × 5.2m × 5m)
**Propulsion** 1 shaft, diesel-electric drive; 5,000 shp = 10 knots (surface), 22 knots (submerged)
**Armament** 8 × 21in (533mm) torpedo tubes (16 torpedoes carried)
**Complement** 31 officers and men

This new type of compact submarine is an export variant of the various IKL (Ingenieurkontor Lübeck) designs produced for the Federal German Navy (FGN) under the aegis of Professor Ulrich Gabler. Although small and hardly ideal for extended operations, they have proved very popular with overseas navies and many are being built.

The basic difference between the Type 209 and the FGN designs is size, since the restrictions imposed on West German operations by Baltic conditions do not apply. Many of the features are common, however, particularly the heavy bow salvo of eight torpedo tubes. Despite the small hull a full outfit of reloads is carried.

Despite being on the small side, the German IKL Type 209 design has overhauled the British *Oberon* and French *Daphne* types in export markets; to date a total of 27 have been sold. This is the Argentinian *San Luis*, commissioned in 1974 with her sister *Salta*.

## *U.13* class

**Displacement** 450 tons (surface), 500 tons (submerged)
**Dimensions** 48.6m (oa) × 4.7m × 4.0m (159.4ft (oa) × 15.4ft × 13.1ft)
**Propulsion** 1 shaft, diesel-electric drive; 1,800 hp = 10 knots (surface), 17 knots (submerged)
**Armament** 8 × 21in (533mm) torpedo tubes
**Complement** 22 officers and men

18 built for Germany between 1969 and 1975 by Howaldtswerke, Kiel, and Reinstahl, Emden; 3 built for Israel by Vickers at Barrow.

The rebirth of the German Navy has brought about the third generation of U-Boats. Following the successful Type 205 designed by Ingenieurkontor Lübeck under the direction of Professor Gabler, the design was expanded from 370 tons to 400 tons. A total of 18 boats, *U.13-30*, were built, eight by Howaldtswerke, Kiel, and ten by Reinstahl Nordseewerke, Emden, between 1969 and 1975.

During their refits in 1977-78 these boats were fitted with the same minelaying gear as applied to the earlier classes. This is in a unique "annular"

The older *U.10* belongs to the slightly smaller Type 205 class but is otherwise similar to the Type 206 boats. The hull form is of the "teardrop" type but much smaller than its foreign contemporaries. This docking view gives little idea of scale.

*U.18* exercising with a Breguet Atlantic ASW aircraft off Kiel. She and her sisters are the second class of post-war U-Boat designs to emerge from the successful Ingenieurkontor Lübeck (IKL) bureau. Similar boats serve in the Danish and Norwegian navies, and the type is to be developed as a replacement for older boats.

form, with the mines disposed on the outside of the pressure hull in circular stowage. Because of the small size of these boats the crews do not live aboard while in port, and every member is either a commissioned or non-commissioned officer.

The class is to be followed by the 750-ton Type 210, designed in conjunction with the Norwegian Navy as a replacement for the Type 205 and Type 207 boats when they reach the end of their effective lives in the 1980s.

The boats have pennant numbers S 192-199 (*U.13-20*) and S 170-179 (*U.21-30*). They serve in two squadrons, *U.25-30* in the 1st Squadron and *U.13-24* in the 3rd Squadron.

In 1972 a contract was signed with Vickers to allow the British company to build three for Israel. They were built in total secrecy and completed as the *Gal*, *Tanin* and *Rahav* in 1977. They are the only submarines to have the British Slam anti-aircraft defence system, based on the Short Blowpipe missile.

A special feature of this class and the earlier U-Boats is the non-magnetic steel alloy used in the hull. This was developed in response to the risk from magnetic mines in the shallow waters of the Baltic, but when first introduced it suffered from corrosion. These boats are so small that there is no room for the conventional torpedo loading hatch; they trim down by the stern to allow the torpedoes to be loaded through the bow doors.

# Cruisers

The definition of a cruiser has always been difficult, varying according to fashion and almost from decade to decade. The cruiser as we know it began as the frigate of the 18th and 19th centuries, first sail-driven and then steam-powered. Its prime attribute was the ability to operate independently of the main fleet, either protecting friendly commerce or "cruizing" to attack enemy shipping.

Not until the mid-1880s did design stabilise, and then two main types emerged, one intended to protect commerce on the high seas and a series of smaller ships intended to scout for the main fleet. They also divided into "armoured" cruisers, clad with vertical armour, and "protected" cruisers carrying horizontal armour only. The complex grading system of further dividing protected cruisers into three classes had been all but abolished by 1914 and replaced by the term "light" cruiser. A complication was the battlecruiser, originally conceived by the fertile brain of Lord Fisher as a turbine-driven successor to the armoured cruiser but rapidly (and prematurely) upgraded to the status of a fast battleship.

The experience of the First World War showed that armoured cruisers had outlived their usefulness, but the light cruiser proved extremely battleworthy. Nevertheless, after the war there was a return to the big, well armed but under-armoured cruiser. This came about because the United States and Japan needed cruisers with good endurance and long-range armament (8in guns) for the Pacific, and so the Washington Treaty of 1922 fixed the limit at 10,000 tons and 8in guns. Inevitably the world's navies rapidly built up to the limits allowed, although the Europeans continued to press for smaller cruisers armed with 6in guns. Successive treaties got the limit for light cruisers down to 8,000 tons, but it was all to little avail in the face of the Axis powers' determination to pursue policies of military expansion.

Although the limitations of the pre-war treaties have long since been discarded, the artificial distinction between "heavy" cruisers with 8in guns and "light" cruisers with 6in guns persisted as long as gun-armed cruisers remained in service. A new category introduced in the late 1930s was the anti-aircraft cruiser, generally smaller and armed with guns of less than 6in calibre.

For a while after the Second World War it looked as if the cruiser might follow the battleship into oblivion, but during the Korean War both types showed that gunfire was a cheaper and more effective means of coastal bombardment than air strikes. Another attractive feature of the cruiser was that it was cheaper to run than a capital ship while having the space for command facilities, and several cruisers survived into the 1960s as flagships.

The growing threat from the air and the availability of guided missiles from the mid-1950s led to the conversion of several cruisers so that they could fire guided weapons. The missiles were purely for fleet defence at first, and only cruisers were big enough to carry first-generation missiles such as Terrier. In 1960, however, the Soviet Navy laid down the first of a new type of "rocket cruiser," known subsequently to Nato as the Kynda class, with a main armament of surface-to-surface missiles.

Although a few Western cruiser hulls left over from the 1939-45 construction programmes were completed to modern designs, it was generally assumed that no new cruisers would be built. But in 1957 the US Navy laid down a 14,000-ton nuclear-powered missile ship, the *Long Beach*, and rated her as a guided-missile cruiser (CGN). At about the same time a series of smaller ships was built, and these were rated first as destroyer leaders (DL) and then as frigates (retaining the DL designation). The building of missile-armed versions in this category produced the DLG and the nuclear-powered DLGN, but in mid-1975 the bigger ships in this category were reclassified as cruisers. These included the nuclear-powered *Bainbridge* and *Truxtun*, the steam-driven *Belknap* and *Leahy*, and subsequent nuclear ships.

Thanks to the lead given by the US Navy the word "cruiser" has returned to use, and although the DLG equivalents in other navies such as the British and French either retain the designation or call themselves *frégates*, they are unofficially regarded as cruisers. Similarly, although the Soviet Navy groups its ships under the blanket designation *Bolshoi Protivo Lodochny Korabl* (large anti-submarine ships), they are generally referred to in both Russian and Western sources as cruisers.

One school of thought maintains that the existence of big destroyers based on the *Spruance* design (DDG-47) makes the cruiser redundant. This would seem to be a premature judgment, for the essential qualities of the modern cruiser are her combination of long endurance and comprehensive array of offensive and defensive weapons. A destroyer is by definition a less capable ship, and perhaps it is the DDG-47 which should be reclassified as a light cruiser.

## *California* and *Virginia* classes

| Name | Number | Laid down | Launched | Completed | Builder |
|---|---|---|---|---|---|
| ***California*** | CGN-36 | 23 Jan 1970 | 22 Sep 1971 | 16 Feb 1974 | Newport News SB & DD Co |
| ***South Carolina*** | CGN-37 | 1 Dec 1970 | 1 Jul 1972 | 25 Jan 1975 | Newport News SB & DD Co |
| ***Virginia*** | CGN-38 | 19 Aug 1972 | 14 Dec 1974 | 11 Sep 1976 | Newport News SB & DD Co |
| ***Texas*** | CGN-39 | 18 Aug 1973 | 9 Aug 1975 | 10 Sep 1977 | Newport News SB & DD Co |
| ***Mississippi*** | CGN-40 | 22 Feb 1975 | 31 Jul 1976 | 5 Aug 1978 | Newport News SB & DD Co |
| ***Arkansas*** | CGN-41 | 17 Jan 1977 | 26 Aug 1978 | 1980 | Newport News SB & DD Co |

**Displacement** (*California*) 11,100 tons (full load)
(*Virginia*) 10,000 tons (full load)
**Dimensions** (C) 181.7m (oa) × 18.6m × 9.6m (596ft (oa) × 61ft × 31.5ft)
(V) 177.3m (oa) × 18.9m × 9.0m (585ft (oa) × 63ft × 29.5ft)
**Propulsion** 2 shafts, geared steam turbines, 2 pressurised water-cooled D2G nuclear reactors; 60,000 shp = 30+ knots
**Aircraft** (C) Pad for helicopter
(V) 2 helicopters, hangar under quarterdeck pad
**Armament** (C) 2 single Tartar-D SAM launchers (Standard MR Mk 13 Mod 3), 2 single 5in (127mm) 54-cal guns, 1 Asroc

The spare lines of modern warships are epitomised by the nuclear cruiser USS *Virginia* (CGN-38), her 585ft hull carrying only two twin missile launchers and two 5in guns. She is nonetheless one of the most powerful warships afloat.

8-tube ASM launcher, 4 × 12.7in (324mm) Mk 32 torpedo tubes
(V) 2 twin Tartar D/Asroc SAM/ASM launchers (Standard MR Mk 26), 2 single 5in (127mm) 54-cal guns, 2 triple 12.7in (324mm) Mk 32 torpedo tubes
**Complement** (C) 28 officers, 512 enlisted men
(V) 27 officers, 415 enlisted men

These two classes are treated together because they are so similar in conception and configuration. They form one of the most powerful groups of warships afloat, and represent the high-water mark of the US Navy's efforts to go all-nuclear.

In the early 1960s experience with the nuclear carrier *Enterprise* showed that the ability to steam at high speed for practically unlimited periods was of little use if the carrier's escorts could not keep up and had to be regularly refuelled. As early as Fiscal Year 1957 Congress had authorised the big nuclear cruiser *Long Beach*, followed by the "frigates" *Bainbridge* and *Truxtun*. But the enormous expense of nuclear propulsion was a stumbling block, even if the advantage of cheaper maintenance was taken into account. But nuclear propulsion returned to favour, and when the carrier *Nimitz* was ordered in 1967 she was followed by two nuclear frigates (DLGN). Named *California* and *South Carolina*, they were reclassified as nuclear missile cruisers (CGN) shortly after commissioning. Burgeoning costs led to the cancellation of a third ship authorised in FY 1968.

The design is a development of the *Truxtun*, but with a flush deck built up to provide a helicopter landing pad. In place of the earlier ship's low superstructure and lattice masts the *California*s were given two pyramidal towers to support their multiplicity of radar and ECM arrays. Their armament appears insignificant by comparison: two small Mk 45 5in gun mountings, an Asroc "pepperbox" A/S missile launcher, and two single-arm Mk 13 Tartar/Standard SAM launchers.

Appearances are deceptive, however, and the effectiveness of such ships lies in their ability to co-ordinate the weapons with the information provided by sensors. The Naval Tactical Data System (NTDS) co-ordinates raw data from the sonar, surface radars and air-warning radars and can also cope with data from other ships passed through a data link. After processing the information is displayed to allow the commander to use his guns and missiles to the best advantage.

The decision to order two more *Nimitz*-class carriers led to orders for a further class of four CGNs in FYs 1970, 1971, 1972 and 1975. These emerged as the *Virginia* class, a modification of the *California* design. They have the same basic configuration but could be described as a "cleaned up" version, with the new twin Mk 26 missile launcher, capable of firing both Asroc and Standard missiles, and a helicopter hangar under the stern. The US Navy has now been reconvinced of the value of small shipborne helicopters for anti-submarine work, and there is ample space for a hangar in such large ships.

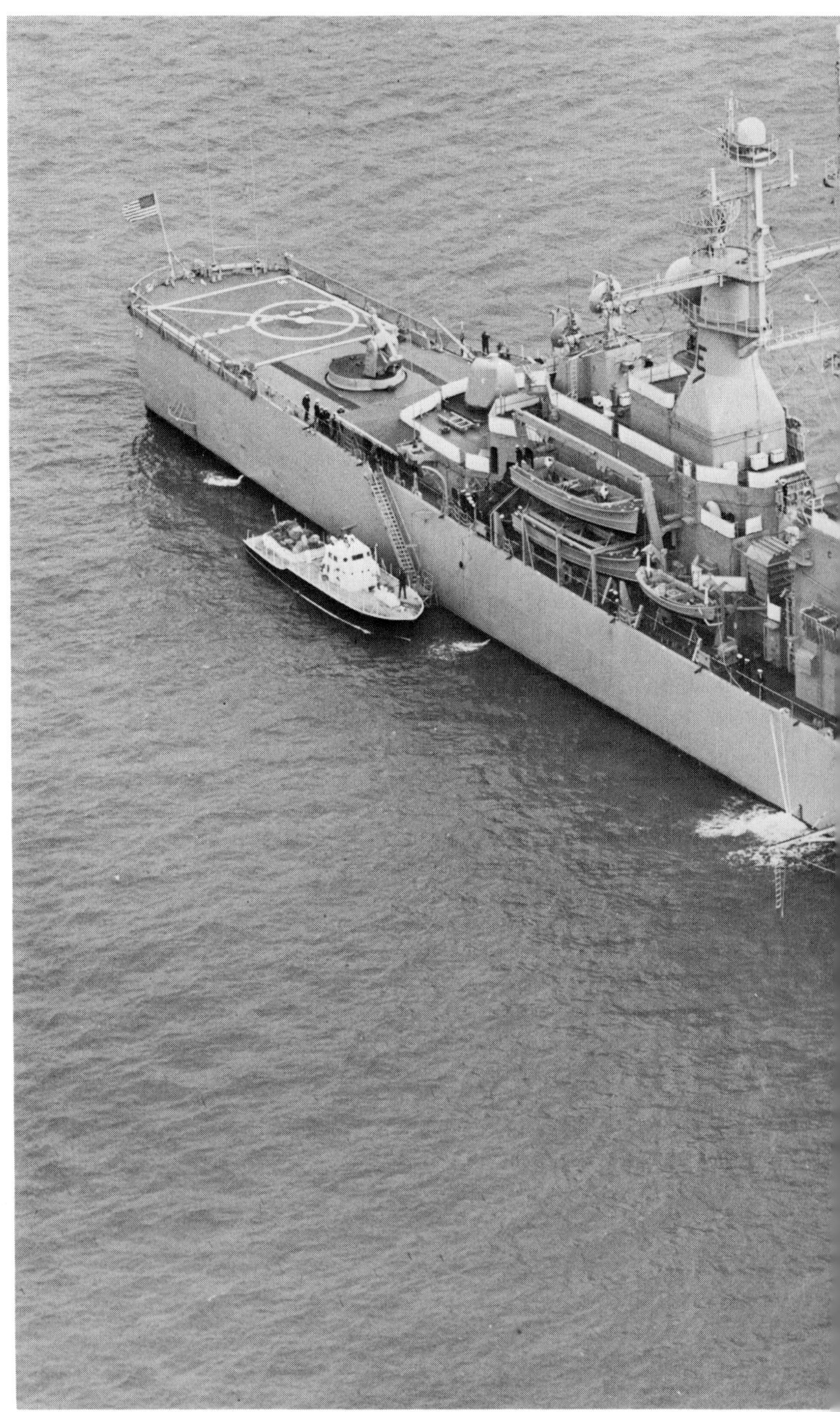

The NTDS is an improved version of that in the earlier CGNs, with more centralisation and integration to permit more rapid evaluation of threats.

As with the nuclear submarines, the building of these ships has been affected by long delays, cost overruns and squabbles between the Department of Defence and the shipyard. A fifth ship of the *Virginia* class (CGN-42) was not approved in FY 1976, but for FY 1980 the same hull number has been allocated to an "Improved *Virginia*" equipped with the Aegis fleet defence system. This is a very-high-performance planar-array radar backed up by the new Standard Extended Range (ER) missile, and it promises to provide greatly improved defence against aircraft and missiles.

The USS *California* (CGN-36) has the characteristics of a design slightly older than the *Virginia*: a separate Asroc ASW missile system forward of the bridge in place of the dual-purpose Mk 26 launcher, and no helicopter hangar under the quarterdeck. In other respects they have very similar capabilities.

# Long Beach

| Name | Number | Laid down | Launched | Completed | Builder |
|---|---|---|---|---|---|
| ***Long Beach*** | CGN-9 | 2 Dec 1957 | 14 Jul 1959 | 9 Sep 1961 | Bethlehem Steel Co, Quincy, Mass |

The world's first nuclear-powered cruiser, the USS *Long Beach* is now rather dated, and as she has not received a full mid-life modernisation she is less effective than some smaller ships. The "billboard" planar radars around the square bridge are unmistakable recognition features.

**Displacement** 14,200 tons (standard), 17,100 tons (full load)
**Dimensions** 219.8m (oa) × 22.3m × 9.5m (721.2ft (oa) × 73.2ft × 31ft)
**Propulsion** 2 shafts, geared steam turbines, 2 pressurised water-cooled C1W nuclear reactors; approx 80,000 shp = 30 knots
**Protection** None
**Aircraft** Pad for helicopter
**Armament** 1 twin Talos SAM launcher, 2 twin Terrier Standard ER SAM launchers, 2 single 5in (127mm) 38-cal guns, 1 Asroc 8-tube ASM launcher, 2 triple 12.7in (324mm) Mk 32 torpedo tubes
**Complement** 79 officers, 1,081 enlisted men

This ship was the first cruiser to be built for the US Navy after the Second World War, the first ship with an all-missile armament and, most important of all, the first nuclear-powered surface warship. As such she suffers from the comparative lack of nuclear sophistication in the mid-1950s and from the prevailing uncertainty about which direction to follow.

The design is somewhat extravagant, having started as a 7,800-ton frigate and grown to nearly double the displacement to allow for such luxuries as the Regulus II cruise missile (later cancelled), a Talos long-range SAM system, and even eight Polaris SLBM launch tubes (space was allocated but not taken up). A contemporary of the *Enterprise*, she was given similar "billboard" fixed radar arrays around her block superstructure and was the only other ship to have such antennas.

The ship is now past her mid-life point, and although scheduled for modernisation she is not regarded as worthy of a full rebuild. This means that she will get Harpoon SSMs in place of the cumbersome Talos SAMs, and Mk 26 Asroc/Standard twin launchers in place of the separate Terrier and Asroc launchers, but will not get the Aegis fleet defence system. Even so, the three-year conversion will cost an estimated $267 million. The main drawbacks to this otherwise successful ship are the short core life of the C1W pressurised-water reactors, compared with the D2G type in later CGNs, and the fact that she needs 1,160 men to run her, against 540 for the *California*.

# *Albany* class

| Name | Number | Laid down | Launched | Completed | Builder |
|---|---|---|---|---|---|
| *Albany* | CG-10 | 6 Mar 1944 | 30 Jun 1945 | 15 Jun 1946 | Bethlehem Steel Co Fore River |
| *Chicago* | CG-11 | 28 Jul 1943 | 20 Aug 1944 | 10 Jan 1945 | Philadelphia Navy Yard |

**Displacement** 13,700 tons (standard), 18,000 (full load)
**Dimensions** 205.4m (oa) × 21.6m × 9.1m (674ft (oa) × 70ft × 30ft)
**Propulsion** 4 shafts, geared steam turbines, 4 boilers; 120,000 shp = 32 knots
**Protection** ?6in (152mm) side, ?3in (76mm) deck
**Aircraft** Pad for helicopter
**Armament** 2 twin Talos SAM launchers, 2 twin Tartar SAM launchers, 2 single 5in (127mm) 38-cal guns, 1 Asroc 8-tube ASM launcher, 2 triple 12.7in (324mm) torpedo tubes
**Complement** 72 officers, 1,150 enlisted men

In the mid-1950s the heavy cruisers *Boston* and *Canberra* were converted into the world's first missile cruisers, with Terrier SAMs in place of the after 8in turret. Following this successful conversion six of the *Cleveland*-class light cruisers were similarly converted. Although a further series of from-the-keel-up cruisers was planned, commencing with the *Long Beach* in 1957, it was clear that more interim ships would be needed.

To bridge the gap and to provide more thorough conversions, three heavy cruisers of the *Baltimore* and *Oregon City* classes were earmarked for a full conversion, with a "double-ended" missile armament and new superstructure. The ships chosen were the *Albany*, *Chicago* and *Fall River*; the *Columbus* subsequently replaced the *Fall River*. The three ships were completely stripped, and as they had identical hulls and machinery the original differences in appearance virtually disappeared.

The conversions took from 1959 to 1964, and the ships were given twin Talos long-range SAM launchers forward and aft, and twin Tartar medium-range SAM launchers on either side of the bridge. A huge aluminium bridge and two tall "macks", combining funnels and masts into one, were added. Although this was a compact arrangement it caused more trouble than it was worth; the mixture of hot gases and cold air caused distortion of radar aerials and fixtures near the smoke pipe on the rear face of the mack.

The "Tall Ladies" have given sterling service, but their hulls are now well over 30 years old. The *Columbus* (CG-12) was decommissioned in 1975 and stricken the following year. The other two will not remain in service much longer, and their Talos systems are being cannibalised for other ships.

The class should be seen as an attempt to produce the qualities of the *Long Beach* by conversion rather than new building. Although an effective interim measure, this programme undoubtedly worked out far more expensive than expected. Many of the features of the *Long Beach* design were duplicated in these ships; for example, there was provision for eight Polaris missiles and Regulus II, and after completion a pair of single 5in DP guns had to be added to provide for gunfire support.

The USS *Albany* (CG-10) bears no resemblance to the heavy cruiser she once was. The lofty "macks" (combined mast/funnels) earned the class the nickname the "Tall Ladies". Note the single 5in gun mounted at the base of the after mack, installed for gunfire-support purposes during the Vietnam War.

## *Des Moines* class

| Name | Number | Laid down | Launched | Completed | Builder |
|---|---|---|---|---|---|
| ***Des Moines*** | CA-134 | 28 May 1945 | 27 Sep 1946 | 16 Nov 1948 | Bethlehem Steel Co, Fore River |
| ***Salem*** | CA-139 | 4 Jul 1945 | 25 March 1947 | 14 May 1949 | Bethlehem Steel Co, Fore River |
| ***Newport News*** | CA-148 | 1 Oct 1945 | 6 Mar 1947 | 29 Jan 1949 | Newport News SB & DD Co |

**Displacement** 17,000 tons (standard), 21, 470 (full load)
**Dimensions** 218.4m (oa) × 23.3m × 7.9m (716.5ft (oa) × 76.3ft × 26ft)
**Propulsion** 4 shafts, geared steam turbines, 4 boilers; 120,000 shp = 33 knots
**Protection** 8in (203mm) side, 5in (127mm) deck
**Armament** 3 triple 8in (203mm) guns, 6 twin 5in (127mm) 38-cal guns, 10 twin 3in (76mm) 50-cal guns
(*Newport News*) 2 triple 8in (203mm) guns, 6 twin 5in (127mm) 38-cal guns, 1 twin 3in (76mm) 50-cal guns
**Complement** 115 officers, 1,623 enlisted men

These ships represent the ultimate development of the gun-armed cruiser of the Second World War. They were a

logical expansion of the *Baltimore* and *Oregon City* classes, with a much more effective anti-aircraft battery and a rapid-firing 8in gun using "fixed" ammunition with metal cartridge cases. In their latter days their spacious accommodation found them employment as flagships, and her 8in guns made the *Newport News* exceptionally useful for gunfire support during the Vietnam War.

All three served as flagships in their heyday, but they required very large crews. *Salem* decommissioned in 1959 and *Des Moines* followed her in 1961. The *Newport News* served for many years as flagship of the Second Fleet in the Atlantic and underwent a number of modifications, including the addition of deckhouses amidships for extra accommodation and the installation of new communications equipment.

While on the "gun line" off Vietnam in October 1972 *Newport News* suffered a premature shell detonation in the centre barrel of No 2 turret. The gun was destroyed and the turret was wrecked, but because of the age of the ship the mounting was never repaired. The Mk 16 8in/55-cal gun fired 10 rounds a minute, and at 41° elevation could range to 14 miles with conventional shells. During the Vietnam War Rocket-Assisted Projectiles (RAP) achieved ranges of up to 35 miles. *Des Moines* and *Salem* are now laid up at Philadelphia, while *Newport News* was deleted in 1978. With the passing of the battleship *Des Moines* and *Salem* are the most powerful gun-armed ships in the world.

A more traditional cruiser profile: the USS *Newport News* at Portsmouth, UK. The centre 8in gun is missing from "B" turret, having been removed after it was wrecked by a premature detonation during the Vietnam War. In their day she and her sisters were the most powerful cruisers ever built.

# *Tiger* class

| Name | Number | Laid down | Launched | Completed | Builder |
|---|---|---|---|---|---|
| ***Tiger*** | C 20 | 1 Oct 1941 | 25 Oct 1945 | 18 Mar 1959 | John Brown, Clydeside |
| ***Blake*** | C 99 | 17 Aug 1942 | 20 Dec 1945 | 8 Mar 1961 | Fairfield SB & E Co, Govan |

**Displacement** 9,500 tons (standard), 12,080 tons (full load)
**Dimensions** 172.8m (oa) × 19.5m × 7.0m (566.5ft (oa) × 64ft × 23ft)
**Propulsion** 4 shafts, geared steam turbines, 4 boilers; 80,000 shp = 30 knots
**Protection** 3.2-3.5in (83-89mm) side, 2in (51mm) deck
**Aircraft** 4 Sea King A/S helicopters
**Armament** 2 quad Seacat SAM launchers, 1 twin 6in (152mm) guns, 1 twin 3in (76mm) guns
**Complement** 85 officers, 800 men

The successful *Fiji* or "Colony" class, modified with greater beam to offset topweight, was selected for production during the Second World War, but only the *Swiftsure*, *Minotaur* and *Superb* had been completed by 1945. Most of the programme were cancelled, leaving three hulls incomplete. It was decided to complete them to a different design, using the advanced Mk 26 twin 6in dual-purpose mounting originally developed for a 15,000-ton design known as the *Minotaur* class, and a rapid-firing 3in/70-cal Mk 6 anti-aircraft gun.

The need to adapt these weighty mountings and their fire control to the much smaller *Bellerophon* hull (nearly 100ft shorter and 13ft narrower) meant that only two 6in mountings and three 3in could be squeezed in. However, each mounting was given its own MRS.3 fire-control system, allowing simultaneous engagement of five targets at all angles. Authority to start the conversion was announced in 1954 but the three ships did not appear until 1959-61.

The design was somewhat dated, although the automatic 6in and 3in guns

◀ HMS *Tiger* and her sister *Blake* started life with twin 6in guns aft as well as forward, and twin 3in guns amidships. In 1965–72 a large hangar and flight deck were installed aft, permitting these ships to operate four Sea King helicopters but without sacrificing their command and gunfire support facilities.

▲ HMS *Blake* completed in 1969 with shorter funnels than the *Tiger*; *Blake*'s funnels were lengthened in 1977. This view shows how ungainly the hangar and flight deck appear, marring what was once a handsome design. The conversion provided valuable experience in ASW, however, and made the class more flexible.

were formidable weapons. To extend the role of the ships they were altered to "helicopter command cruisers," each with her after 6in turret replaced by a hangar and flight deck for four Sea King ASW helicopters. *Blake* was converted between 1965 and 1969, and *Tiger* followed in 1968-72, But the cost was so high that *Lion* was laid up unconverted and finally scrapped in 1965.

The two survivors are good flagships for the new task groups based on the nuclear hunter-killer submarines, with first-class communications and a good anti-submarine capability by virtue of their helicopters. They also form good bargaining counters with the Treasury, and could be traded off against the *Invincible*-class carriers, which will perform all of their functions and a few more besides. In any case, they make great demands on skilled manpower and would have to be paid off to provide crews for the carriers.

The conversion involved the provision of a hangar at the old "X" turret level and a wide flight deck built over the old quarterdeck. The midships 3in turrets were replaced by quadruple Seacat SAMs to offset the topweight, with the result that two different calibres of gun are mounted forward. As completed, *Blake* differed from *Tiger* in having shorter funnels with the original clinker screens; *Tiger* was given taller funnels with different caps and in 1977 *Blake* was similarly modified so that fumes would be carried clear of the radar arrays on the mainmast.

These ships are the last traditional cruisers in the RN, and although they now seem to be white elephants they have rendered useful service. The original design gave rise to one of the most ingenious and cost-effective cruisers of the Second World War.

# Colbert

| Name | Number | Laid down | Launched | Completed | Builder |
|---|---|---|---|---|---|
| *Colbert* | C 611 | Dec 1953 | 24 Mar 1956 | 5 May 1959 | Brest Dockyard |

**Displacement** 8,500 tons (standard), 11,300 tons (full load)
**Dimensions** 180.8m (oa) × 20.2m × 7.7m (593.2ft (oa) × 66.1ft × 25.2ft)
**Propulsion** 2 shafts, geared steam turbines, 4 boilers; 86,000 shp = 31.5 knots
**Protection** 2-3.1in (50-80mm) side, 2in (50mm) deck
**Armament** 1 twin Masurca SAM launcher, 2 single 3.9in (100mm) guns, 6 twin 57mm guns
**Complement** 24 officers, 536 men

This ship was ordered in 1953 as an improved *de Grasse* type, with a smaller layout of light anti-aircraft guns but a different internal arrangment of machinery and protection. As completed, the *Colbert* had a heavy AA battery of eight twin 5in DP guns and ten twin 57mm Bofors guns, plus accommodation for 2,400 men and equipment. Although she retained the single funnel of the *de Grasse* her turbines and boilers were divided on the unit system into two engine rooms separated by an 18m watertight bulkhead.

Between 1970 and 1972 she was converted into a missile cruiser, with a twin Masurca medium-range SAM launcher aft, new radars and fire control, and 100mm DP guns in place of the 5in (127mm) weapons. Plans to install four MM.38 Exocet SSMs were dropped, and four of the twin 57mm mountings were removed. Data are handled by the SENIT action-data information system, which is based on the American NTDS.

With the passing of the *de Grasse* the *Colbert* is the last big cruiser in the French Navy. As such she is a very useful command ship and is likely to remain in service for some years.

In 1970–72 the *Colbert* lost her after guns to make way for a twin Masurca SAM system, two directors and a long-range surveillance radar. The original 5in guns were replaced by 100mm (3.9in) units and the other radars were modernised at the same time.

## Kresta II and Kara classes

**Displacement** (Kresta II) 6,000 tons (standard), 7,500 tons (full load) (Kara) 8,200 tons (standard), 10,000 tons (full load)
**Dimensions** (K II) 158.5m (oa) × 16.8m × 6.0m (519.9ft (oa) × 55.ft × 19.7ft)
(K) 173.8m (oa) × 18.3m × 6.2m (570ft (oa) × 60ft × 20ft)
**Propulsion** (K II) 2 shafts, geared steam turbines, 4 boilers; 100,000 shp = 35 knots
(K) 2 shafts, geared gas turbines; 120,000 shp = approx 34 knots
**Aircraft** 1 Hormone-A or B A/S helicopter
**Armament** (K II) 2 twin SA-N-3 SAM launchers, 2 twin 57mm guns, 4 Gatling-type ?30mm guns, 2 quad SS-N-13 ASM launchers, 2 × 12-barrel MBU-2500A A/S rocket launchers, 2 × 6-barrel MBU-4500A A/S rocket launchers, 2 quint 21in (533mm) torpedo tubes
(K) 2 twin SA-N-3 SAM launchers, 2 twin SA-N-4 SAM launchers, 2 twin 76mm guns, 4 Gatling-type ?30mm guns, 2 quad SS-N-14 ASM launchers, 2 × 12-barrel MBU-2500A A/S rocket launchers, 2 × 6-barrel MBU-4500A A/S rocket launchers, 2 quint 21in (533mm) torpedo tubes
**Complement** (K II) Approx 500 officers and men
(K) Approx 500 officers and men

| **Kresta II** | **Commissioned** |
|---|---|
| *Kronstadt* | 1970 |
| *Admiral Isakov* | 1971 |
| *Admiral Nakhimov* | 1972 |
| *Admiral Makarov* | 1973 |
| *Marshal Voroshilov* | 1973 |
| *Admiral Oktyabrsky* | 1974 |
| *Admiral Isachenkov* | 1975 |
| *Marshal Timoshenko* | 1976 |
| *Vasiliy Chapaev* | 1977 |
| *Admiral Yumaschev* | 1978 |

| **Kara** | **Commissioned** |
|---|---|
| *Nikolaiev* | 1973 |
| *Ochakov* | 1974 |
| *Kerch* | 1975 |
| *Azov* | 1976 |
| *Petropavlovsk* | 1977 |
| *Tashkent* | 1978 |
| *Tallin* | 1979 |

▶ The Kresta II missile cruiser *Admiral Isachenkov* north of the Hebrides. She has SAMs forward and aft, stand-off anti-submarine missiles abreast of the bridge, torpedoes just abaft the funnel and a helicopter hangar aft. Soviet radar antennas are massive and complex by comparison with Western arrays.

▼ Another of the class, the *Admiral Makarov*, shadowing HMS *Ark Royal* during a Nato exercise in 1978. This view clearly shows the rakish profile and the SS-N-14 anti-submarine missiles. The heavily raked bow keeps the anchors clear of the bow sonar.

These two classes permit an interesting comparison of two successive Soviet missile-cruiser designs. The 6,000-ton Kresta IIs (possibly known to the Russians as the *Kronstadt* class) were built as large anti-submarine ships (*Bolshoi Protivo Lodochny Korabl*) and ten have appeared since 1970. The bigger Kara class (possibly the *Nikolaiev* class) appeared about three years later, in 1973.

Now that the SS-N-14 has been identified as a long-range anti-submarine weapon rather than a 300-mile range cruise missile, there is less scepticism about the Russian designation. What is interesting, however, is the fact that neither class incorporates any reload gear for the eight launch tubes housed abreast of the forward superstructure. This suggests that topweight problems were encountered with Kresta I. The extra size of the Kara permits the mounting of twin 76mm guns amidships, but in other respects this class is similar to Kresta II, apart from having gas-turbine propulsion instead of steam.

As in other Soviet designs, no space is left uncluttered and these ships carry five separate missile systems, to say nothing of guns, torpedoes, depth-charge projectors and ASW rockets. This looks very impressive but must make tremendous space demands, adversely affecting habitability and computer processing capacity. Another feature whch strikes Western observers as a retrograde step is the tiny wheelhouse, much of which is already taken up by the supports for the Head Light radar array for the SA-N-3 area-defence missiles. Another quaint feature is the half-sunken helicopter hangar aft, which must be one of the most inconvenient arrangements afloat.

At the time of writing (1979) 10 Kresta IIs are reported to have been built at the Zhdanov yard, Leningrad, since 1968, with possibly one more fitting out. Seven Karas have been seen since 1973 and there are reports of three more building at Nikolaiev on the Black Sea. *Petropavlovsk*, *Tashkent* and *Azov* are reported to have a new surface-to-air missile system.

▶ The *Kara* class can be distinguished from the Kresta IIs from ahead or astern by reference to the prominent Owl Screech directors controlling the 76mm guns amidships. Both classes sport the massive Top Sail 3-D radar, necessary to give a complete air-defence plot.

▼ The *Kerch* shows clearly how the somewhat cluttered superstructure of the Kresta I and II has been cleaned up. A big funnel is needed to vent the heat from her gas turbines, and so the Top Sail 3-D radar has been moved to a separate tower. The extra length also allows a pair of twin 76mm guns to be fitted in.

539

## *Sverdlov* class

**Displacement** 16,000 tons (standard), 18,000 tons (full load)
**Dimensions** 210.0m (oa) × 22.0m × 7.5m (689ft (oa) × 72.2ft × 24.5ft)
**Propulsion** 2 shafts, geared steam turbines, 6 boilers; 110,000 shp = 30 knots
**Protection** 3.9-4.9in (100-125mm) side, 2-3in (50-75mm) deck
**Aircraft** (*Zhdanov*) Helicopter pad (*Senyavin*) Helicopter hangar and pad
**Armament** 4 triple 6in (152mm) guns, 6 twin 3.9in (100mm) guns, 8 twin 37mm guns, 150 mines
(Z) 1 twin SA-N-4 SAM launcher, 3 triple 6in (152mm) guns, 6 twin 3.9in (100mm) guns, 4 twin 30mm guns
(S) 1 twin SA-N-4 SAM launcher, 2 triple 6in (152mm) guns, 6 twin 3.9in (100mm) guns, 8 twin 30mm guns
(*Dzerzhinski*) 1 twin SA-N-2 SAM launcher, 3 triple 6in (152mm) guns, 6 twin 3.9in (100mm) guns, 8 twin 37mm guns, 150 mines
**Complement** Approx 1,000 officers and men

*Admiral Lazarev*, *Admiral Senyavin*, *Admiral Ushakov*, *Aleksandr Nevski*, *Aleksandr Suvorov*, *Dmitri Pozharski*, *Dzerzhinski*, *Mikhail Kutusov*, *Murmansk*, *Oktyabrskaya Revolutsiya*, *Sverdlov* and *Zhdanov* built by Baltiski, Leningrad; Nikolaiev; and Komsomolsk from 1950 to 1958.

In their day this class of cruisers caused as much consternation as the *Kiev* and *Minsk* do today. When the *Sverdlov* appeared at Spithead in 1953 for the Royal Navy's Coronation Naval Review she was hailed as a wonder ship with some special secret method of manoeuvring.

The *Zhdanov* about to drop anchor at Messina in September 1976. The big double optical rangefinders on the director control tower are part of the original design but the lattice mast was added around 1972. The "horns" on the new mast are probably communications antennas.

◀ The *Sverdlov* in 1976, still unmodified apart from the big Knife Rest radar aft. Although the fire-control system is German in style, the layout and appearance clearly reflect pre-war Italian ideas, especially the *Zara* and *Bolzano* types. Note the minelaying chutes aft.

▼ Looking along the shelter deck of the *Dzerzhinski*, with twin 37mm AA guns in the foreground and the starboard secondary fire control and two 100mm turrets behind. In a modernisation programme "X" turret gave way to a SAM launcher, the blast screen of which can be seen over the 100mm turret roofs.

The fact that the ship looked exactly what she was, a big 6in-gunned cruiser developed from a pre-war Italian design, (the *Chapaev* class) was lost on everybody. Her armament of four triple 15cm guns controlled by ex-German optical rangefinders was obsolescent, as was the concept of using cruisers on the trade routes. The RN even designed a 38-knot "*Sverdlov*-killing" destroyer armed with rapid-firing 5in guns, a lunatic project which was fortunately strangled in its cradle by Lord Mountbatten, the new First Sea Lord. Although Soviet leader Nikita Khrushchev was undoubtedly premature in declaring them fit for the scrapheap, in the long run his cutback of this cruiser programme probably helped Admiral Gorshkov's plans for expansion rather than hindered them.

The original programme called for 24 ships, of which 20 were laid down before the Khrushchev "axe" in 1956; three of these were broken up on the slip and three more were scrapped incomplete. Twelve of the original 14 ships survive; *Ordzonikidze* became the Indonesian *Irian* in 1962 and was scrapped on her return in 1972, and *Admiral Nakhimov* was stricken in 1969.

Nine of the ships retain their full gun armament, the other three having undergone conversion. In 1972 *Admiral Senyavin* appeared after a refit minus "X" and "Y" turrets and fitted with a large helicopter hangar, four 30mm twin mountings and a twin SA-N-4 SAM launcher. Shortly afterwards the *Zhdanov* appeared with a slightly different arrangement: "X" turret was removed and replaced by a lower deckhouse and SA-N-4 launcher. *Dzerzhinski* has "X" turret replaced by a twin SA-N-2 launcher, and is rated by Western intelligence sources as the only CG, the others being command ships. It seems that the missile conversions were not an outstanding success, and some sources suggest that there are many problems in providing a stable platform for the flapping Fan Song radar used to control the SA-N-2 Guideline missile. The SA-N-4 system may well have been installed for trials; big ships make good experimental test beds as they have accommodation for the extra personnel involved.

The value of the remaining *Sverdlovs* is quite low, but presumably they are retained for training and, in the case of the *Senyavin* and *Zhdanov*, to act as flagships in the Pacific and Black Sea respectively.

## *Mysore* and *Capitan Quiñones* classes

| Name | Number | Laid down | Launched | Completed | Builder |
|---|---|---|---|---|---|
| ***Mysore*** (ex-***Nigeria***) | C 60 | 8 Feb 1938 | 18 Jul 1939 | 23 Sep 1940 | Vickers-Armstrong, Tyne |
| ***Capitan Quiñones*** (ex-***Almirante Grau***, ex-***Newfoundland***) | CL 83 | 9 Nov 1939 | 19 Dec 1941 | 31 Dec 1942 | Swan Hunter & Wigham Richardson Ltd, Wallsend |
| ***Coronel Bolognesi*** (ex-***Ceylon***) | CL 82 | 27 Apr 1939 | 30 Jul 1942 | 13 Jul 1943 | Alexander Stephen, Govan |

**Displacement** (*Mysore*) 8,700 tons (standard), 11,040 tons (full load); (*Capitan Quiñones*) 8,800 tons (standard), 11,090 tons (full load)
**Dimensions** (M) 169.3 (oa) × 18.9m × 6.4m (555.5ft (oa) × 62ft × 21ft) (CQ) 169.9m (oa) × 19.4m × 6.2m (555.5ft (oa) × 63.6ft × 20.5ft)
**Propulsion** 4 shafts, geared steam turbines, 4 boilers; 72,500 shp = 31.5 knots
**Protection** 3½in (89mm) side, 2in (51mm) deck
**Armament** 3 triple 6in (152mm) guns, 4 twin 4in (102mm) guns, 12-18 ×40mm guns
**Complement** Approx 750-800

These are the only survivors of the Royal Navy's *Fiji* or "Colony" class, ordered in 1938 as a new type of compact light cruiser with good protection and armament. As such they were highly successful and a total of 14 were built.

The outstanding features of the design were the economical distribution of armour and the transom stern, which not only saved weight but improved speed and manoeuvrability. Two ships, the *Fiji* and *Trinidad*, were sunk, the *Uganda* and *Minotaur* became the Canadian *Quebec* and *Ontario*, and the rest were sold or scrapped. In April 1954 HMS *Nigeria* was sold to India and three years later she commissioned as INS *Mysore*. In December 1959 the *Newfoundland* was acquired by Peru and became the *Almirante Grau*, and two months later she was joined by her sister, *Coronel Bolognesi* (ex-HMS *Ceylon*). The *Grau* was subsequently renamed *Capitan Quiñones* to release the name for another cruiser.

All three were modernised to about the same standard while still in RN hands, with lattice masts and Mk 6 anti-aircraft fire control. Although now elderly and expensive to run they provide good training facilities and have much prestige value as flagships. As they have seen comparatively little service in recent years – apart from the *Mysore*, which played an active part in the war between India and Pakistan – they are likely to last for some years unless the manpower problem becomes acute. The worst aspect of maintaining such ships is the number of skilled technicians, such as electrical specialists, which they absorb.

The Peruvian *Coronel Bolognesi* was completed in 1943 as HMS *Ceylon* and was transferred after modernisation. This included provision of an enclosed bridge, a uniform light AA armament of 40mm Bofors guns, and a lattice foremast. The upright funnels and masts were intended to complicate visual estimates of bearing.

# *General Belgrano* and *Capitan Prat* classes

| Name | Number | Laid down | Launched | Completed | Builder |
|---|---|---|---|---|---|
| ***General Belgrano*** (ex-***17 de Octobre***, ex-***Phoenix***) | C4 | 15 Apr 1935 | 12 Mar 1938 | 18 Mar 1939 | New York SB Co |
| ***Nueve de Julio*** (ex-***Boise***) | C5 | 1 Apr 1935 | 3 Dec 1936 | 1 Feb 1939 | Newport News SB & DD Co |
| ***Almirante O'Higgins*** | 02 | 12 Mar 1935 | 30 Nov 1936 | 18 Jul 1938 | New York Navy Yard |
| ***Capitan Prat*** (ex-***Nashville***) | 03 | 24 Jan 1935 | 2 Oct 1937 | 25 Nov 1938 | New York SB Co |

**Displacement** 10,000-10,800 tons (standard), 13,500-13,645 tons (full load) **Dimensions** 185.4m (oa) × 21.0m × 7.3m (608.3ft (oa) × 69ft × 24ft) **Propulsion** 4 shafts, geared steam turbines, 8 boilers; 100,000 shp = 32.5 knots **Protection** 1.5-4in (38-102mm) side, 2-3in (51-76mm) deck **Aircraft** (*General Belgrano*) 2 helicopters (*Capitan Prat*) 1 helicopter

**Armament** (GB) 2 quad Seacat SAM launchers, 5 triple 6in (152mm) guns, 8 single 5in (127mm) 25-cal guns, 2 twin 40mm guns
(*Nueve de Julio*) 5 triple 6in (152mm) guns, 8 single 5in (127mm) 25-cal guns, 4 twin 40mm guns
(CP) 5 triple 6in (152mm) guns, 8 single 5in (127mm) guns, 28 × 40mm guns, 24 × 20mm guns
**Complement** Approx 1,000 officers and men

When the Japanese *Mogami*-class light cruisers appeared in 1935 the US Navy was forced to build a reply. This took the form of the seven *Brooklyn*-class ships, each armed with 15 6in guns in a similar disposition.

The new ships incorporated several innovations. They had high freeboard and a flush deck so that two floatplanes and spares for another two could be accommodated under the "fantail" or quarterdeck. This proved not to be feasible, however, and in practice the two floatplanes were carried on the catapults at all times, leaving the hangar for use as a workshop. The fifth turret, sandwiched between No 2 and the bridgework, was badly placed, the open AA battery in the waist of the ship was weak, and during the war the *Brooklyn*s suffered from excess topweight. But they had a first-class fighting record and took part in many actions.

After the war they were surplus to US Navy requirements as so many *Cleveland*-class ships had been built, and so they were offered for sale. To avoid rivalry between the three major South American countries, in 1951 a special agreement was drawn up under which Argentina, Brazil and Chile each bought two cruisers at a cost of $7.8 million, representing 10 per cent of their original cost plus the expense of refitting them. Thus Argentina received the *Phoenix* and *Boise*, Brazil got the *Philadelphia* and her half-sister *St Louis*, and Chile had the *Brooklyn* and *Nashville*. The remaining two ships were scrapped in 1960. Since then both Brazilian ships have been scrapped, while the Chilean *Almirante O'Higgins* has been repaired after running aground. The remaining four are retained for their prestige value and for training, although they must make heavy demands on skilled manpower and the difficulties of obtaining spares must now be acute.

Although recently scrapped, the Brazilian *Tamandaré* gives a good impression of her surviving sisters in the Argentinian and Chilean navies. Note the long, flush forecastle deck, the boat crane aft (originally intended to serve catapults and a hangar under the quarterdeck) and the cramped position of the third 6in turret.

## *Almirante Grau* class

| Name | Number | Laid down | Launched | Completed | Builder |
|---|---|---|---|---|---|
| ***Almirante Grau*** (ex-***de Ruyter***) | CL81 | 5 Sep 1939 | 24 Dec 1944 | 18 Nov 1953 | Wilton-Fijenoord, Schiedam |
| ***Aguirre*** (ex-***de Zeven Provincien***) | CL84 | 19 May 1939 | 22 Aug 1950 | 17 Dec 1953 | Rotterdamse Droogdok Maatschippij |

**Displacement** 9,529 tons (standard), 11,850 tons (full load)
**Dimensions** 187.6m (oa) × 17.3m × 6.7m (609ft (oa) × 56.7ft × 22ft)
**Propulsion** 2 shafts, geared steam turbines, 4 boilers; 85,000 shp = 32 knots
**Protection** 3-4in (76-102mm) side
**Aircraft** (*Aguirre*) 4 helicopters
**Armament** (*Almirante Grau*) 4 twin 6in (152mm) guns, 4 twin 57mm guns, 4 twin 40mm guns
(*Aguirre*) 2 twin 6in (152mm) guns, 3 twin 57mm guns, 4 × 40mm guns
**Complement** (AG) 926 officers and men

Two cruisers were ordered for the Royal Netherlands Navy on 1937-38, to be named *de Zeven Provincien* and *Kijkduin* and to be armed with twin and triple 15cm (5.9in) guns supplied by Bofors AB. Little more than the keel-laying had taken place when the first German troops crossed the border, and there was no

time to destroy them. Work proceeded slowly on completion for the *Kriegsmarine*, although the main armament had never been delivered from Sweden. The two hulls escaped serious damage and fell into Allied hands late in 1944.

There was no point in finishing the two ships to the old design, and in any case the two triple and four twin turrets completed had been bought from Bofors by the Royal Swedish Navy to arm the *Tre Kronor* and *Gota Lejon*. The designer and his team asked for technical assistance from the Royal Navy in revising the design, and a totally new armament of four twin 6in and 57mm Bofors guns was bought. The original three-shaft machinery was replaced by two-shaft turbines in a unit arrangement, and the single short funnel was replaced by two widely spaced tall funnels.

Work began in 1947, and when the second ship was launched in 1950 she changed names with her sister, becoming *de Zeven Provincien* while her sister took the name of *de Ruyter* to commemorate a war loss. The two ships were completed in 1953 and subsequently saw extensive service under Nato command.

In the early 1960s there were plans to convert both ships to missile cruisers, using Terrier medium-range SAMs and fire control supplied from the United States. The cost meant that only one ship could be converted and *de Ruyter* remained unaltered; her sister emerged totally rebuilt in 1964. The *de Ruyter* was stricken in 1973 and sold to Peru the same year; she recommissioned as the *Almirante Grau* in March that year and sailed for Callao three months later.

In August 1975 *de Zeven Provincien* was also laid up as an economy measure, being expensive to man, and in August 1976 she was bought by Peru and renamed *Aguirre*. Under Nato and MDAP rules the missile gear remained the property of the United States, however, and so it had to be removed before the ship was handed over. The Peruvians have added a flight deck and hangar aft to accommodate three Sea King ASW helicopters.

The ships are easily distinguishable. The *Aguirre* has a large box hangar and a plated "mack" in place of her second funnel, while the forecastle deck has been extended aft to form a flight deck. Her sister remains as completed, with two tall funnels and lattice masts; she is reported to have been armed with four MM.38 Exocet SSMs but it is not known whether any gun mountings have been removed.

The *Almirante Grau* is practically unchanged since her days in the Royal Netherlands Navy. The original design was a total recasting of a pre-war layout. When completed in 1953 she and her sister had the mainmast stepped abaft the funnel, but ultimately the mast had to be shifted to avoid interference from smoke.

# Vittorio Veneto

| Name | Number | Laid down | Launched | Completed | Builder |
|---|---|---|---|---|---|
| *Vittorio Veneto* | C 550 | 10 Jun 1965 | 5 Feb 1967 | 12 Jul 1969 | Castellammare |

**Displacement** 7,500 tons (standard), 8,850 tons (full load)
**Dimensions** 179.6m (oa) × 19.4m × 6m (589ft (oa) × 63.6ft × 19.7ft)
**Propulsion** 2 shafts, geared steam turbines, 4 boilers; 73,000 shp = 32 knots
**Aircraft** 9 Agusta-Bell AB.204B A/S helicopters
**Armament** 1 combined twin Terrier/Asroc SAM/ASM launcher, 8 single 3in (76mm) guns, 2 triple 12.7in (324mm) Mk 32 torpedo tubes
**Complement** 60 officers, 500 men

Following the introduction of the *Andrea Doria*-class missile cruisers the Italian Navy decided to develop the type into a hybrid missile-armed helicopter cruiser. The design was recast several times after she was authorised under the 1959-60 New Construction Programme, and it was another six years before the keel of the *Vittorio Veneto* was laid.

As with other Italian designs there is a great deal of ingenious weight-saving, aided by the reduced requirements for habitability and range for Mediterranean operations. For example, she carries a twin Terrier/Asroc launcher forward, an Italian innovation later introduced into the USN as the Mk 26 launcher, and eight lightweight 76mm guns. The lack of individual directors for four of the guns is a weakness, however.

The ship has embarked nine AB.204B ASW helicopters, soon to be replaced with the latest AB.212ASW anti-submarine and strike helicopter. *Vittorio Veneto* has proved successful, although several proposals for a larger ship

▲ The Italian helicopter cruiser *Vittorio Veneto* has a unique silhouette, with freeboard raised amidships. Apart from her Terrier/Asroc missile launcher forward, she relies solely on single 76mm guns for defence. Each pair of mountings has its own Orion radar-controlled director.

capable of operating Sea Kings have been made. These have at last culminated in the *Giuseppe Garibaldi*, which is to replace the *Andrea Doria* in the late 1980s. Until then the *Vittorio Veneto* will presumably continue to serve as fleet flagship.

Critics of the ship say that she is a large and expensive platform for a single SAM system and a few light helicopters. She is a classic example of a lot being attempted on a small hull, and must be rated as a qualified success which just missed being much better.

◀ This view of the *Vittorio Veneto* gives some impression of her beaminess, which was built in primarily to provide a stable platform for helicopter operations. The Terrier fire control and guidance are standard US Navy equipment but the Italians took the lead in designing a dual Asroc/Terrier loading system.

## *Andrea Doria* class

| Name | Number | Laid down | Launched | Completed | Builder |
|---|---|---|---|---|---|
| *Andrea Doria* | C 553 | 11 May 1958 | 27 Feb 1963 | 23 Feb 1964 | Cantieri del Tirreno |
| *Caio Duilio* | C 554 | 16 May 1958 | 22 Dec 1962 | 30 Nov 1964 | Castellammare |

**Displacement** 5,000 tons (standard), 6,500 tons (full load)
**Dimensions** 149.3m (oa) × 17.2m × 5.0m (489.8ft (oa) × 56.4ft × 16.4ft)
**Propulsion** 2 shafts, geared steam turbines, 4 boilers; 60,000 shp = 31 knots
**Aircraft** 4 Agusta-Bell AB.204B A/S helicopters
**Armament** 1 twin Terrier SAM launcher, 8 single 3in (76mm) guns, 2 triple 12.7in (324mm) Mk 32 torpedo tubes
**Complement** 45 officers, 440 men

In 1958 the Italians yet again broke new ground by ordering two of a new type of "escort cruiser". In reality they were missile-armed large destroyers with a helicopter deck aft, but they showed the way to other navies and the type is now common.

The layout is straightforward, with a twin Terrier SAM launcher and two fire-control systems forward, single 76mm guns in the waist at two levels, and a broad flight deck and hangar aft. Four light helicopters are carried, currently the Agusta-Bell AB.204B but soon to be the new AB.212ASW.

*Andrea Doria* and her sister, *Caio Duilio*, entered service in 1964, when the Italian Navy was expanding to meet its Nato commitments. Since then they have been superseded by the bigger *Vittorio Veneto*, probably a more cost-effective ship. Their cramped hangars have proved too small for efficient helicopter operations, and although the *Andrea Doria* handled the Harrier V/Stol aircraft in a series of trials in 1969 she could not operate such an aircraft. Another drawback is the weak anti-ship armament, which could only be rectified by replacing the Terriers with Standard (MR) missiles, which have a limited surface-to-surface capability.

Both ships are to be replaced by the sea-control ship *Giuseppe Garibaldi* in the late 1980s, by which time they will be near the end of their hull lives. They demonstrate both the virtues and vices of a compact design, as any major improvement to their capabilities would be very expensive.

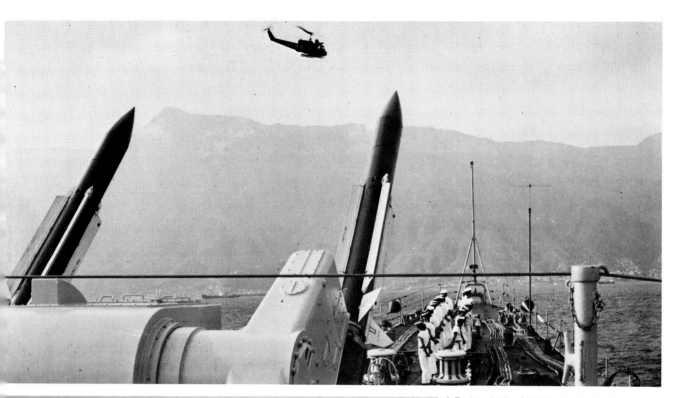

▲ Terrier missiles frame the *Andrea Doria*'s Agusta-Bell AB.204B helicopter. She and her sister introduced the idea of a small missile cruiser with anti-submarine helicopters some years before other navies took up the concept. It is thus not surprising that they are only a qualified success.

◀ The *Caio Duilio* has the same gun armament and Orion radar-controlled directors as the bigger *Vittorio Veneto* but lacks Asroc anti-submarine missiles. The two separate funnels seen in this view took up a large amount of deck space and were replaced with macks in the later ship.

# *Bainbridge* and *Truxtun*

| Name | Number | Laid down | Launched | Completed | Builder |
|---|---|---|---|---|---|
| ***Bainbridge*** | CGN-25 | 15 May 1959 | 15 Apr 1961 | 6 Oct 1962 | Bethelehem Steel Co, Quincy, Mass. |
| ***Truxtun*** | CGN-35 | 17 Jun 1963 | 19 Dec 1964 | 27 May 1967 | New York SB Co, Camden, New Jersey |

**Displacement** (*Bainbridge*) 7,600 tons (standard), 8,580 tons (full load) (*Truxtun*) 8,200 tons (standard), 9,127 tons (full load)

**Dimensions** (B) 172.2m (oa) × 17.6m × 9.5m (565ft (oa) × 57.9ft × 31ft) (T) 171.9m (oa) × 17.7m × 9.4m (564ft (oa) × 58ft × 31ft)

**Propulsion** 2 shafts, geared steam turbines, 2 pressurised water-cooled D2G nuclear reactors; approx 60,000 shp = 30+ knots

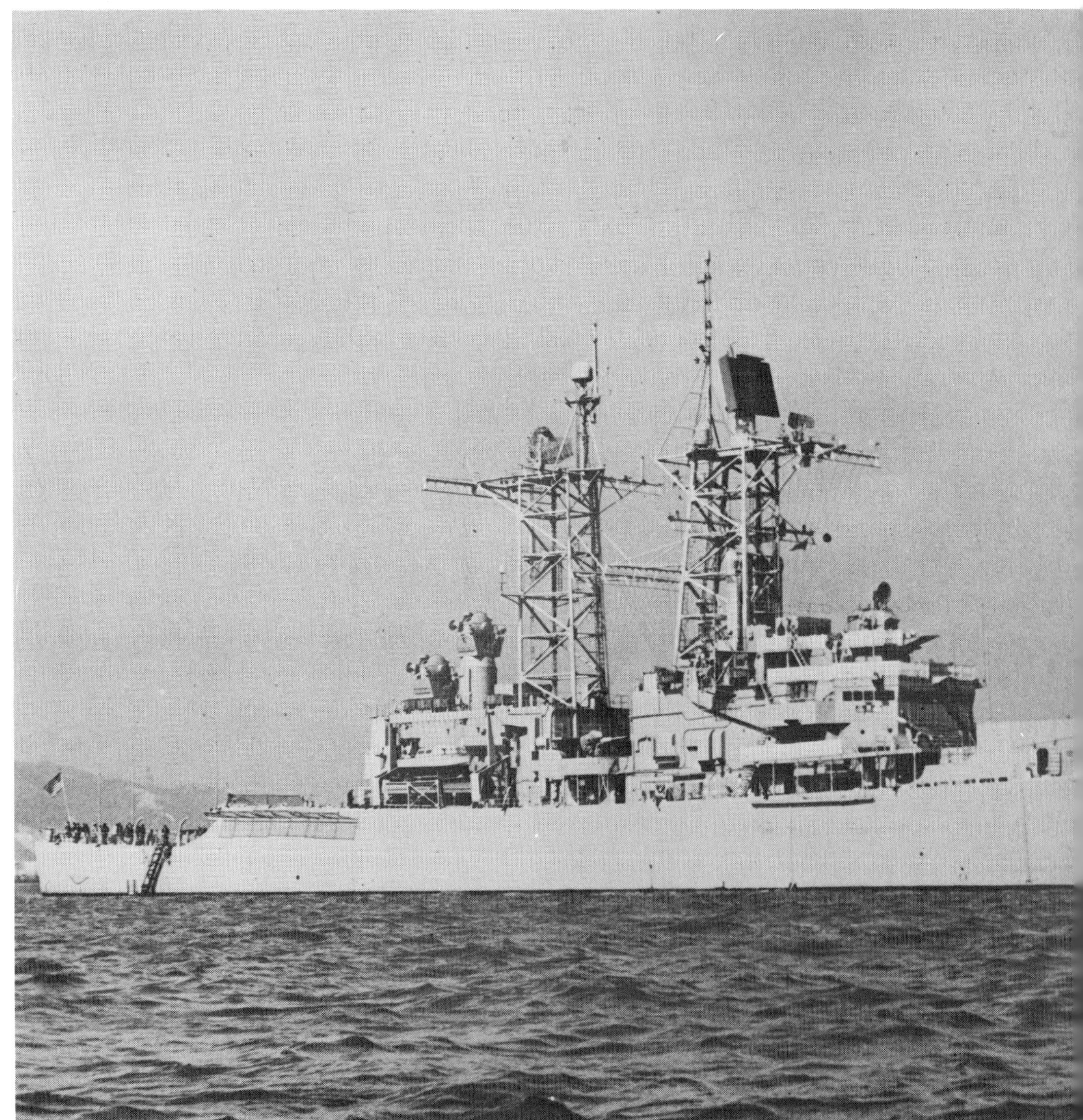

**Aircraft** Hangar for helicopter (pad only in *Bainbridge*)
**Armament** (B) 2 twin Terrier Standard ER SAM launchers, 2 twin 3in (76mm) 50-cal guns, 1 8-tube Asroc ASM launcher, 2 triple 12.7in (324mm) Mk 32 torpedo tubes
(T) 1 twin Standard ER/Asroc SAM/ASM launcher, 1 single 5in (127mm) 54-cal gun, 2 single 20mm guns, 4 × 12.7in (324mm) Mk 32 torpedo tubes
**Complement** (B) 34 officers, 436 enlisted men
(T) 36 officers, 456 enlisted men

Following its experiences with the cruiser *Long Beach* and carrier *Enterprise*, the US Navy decided to build a third nuclear-powered surface ship, a smaller DLG or frigate without the "extras" of the *Long Beach*. The design was based on the contemporary steam-powered *Leahy* class and she was authorised in FY 1956.

The ship was originally armed with two twin Terrier SAM systems and an eight-cell Asroc launcher; after completion she was given two twin 3in AA guns amidships. In 1976 these weapons were replaced by single 20mm Oerlikon guns and the Terriers are shortly to be replaced by Standard (ER) missiles. The addition of Harpoon SSMs will give her a much-needed surface strike capability, but her most serious lack is any facility for operating a helicopter.

The ship underwent an Anti-Air Warfare (AAW) modernisation in 1974-76, when she was fitted with NTDS and improved fire-control for her SAMs.

FY 1962 saw the authorisation of a second nuclear frigate, the slightly longer *Truxtun*. This ship resembles the slightly later *Belknap*-class steam-powered frigates, but with the gun and missile armament reversed and two massive lattice masts. Major improvements over the *Bainbridge* include a combined Terrier/Asroc missile launcher with improved loading arrangements and a helicopter hangar. There is also a 5in gun to provide the gunfire support which proved so useful in Vietnam.

The helicopter hangar was provided to allow the ship to operate the Drone Anti-Submarine Helicopter (Dash), but this system proved unreliable and was withdrawn. Now the renewed interest in helicopters means that the ship can operate the SH-2 Lamps light helicopter after strengthening of the flight deck, leading to a great increase in her ASW effectiveness.

Like the *Bainbridge*, she will probably receive Harpoon SSMs, and it is reported that two 20mm Vulcan Phalanx Close-In Weapon Systems (CIWS) will be fitted for defence against sea-skimming missiles.

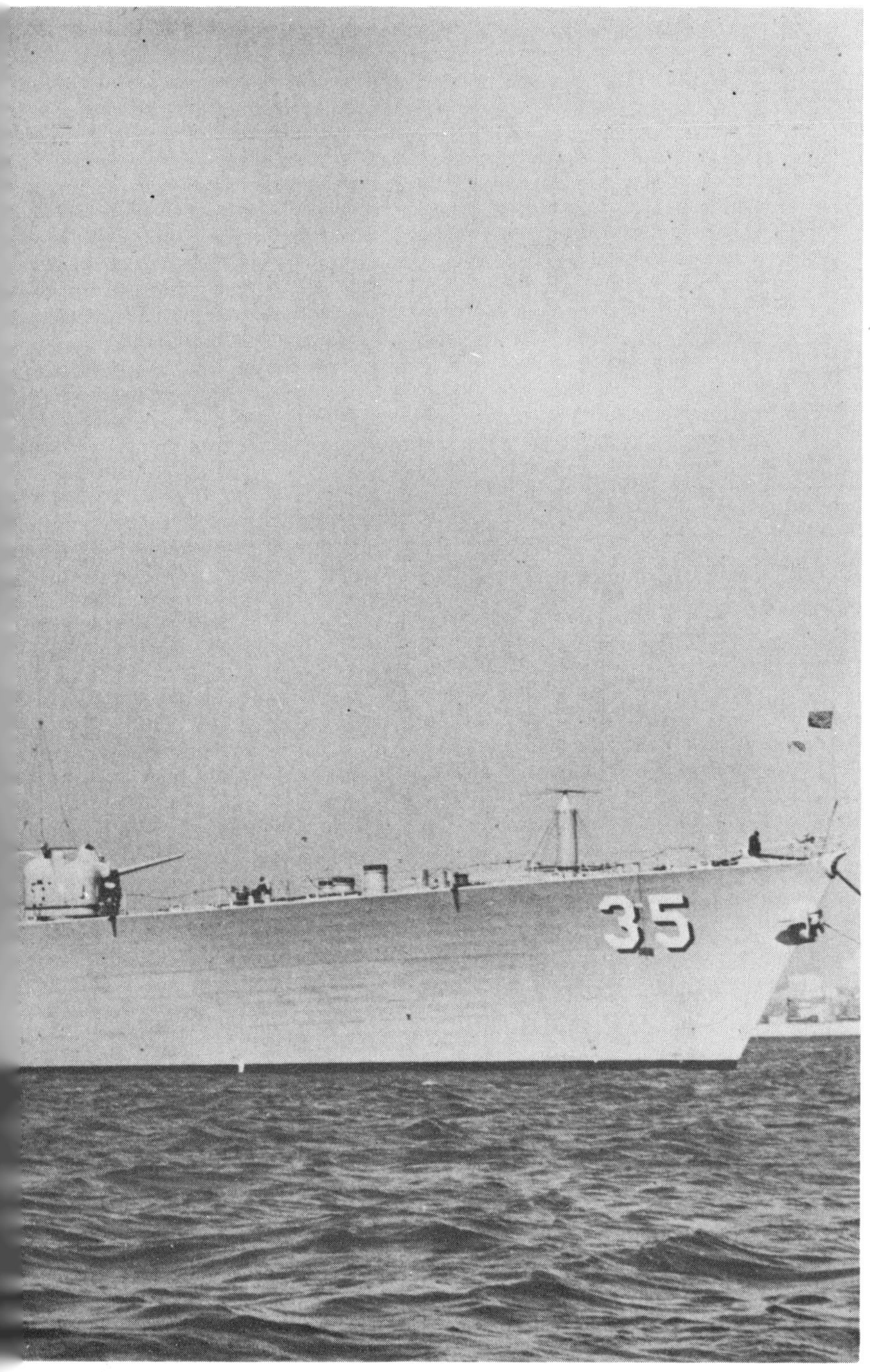


The *Truxtun*, the world's fourth nuclear-powered surface warship, is recognisable by her massive lattice masts. The massive deckhouse forward is the reloading system for the Asroc launcher. The after deckhouse includes a hangar intended for the defunct Dash drone ASW helicopter.

## *Leahy* and *Belknap* classes

**Displacement** (*Leahy*) 5,670 tons (standard), 7,800 tons (full load) (*Belknap*) 6,570 tons (standard), 7,930 tons (full load)
**Dimensions** (L) 162.5m (oa) × 16.6m × 7.9m (533ft (oa) × 54.9ft × 26ft) (B) 166.7m (oa) × 16.7m × 8.7m (547ft (oa) × 54.8ft × 28.8ft)
**Propulsion** 2 shafts, geared steam turbines, 4 boilers, 85,000 shp = 34 knots
**Aircraft** (L) Pad for helicopter (B) 1 Lamps A/S helicopter
**Armament** (L) 2 twin Standard ER SAM launchers, 2 twin 3in (76mm) 50-cal guns, 1 8-tube Asroc ASM launcher, 2 triple 12.7in (324mm) Mk 32 torpedo tubes
(B) 1 twin Standard ER/Asroc SAM/ASM launcher, 1 single 5in (127mm) 54-cal gun, 2 single 3in (76mm) 50-cal guns, 2 triple 12.7in (324mm) Mk 32 torpedo tubes
**Complement** (L) 32 officers, 381 enlisted men
(B) 31 officers, 387 enlisted men

*Dale, England, Gridley, Halsey, Harry E. Yarnell, Leahy, Reeves, Richmond K. Turner* and *Worden* built 1959-64.
*Belknap, Biddle, Fox, Horne, Josephus Daniels, Jouett, Sterett, Wainwright* and *William H. Standley* built 1962-67.

Two classes of steam-powered frigates were built for the US Navy, the nine "double-ended" *Leahys* and the nine "single-enders" of the *Belknap* class. They bear the same relation to one another as the nuclear-powered *Bainbridge* and *Truxtun*, of which they are smaller versions.

The *Leahy* introduced the "mack," or combined mast and stack, into the US Navy, with smoke pipes emerging on the rear side of two plated masts. The system saved much-needed topweight and

space but was more trouble than it was worth, as the resulting temperature fluctuations caused distortion of metal components.

The *Leahy* class was fitted with two Terrier SAM launchers, while the *Belknaps* have a Mk 10 launcher for Terrier and Asroc; the Mk 10 is reloaded from a ramp, beneath which is housed a triple revolving magazine containing 20 Asroc rounds in one drum and 40 Terriers in the other two. Aft is a Mk 42 5in DP gun and a Dash drone helicopter hangar and flight deck. The helicopter facilities fell into disuse after the failure of Dash in the late 1960s, but now they have been brought back into service for the SH-2 Lamps ASW helicopter.

On 22 November 1976 the *Belknap* was involved in a bad collision with the carrier *John F. Kennedy* in the Ionian Sea. The carrier's overhang sliced into the cruiser's superstructure and a fractured fuel pipe drenched her with thousands of gallons of JP-5 aviation fuel. Sparks then ignited the fuel, and as the superstructure was entirely made of aluminium it melted down to the weather deck. Despite the appalling damage done to the topsides, only eight men were killed and the ship did not sink. She is being rebuilt and is almost ready to rejoin the fleet.

The *Sterett* has been rearmed with Harpoon SSMs, and the others will get them in due course. They are mounted amidships in place of the 3in guns, which are being removed from all ships. In 1977 the *Fox* was fitted with a twin Tomahawk cruise missile launcher for evaluation and combat tests.

Both classes were re-rated as guided missile cruisers (CG) in June 1975, a more appropriate rating for such imposing and well-armed ships.

The USS *Leahy* and her sisters were the first American warships to be designed with macks. The deck space thus saved was devoted to a second Terrier SAM system forward, one more than in the *Coontz*-class DLGs. The higher freeboard also helps to make the *Leahys* look bigger, with the result that they were re-rated as cruisers in 1975.

ROYAL NAVY
ROYAL NAVY
ROYAL NAVY
003

## *Coontz* class

**Displacement** 4,700 tons (standard), 5,800 tons (full load)
**Dimensions** 156.2m (oa) × 15.9m × 7.6m (512.5ft (oa) × 52.5ft × 25ft)
**Propulsion** 2 shafts, geared steam turbines, 4 boilers; 85,000 shp = 34 knots
**Aircraft** Pad for helicopter
**Armament** 1 twin Terrier/Standard ER SAM launcher, 1 5in (127mm) 54-cal gun, 1 8-tube Asroc ASM launcher, 2 triple 12.7in (324mm) Mk 32 torpedo tubes
**Complement** 21 officers, 356 enlisted men

*Coontz, Dahlgren, Dewey, Farragut, King, Luce, Macdonough, Mahan, Preble* and *William V. Pratt* built 1957-61.

Following the construction of two very large destroyer types, the *Norfolk* (DL-1) and the *Mitscher* class (DL-2-5) armed with guns, the first generation of missile-armed frigates was planned in the early 1950s. Ten were built (DLG-6-15) and in June 1975 they were reclassified as missile-armed destroyers (DDG-37-46).

In fact they are an anomaly. Although they are nothing more than a much bigger version of the *Charles F. Adams*-class destroyers, with the classic American look of tall capped funnels and a graceful flush weather deck, they were given the medium-range Terrier SAM system. The *Leahy* class is nothing more than a "cleaned-up" version with the same powerplant and a remodelled superstructure, yet the *Leahy*s are now cruisers while their half-sisters have been downgraded to destroyers. However, they *look* more like destroyers, which presumably influenced the decision.

Since completion the ships have undergone various modifications. They have been progressively fitted with NTDS and improved missile guidance, and will receive Standard (ER) in place of Terrier missiles. The *Farragut* was given an Asroc reloading position forward of the bridge, while the *King* has a prototype Vulcan Phalanx 20mm Gatling gun mounting at the after end of the fantail.

The DLG USS *McDonough* is almost exactly the same size as the *Leahy* but retains the essentially light appearance of a destroyer. She is seen here wearing her new DDG pennant number (formerly DLG-8) and closing HMS *Ark Royal* during a Nato exercise in October 1977.

# *Devonshire* class

| Name | Number | Laid down | Launched | Completed | Builder |
|---|---|---|---|---|---|
| ***Devonshire*** | D 02 | 9 Mar 1959 | 10 Jun 1960 | 15 Nov 1962 | Cammell Laird, Birkenhead |
| ***Kent*** | D 12 | 1 Mar 1960 | 27 Sep 1961 | 15 Aug 1963 | Harland & Wolff, Belfast |
| ***London*** | D 16 | 26 Feb 1960 | 7 Dec 1961 | 4 Nov 1963 | Swan Hunter & Wigham Richardson, Wallsend |
| ***Antrim*** | D 18 | 20 Jan 1966 | 19 Oct 1967 | 14 Jul 1970 | Fairfield SB & E Co, Govan |
| ***Fife*** | D 20 | 1 Jun 1962 | 9 Jul 1964 | 21 Jun 1966 | Fairfield SB & E Co, Govan |
| ***Glamorgan*** | D 19 | 13 Sep 1962 | 9 Jul 1964 | 11 Oct 1966 | Vickers-Armstrong, Tyne |
| ***Norfolk*** | D 21 | 15 Mar 1966 | 16 Nov 1967 | 7 Mar 1970 | Swan Hunter & Wigham Richardson, Wallsend |

**Displacement** 5,440 tons (standard), 6,200 (full load)
**Dimensions** 158.7m (oa) × 16.5m × 6.1m (520.5ft (oa) × 54ft × 20ft)
**Propulsion** 2 shafts, geared steam turbines and gas turbines (COSAG), 2 boilers; 60,000 shp = 30 knots
**Aircraft** 1 Wessex A/S helicopter
**Armament** (Group I) 1 twin Seaslug I SAM launcher, 2 quad Seacat SAM launchers, 2 twin 4.5in (114mm) guns, 2 single 20mm guns
(Group II) 1 twin Seaslug II SAM launcher, 2 quad Seacat SAM launchers, 4 Exocet SSM launchers, 1 twin 4.5in (114mm) guns, 2 single 20mm guns
**Complement** 33 officers, 438 men

Better known as the County class, these handsome ships were the first British warships to be equipped with guided weapons. They also introduced the then-revolutionary Combined Steam and Gas Turbine (COSAG) propulsion system, with a gas turbine for starting and boost, and a steam turbine for main power.

The origin of the class is not without interest. Obsessed with the nightmare of *Sverdlov* cruisers roaming at will about the trade routes, the Admiralty designed a cruiser-destroying ship capable of 38

knots and armed with three 5in guns capable of firing 80 rounds a minute. It would in theory have used its speed to close and overwhelm a *Sverdlov* with a hail of shells . . . All that survived of this interesting if misconceived design was the machinery, for Lord Louis Mountbatten refused to accept a ship with no guided weapons for defence against aircraft.

In fact the guided-weapon system has been the major drawback of this class since its inception. The Seaslug is a cumbersome beam-rider guided by a somewhat primitive radar, and its Ministry of Supply-designed launcher weighs as much as a gun mounting. Because the missiles have to be stowed horizontally the magazine capacity is very low for such big ships (the usually quoted figure of 36 is believed to be exaggerated), and the entire interior of the forecastle deck is taken up with a tunnel down which the Seaslugs travel from the hoist to the launcher.

On the other hand, the Counties are superb sea-going vessels with good command facilities, and in a navy which is all too short of big ships they act as useful flagships for task groups. The faults of Seaslug were supposed to have been remedied in Seaslug II, which is reputed to have a "limited" surface-to-surface capability, but the limitations of the Type 901 radar make this a dubious claim. The second four, the *Antrim* group, have Seaslug II and the more comprehensive AKE-2 double Type 965 long-range radar. To improve their anti-ship capability the *Antrim* group have also been given four Exocet SSMs in place of the second 4.5in gun mounting.

Although the COSAG plant was highly regarded in its day, it is now considered to suffer the inconveniences of steam without offering the benefits of a modern marine gas turbine. This was one of the reasons for the early scrapping of *Hampshire* in 1976, and explains the big demands which these ships make on manpower.

In view of the success of Sea Dart and the *Sheffield* class, the remaining seven ships will not be modernised. The configuration dictated by Seaslug, with its antiquated horizontal loading, in any case rules out any change to Sea Dart. The Egyptian Navy has expressed some interest in the purchase of *Devonshire*, with an eye to converting her to a helicopter carrier. This may sound bizarre, but the tunnel for the missiles could easily be opened up and converted to a hangar for Lynx helicopters. Though the deal is reported to have fallen through, it could have led to an interesting adaptation of a valuable hull. Conversion of one to a minelayer is under consideration.

The "County"-class DLGs are still impressive ships, with their long forecastle deck carried right aft. HMS *Antrim* is seen coming up the Clyde in 1977, with her recently installed MM.38 Exocet surface-to-surface missiles forward of the bridge. The earlier ships retain the "B" 4.5in gun mounting and have a single "bedstead" radar.

# Bristol

| Name | Number | Laid down | Launched | Completed | Builder |
|---|---|---|---|---|---|
| ***Bristol*** | D 23 | 15 Nov 1967 | 30 Jun 1969 | 31 Mar 1973 | Swan Hunter & Wigham Richardson, Wallsend |

**Displacement** 6,100 tons (standard), 7,100 tons (full load)
**Dimensions** 154.5m (oa) × 16.8m × 7m (507ft (oa) × 55ft × 23ft)
**Propulsion** 2 shafts, geared steam and gas turbines (COSAG), 2 boilers; 74,600 shp = 30 knots
**Aircraft** Pad for helicopter
**Armament** 1 twin Sea Dart SAM launcher, 1 single 4.5in (114mm) Mk 8 gun, 1 single Ikara ASM launcher, 1 3-barrel Limbo A/S mortar
**Complement** 29 officers, 378 men

This ship had her origins in the ill-fated British carrier replacement programme. Four Type 82 DLGs or cruisers were planned to escort the carriers CVA 01 and CVA 02, armed with the new Sea Dart area-defence SAM system and using a new Anglo-Dutch 3-D radar. The emphasis was on endurance to give the escorts the ability to keep pace with the carriers for as long as possible.

It is a measure of the expediency of politicians that the administration which cancelled CVA 01 refused to cancel the Type 82 DLGs, in spite of an MoD request that the four ships be dropped in favour of more frigates. It was held that the public might be "alarmed" if too many ships were axed, and although the last three of the class were later dropped the RN was still saddled with a ship without a role.

Nevertheless, the *Bristol* has excellent command facilities, a good SAM system and a long-range anti-submarine missile system, the Anglo-Australian Ikara. Her size made her ideal for the role of trials ship for Ikara and Sea Dart. But because she spent so long on that task she never received any significant updating of equipment. Another drawback is her lack of a helicopter hangar, a result of the fact that she was intended to operate at all times with carriers; this may well be remedied at her half-life modernisation.

The *Bristol* suffered a very bad boiler-room fire in 1975, and there was talk of her being paid off into reserve. But her importance as trials ship for Sea Dart and Ikara, as well as the fact that she could still run on her two Olympus TM1A gas turbines, meant that she soldiered on until the trials programme was finished. Her steam machinery has now been repaired, and she is scheduled for a modernisation during which she may receive the Dutch 3-D radar originally intended for her, in place of the ageing AKE-2 "bedstead".

The peculiar three-funnel layout of the *Bristol* results from the need for removal routes for the Olympus gas turbines. A hatchway is provided between the two after funnels to allow the turbines to be lifted out.

Though the *Bristol* has had a chequered career, her reputation for being a failure is quite unjustified. The disappearance of her role does not prevent her from providing area defence and command facilities for a task group, and she will remain a powerful unit for many years.

*Bristol*'s broad quarterdeck, with the three-barrelled Limbo Mk 10 anti-submarine mortar in its well. The steam turbines are located forward and the gas turbines aft, with an exhaust trunk coming up between the after funnels. Sea Dart is loaded vertically, as in American missile systems.

HMS *Bristol* is virutally an improved *Devonshire*, avoiding the penalties imposed by the bulky, horizontally loaded Seaslug missile. The diminutive Sea Dart launcher can be seen aft, with its two fire-control directors under their weatherproof domes. The after funnels are divided to allow removal of the gas turbines.

## *Suffren* class

| Name | Number | Laid down | Launched | Completed | Builder |
|---|---|---|---|---|---|
| ***Suffren*** | D 602 | Dec 1962 | 15 May 1965 | Jul 1967 | Lorient Dockyard |
| ***Duquesne*** | D 603 | Nov 1964 | 11 Feb 1966 | Apr 1970 | Brest Dockyard |

**Displacement** 5,090 tons (standard), 6,090 tons (full load)
**Dimensions** 157.6m (oa) × 15.5m × 6.1m (517.1ft (oa) × 50.9ft × 20ft)
**Propulsion** 2 shafts, geared steam turbines, 4 boilers; 72,500 shp = 34 knots
**Armament** 1 twin Masurca SAM launcher, 4 single Exocet SSM launchers, 1 single 3.9in (100mm) gun, 1 single Malafon ASM launcher, 4 × 21in (533mm) torpedo tubes
**Complement** 23 officers, 332 men

Two *frégates* or missile cruisers, the first to have this designation, were built under the French Navy's 1960 programme. They were armed with the Masurca medium-range SAM system and the Malafon anti-submarine missile system.

The French showed even more preference for the mack than other navies, with a low superstructure and a slender mack almost amidships. Other peculiarly French features are the "droop snoot" bow to allow "A" gun to fire at zero elevation without blast damage, and a wide transom stern. The ships are fitted with a big variable-depth sonar, and the DRBI-23 3-D radar is conspicuous under its huge weatherproof "golfball" dome.

The ships are reputed to be very seaworthy, rolling only slightly with very little pitch. Since 1977 both ships have received MM.38 Exocet SSMs on the after superstructure.

The Masurca SAM system is a first-generation weapon, and in view of the announcement that the next group of C70 corvettes will have the Standard SM-1 it is possible that the *Suffren*s could be re-armed. They are still very effective units, however, with good command-and-control facilities to back up their balanced armament. The chief drawback is the lack of a helicopter, though they are armed with the Malafon long-range ASW system.

▶ The French DLG *Duquesne* in 1971, showing the directors for her Masurca SAM system aft and the massive "golfball" hiding the DRBI-23 surveillance radar. The wide, shallow transom stern is cut away to facilitate lowering of the variable-depth sonar. The short lattice mainmast was added after completion.

▼ *Suffren* on completion in 1967, before the mainmast was stepped. The two single 30mm guns on the after deckhouse were replaced by four MM.38 Exocet launchers in 1977–78; two single 20mm guns for "junk-bashing" were added further forward. This view shows the height and slenderness of the mack very well.

# Kynda class

**Displacement** 4,800 tons (standard), 6,000 tons (full load)
**Dimensions** 142m (oa) × 15.8m × 5.3m (465.8ft (oa) × 51.8ft × 17.4ft)
**Propulsion** 2 shafts, geared steam turbines, 4 boilers; 100,000 shp = 35 knots
**Aircraft** Pad for helicopter
**Armament** 1 twin SA-N-1 SAM launcher, 2 quad SS-N-3 SSM launchers, 2 twin 3in (76mm) guns, 2 × 12-barrel MBU-2500A A/S rocket launchers, 2 triple 21in (533mm) torpedo tubes
**Complement** 390 officers and men

*Admiral Fokin*, *Admiral Golovko*, *Grozny* and *Varyag* built 1957-62 at Zhdanov, Leningrad.

These were the first *Raketny Kreyser* (rocket cruisers) built for the Soviet Navy, and that force's first big ships with a powerful armament of long-range surface-to-surface missiles. They could be said to have ushered in the menace of the cruise missile, for the SS-N-3 was originally credited with a range of up to 300 miles and even now is believed capable of 150 to 250 miles. Just how these missiles are to receive mid-course guidance is not satisfactorily explained, as a major enemy warship is not likely to allow a subsonic bomber to loiter while passing target data to the Soviet launch ship.

Construction of the Kynda class, possibly known as the *Varyag* class, got under way in about 1957 at the Zhdanov yard in Leningrad, and the four ships appeared between 1961 and 1962. They are handsome vessels with tall funnels and pyramidal masts, but the fact that production stopped after four units suggests that they were partly experimental. They may have had topweight problems, especially with reload gear in the superstructure forward and aft. The reloading gear may well be cumbersome, which would account for it being dropped subsequently.

The Kyndas set a standard for multiple weapon systems which has since become typical of the Soviet philosophy of warship design. In addition to the eight SS-N-3 Shaddock SSMs there is a twin SA-N-1 Goblet SAM system forward, two twin 76mm gun mountings, two triple torpedo tubes and two 12-barrelled ASW rocket launchers. Initially deployed in the Atlantic, the Kyndas are now in the Pacific. They must now be approaching their mid-life, and it will be interesting to see how any new weapon systems are fitted into a hull that is already at full capacity.

The Kynda-class *Admiral Fokin* at sea with the Red Banner Pacific Fleet. Weapons visible are: two MBU anti-submarine rocket launchers, a twin SA-N-1 Goa SAM launcher and four Shaddock SS-N-3 surface missile launchers on the forecastle, with triple 21in torpedo tubes amidships.

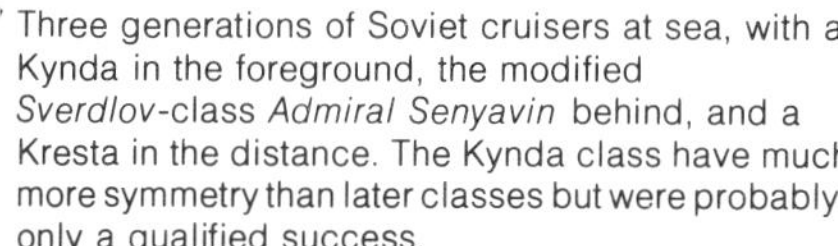

Three generations of Soviet cruisers at sea, with a Kynda in the foreground, the modified *Sverdlov*-class *Admiral Senyavin* behind, and a Kresta in the distance. The Kynda class have much more symmetry than later classes but were probably only a qualified success.

# Destroyers

The destroyer – or, more formally, the torpedo-boat destroyer – was a logical development of the original steam torpedo boat of the 1870s. In much the same way as the anti-ship guided missile has dominated naval thinking in the past decade, the Whitehead "fish" torpedo was regarded as a deadly threat to the large warship exactly a hundred years ago.

Both the British and the French turned their minds to finding a countermeasure to the large numbers of small, fast torpedo boats operated by other navies. The first remedy, the torpedo gunboat, proved too flimsy for the job, and finally the torpedo-boat designers themselves provided the answer. This was a much enlarged torpedo boat with a sturdier hull and a heavy gun armament, a combination which allowed the pursuit of torpedo boats in weather too rough for the smaller craft.

The torpedo-boat destroyer lived up to its name so well that within a few years it had not only driven out the torpedo boat but had taken over its function as well. Thereafter it developed into a fleet escort, using its guns to drive off or sink enemy destroyers before going in to attack the battle line with torpedoes.

Another role for which the destroyer proved highly suitable was that of anti-submarine escort. Its shallow draught and manoeuvrability made the destroyer a difficult target for a U-Boat, and its tight turning circle, good turn of speed and rapid-firing guns gave it a fair chance of hitting or ramming a submarine on the surface or diving. Soon after the outbreak of war in 1914 destroyers began to be fitted with a "tin-opening" spur on the forefoot to facilitate ramming, and throughout the long war against commerce from 1915 to 1918 destroyers were at the forefront of the battle. Their weapons included the hydrophone (the first underwater sensor), a variety of explosive sweeps, and finally the depth charge.

The British, having invented the destroyer, took it to a peak of perfection in the First World War. Although other navies built larger, faster and heavier-armed destroyers, in the famous "V&W" class of 1916 the Royal Navy produced the best balance of guns, torpedoes, speed and weatherliness yet seen. Like the *Dreadnought* in 1907, the V&W class set a new standard all over the world, and formed the basis of all subsequent development.

Although the Germans had taken the lead in producing enlarged *divisions-boote* or divisional leaders as far back as the 1880s, their torpedo boats and destroyers were smaller and less well armed than contemporary British boats. To remedy this and to compensate for the shortage of light cruisers they produced a new type of big destroyer with 15cm (5.9in) guns in 1918. Unfortunately the prototypes, *S.113* and *V.116*, proved deficient in stability and mechanically unreliable, and the big guns proved too unwieldy for such lively platforms.

The Italians also tried to fuse the scout cruiser and the destroyer types in their *esploratori* or scouts, built at the same time. This, combined with the fact that both Italy and France acquired the ex-German large destroyers, led both countries to take matters further. The Italians eventually settled on fast cruisers, but the French continued to develop a generation of super-fast destroyers known as *contre-torpilleurs*. Although costly, fragile and sadly lacking in range, they were among the fastest warships ever built, and the six *Fantasque* class were capable of steaming at 40 knots.

The Franco-Italian rivalry was matched in the Pacific by the Japanese and Americans. In 1928 the first *Fubuki* or Special Type destroyers appeared, massive ships capable of 38 knots and armed with 24in torpedoes. They inspired the Americans to build the *Porter* and *Somers* classes, but nothing could match the Japanese destroyers' secret weapon, the ultra-long-range Long Lance oxygen-driven torpedo. Time and again in the fighting in the Solomons the Japanese had a big tactical advantage because of the Long Lance's phenomenal range and speed.

Learning nothing from their mistakes with *S.113* and *V.116*, the Germans tried once more to give their destroyers 15cm guns, starting with *Z.23* in 1940. These big and imposing destroyers were among the least successful produced by any navy, proving to be top-heavy, mechanically unreliable and too complex for rapid building. In particular, their very-high-pressure boilers and delicate machinery kept them in harbour for much of the time, with the result that German destroyers put in less sea time than their more timidly handled Italian counterparts.

The British stayed aloof from this race to produce ever-larger destroyers, and even their "Tribal" class of 1937 were modest by comparison. The Royal Navy continued to build a simple and relatively cheap standard destroyer, reasoning that numbers and seaworthiness were more important than theoretical qualities.

The destroyer reached a new peak of development in the Second World War, and proved that it was still the flexible and efficient submarine-hunter and fleet escort that it had been 20 years before. New technology in the form of more efficient boilers and longitudinal framing made them more reliable and resistant to battle damage. Outstanding examples were the British *Javelin* and the American *Fletcher* classes. The former paved the way for a further 18 classes of virtually identical design, while the *Fletcher* class ran to 175 units and was then expanded into the 170 *Allen M. Sumner* and *Gearing* classes. With its heavy dual-purpose armament and 6,000-mile endurance, the *Fletcher* was probably the best all-round destroyer ever built, although the Japanese *Kagero* class, with its oxygen-driven Long Lance torpedoes and six dual-purpose 5in guns, must take the palm for the most powerful armament.

But by then the long predominance of the torpedo in surface actions was on the wane. Before the war it had become suicidal to attack battleships with torpedoes in daylight, and by 1943 radar-assisted fire control made night attacks nearly as hazardous. By 1945 the role of surface attack was becoming subordinate to that of anti-submarine and anti-aircraft screening, and the latest destroyers reflected this trend.

In the 1950s a new breed of much larger destroyer appeared, typified by the American *Coontz* and British "County" classes. The increase in size to what had been light cruiser dimensions before the war was caused partly by the need to arm these new ships with long-range guided missile systems but also by the growing volume of radar, plotting and command facilities needed for modern warfare. The term "destroyer" seemed so inappropriate that the clumsy term Destroyer Leader (DLG) was coined for this new breed, and for a while the US Navy toyed with the term "frigate". Although historically appropriate to the very biggest of such ships, as typified by the nuclear-powered DLG *Bainbridge*, it overlapped with the widely used escort designation, and in 1975 it was decided to reclassify the biggest types as cruisers and the smaller types as destroyers (DDGs).

The older gun-armed destroyers continued to serve side by side with the DDGs, though they were more and more dedicated to the anti-submarine role as their size ruled out installation of a big surface-to-air missile system. To extend the life of its *Fletchers*, *Sumners* and *Gearings* the US Navy began the massive Fleet Rehabilitation and Modernisation (FRAM) programme in 1960. Ten years earlier the Royal Navy had begun a similar effort to turn its Emergency Flotillas into specialised A/S ships in the Type 15 and Type 16 frigate conversion programme; subsequently the British ships were reclassified as frigates while the FRAM ships remained destroyers. The FRAMs have now all but disappeared from the USN but are the backbone of many Nato and other small navies.

Today the term destroyer, used in the sense of "submarine destroyer" or "aircraft destroyer," is used as much for its proud traditions and associations as for any other reason. It thus embraces a wide variety of ships. To cite only two examples, at one end of the scale is the extremely compact British *Sheffield* class, armed with an area-defence missile, and at the other extreme there is the American *Spruance* class, twice the size but without any major anti-aircraft system.

The one factor which destroyers have always had in common is high speed. The steam turbine was introduced at the beginning of the century because the rising speeds of destroyers had taken the vertical triple-expansion engine to its limits, and now easily maintained gas turbines are replacing steam turbines. Speed requirements are less onerous than they used to be: a guaranteed 30 knots is recognised as being of more practical value in a warship than a theoretical 36 knots in a wartime destroyer which was actually capable of a sea speed of only 30-31 knots at normal load. An added advantage of gas turbines is their rapid acceleration, which reduces the risk of torpedo attack. A high degree of automation ensures that engine-room complements are smaller than they used to be, and as repairs are done by replacement a machinery overhaul takes a matter of days rather than months. A gas turbine could be lifted from a ship like HMS *Sheffield* and replaced anywhere in the world, given a calm anchorage and a heavy lift from a shore crane or a cargo vessel alongside.

But for all the advantages of the type of powerplant, one prophecy of a few years ago has not come true. It was claimed that the compactness of gas turbines would allow a much heavier weight of armament and less superstructure. But gas turbines require vast quantities of air, which means big air intakes and exhausts to vent the hot gases, while the engine rooms have to be spacious to allow easy removal. As a result, today's destroyers have massive blocks of superstructure and the slim "mack" or combined mast/funnel has once more given way to the traditional exhaust-only funnel.

## *Spruance* and CG-47 classes

**Displacement** (CG-47) 9,055 tons (full load)
(*Spruance*) 7,300 tons (full load)
**Dimensions** (C) 171.1m (oa) × 17.6m × ?m (563.3ft (oa) × 55ft × ?ft)
(S) 171.1m (oa) × 17.6m × 8.8m (563.3ft (oa) × 55ft × 29ft)
**Propulsion** 2 shafts, geared gas turbines; 80,000 shp = 30+ knots
**Protection** (C) 1 in (25mm) side
**Aircraft** 2 Lamps helicopters
**Armament** (C) 2 twin Standard MR/Asroc SAM/ASM launchers, 2 × 8-tube Harpoon SSM launchers, 2 single 5in (127mm) 54-cal guns, 2 × 20mm Phalanx CIWS guns
(S) 2 single 5in (127mm) 54-cal guns, 1 × 8-tube Asroc ASM launcher, 2 triple 12.7in (324mm) Mk 32 torpedo tubes
**Complement** (C) 27 officers, 289 enlisted men
(S) 24 officers, 272 enlisted men

CG-47, 48 ordered 1978-79, 14 more projected 1980-82. 31 *Spruance* class built or building from 1972 onwards by Litton, Pascagoula, Mississippi. All launched by the end of 1979; four fitting out for completion in 1980.

As the nuclear submarine grew in significance during the 1960s and early 1970s, the US Navy's need for more specialised ASW ships led to a requirement for a new mass-produced general-purpose class to replace the FRAM *Fletcher*, *Sumner* and *Gearing* classes. The brilliant designer Dr Reuven Leopold was able to convince the Navy that the time had come for a radically new approach to design, and the result is the bitterly criticised *Spruance* class.

At the heart of Dr Leopold's philosophy is the unpalatable fact that weapon systems, the "payload" of a ship, become obsolete after seven to ten years, whereas the hull or "platform" can last 30 years or more. In recent years warships have had to be scrapped or expensively modified because new equipment and new tactical concepts outgrew the original hull. Therefore, it was argued, the *Spruance* should be built as big as possible to allow for future growth and replacement of the payload. The savings would come from using assembly-line methods in one shipyard instead of following the traditional method of sharing contracts among several yards to secure competitive tendering.

Resulting in an apparently under-armed giant destroyer as big as yesterday's cruisers, the *Spruance* philosophy is in fact already justifying itself. The last six ships are not yet completed, but already an Aegis-equipped derivative, the CG-47, has been laid down and a variant with SAM launcher for area defence has been ordered for Iran. The critics of the *Spruance* claim that she cannot defend herself against heavy air attack, while her proponents contend that she is not intended to operate as a convoy escort and will be screening task forces which already have their own area defence. Her immense size makes for good habitability and seaworthiness, both

Nine *Spruance*-class destroyers at various stages of fitting-out at Pascagoula. Large hull sections are fitted out to an advanced stage, assembled on a giant raft or pontoon, and the hull is then put afloat by sinking the pontoon. Work is speeded up by using modules wherever possible.

The USS *Peterson* (DD-969) on trials, showing her boxlike superstructure and the square funnels offset to port and starboard. Although heavily criticised, these 7,000-tonners have proved exceptionally quiet ASW platforms and magnificent seaboats. The triple A/S torpedo tubes are out of sight, hidden behind sliding doors to protect them from the weather.

vital for a ship intended to hunt nuclear submarines in mid-ocean.

Another revolutionary feature of the *Spruance* design is the adoption of two-shaft gas turbines, the first time this has been done in a large US warship. These powerplants were chosen for their quietness, vital in an ASW ship, and ease of maintenance.

The ships are quite the ugliest afloat, with two staggered funnels surmounted by "stovepipe" exhausts for the gas turbines. The superstructure is merely a series of boxes and even the funnels are square. The ships are prefabricated in a special facility at Litton's shipyard at Pascagoula and moved sideways onto a raft for launching. This method permits maximum use of modules and fitted-out sections.

Six Iranian ships were originally ordered, but the last pair were cancelled. The first two are nearly complete and all four have been taken into the US Navy as the *Kidd* class. Equipped with Standard SAM launchers and USN fire control and radars, they are compatible with any US Navy force.

A fourth variant of the basic design was the DD-997 with a large hangar and flight deck aft for four Lamps III helicopters. But because of mounting costs the "air-capable" part of the design was dropped and she is merely to be a standard *Spruance*.

| Name | Number |
|---|---|
| ***Spruance*** | DD-963 |
| ***Paul F. Foster*** | DD-964 |
| ***Kinkaid*** | DD-965 |
| ***Hewitt*** | DD-966 |
| ***Elliott*** | DD-967 |
| ***Arthur W. Radford*** | DD-968 |
| ***Peterson*** | DD-969 |
| ***Caron*** | DD-970 |
| ***David R. Ray*** | DD-971 |
| ***Oldendorf*** | DD-972 |
| ***John Young*** | DD-973 |
| ***Comte de Grasse*** | DD-974 |
| ***O'Brien*** | DD-975 |
| ***Merrill*** | DD-976 |
| ***Briscoe*** | DD-977 |
| ***Stump*** | DD-978 |
| ***Conolly*** | DD-979 |
| ***Moosbrugger*** | DD-980 |
| ***John Hancock*** | DD-981 |
| ***Nicholson*** | DD-982 |
| ***John Rodgers*** | DD-983 |
| ***Leftwich*** | DD-984 |
| ***Cushing*** | DD-985 |
| ***Harry W. Hill*** | DD-986 |
| ***O'Bannon*** | DD-987 |
| ***Thorn*** | DD-988 |
| ***Deyo*** | DD-989 |
| ***Ingersoll*** | DD-990 |
| ***Fife*** | DD-991 |
| ***Fletcher*** | DD-992 |
| ***Kidd*** (ex-***Kouroosh***) | DDG-993 |
| ***Callaghan*** (ex-***Daryush***) | DDG-994 |
| ***Scott*** (ex-***Ardeshir***) | DDG-995 |
| ***Chandler*** (ex-***Nader***) | DDG-996 |
| unnamed | DD-997 |
| unnamed | CG-47 |

## *Charles F. Adams* class

| Name | Number |
|---|---|
| ***Charles F. Adams*** | DDG-2 |
| ***John King*** | DDG-3 |
| ***Lawrence*** | DDG-4 |
| ***Claude V. Ricketts*** (ex-***Biddle***) | DDG-5 |
| ***Barney*** | DDG-6 |
| ***Henry B. Wilson*** | DDG-7 |
| ***Lynde McCormick*** | DDG-8 |
| ***Towers*** | DDG-9 |
| ***Sampson*** | DDG-10 |
| ***Sellers*** | DDG-11 |
| ***Robison*** | DDG-12 |
| ***Hoel*** | DDG-13 |
| ***Buchanan*** | DDG-14 |
| ***Berkeley*** | DDG-15 |
| ***Joseph Strauss*** | DDG-16 |
| ***Conyngham*** | DDG-17 |
| ***Semmes*** | DDG-18 |
| ***Tatnall*** | DDG-19 |
| ***Goldsborough*** | DDG-20 |
| ***Cochrane*** | DDG-21 |
| ***Benjamin Stoddert*** | DDG-22 |
| ***Richard E. Byrd*** | DDG-23 |
| ***Waddell*** | DDG-24 |
| ***Perth*** (Australia)* | 38 |
| ***Hobart*** | 39 |
| ***Brisbane*** | 41 |
| ***Lütjens*** (West Germany)* | D 185 |
| ***Mölders*** | D 186 |
| ***Rommel*** | D 187 |

* Hull numbers DDG-25-30 allocated for accounting purposes.

**Displacement** 3,370 tons (standard), 4,500 tons (full load)
**Dimensions** 133.2m (oa) × 14.3m × 6.1m (437ft (oa) × 47ft × 20ft)
**Propulsion** 2 shafts, geared steam turbines, 4 boilers; 70,000 shp = 31+ knots
**Armament** 1 twin (DDG 2-14) or single (DDG 15-24) Tartar SAM launchers, 2 × 5in (127mm) 54-cal guns, 1 × 8-tube Asroc ASM launcher, 2 triple 12.7in (324mm) Mk 32 torpedo tubes
**Complement** 24 officers, 330 enlisted men

23 *Charles F. Adams* built 1958-64 by Bath Iron Works; New York SB Co; Defoe SB Co; Todd Shipyards, Seattle; Avondale Shipyards; Puget Sound Bridge & DD Co. 3 *Perth*-class built 1962-67 for Australia by Defoe SB Co. 3 *Lütjens*-class built 1966-70 for Germany by Bath Iron Works.

These successful destroyers, with good seakeeping, reliable machinery and a balanced anti-aircraft, anti-submarine and anti-ship armament, form the backbone of the US Navy's carrier-screening forces. The design is a development of the *Forrest Sherman* class, with missiles replacing part of the gun armament. They were originally given hull numbers following the *Forrest Shermans* (DD-952-959) but in 1964 were renumbered in the new DDG series.

In appearance they resemble scaled-down *Coontz*-class DLGs, but without the massive lattice masts and with the Asroc launcher amidships. Three ships of almost identical design were built for Australia and a heavily modified version was produced for West Germany (the *Perth* and *Lütjens* classes).

The *Biddle* was renamed *Claude V. Ricketts* in July 1964 and took part in the famous Nato mixed-manning experiment, in which contingents from various alliance countries made up part of the complement for some months. The idea was to test the feasibility of a mixed-manned Nato surface deterrent force, and although the personnel aspects proved completely workable the plan fell through when the British and French went ahead with their SSBN programmes.

The last five ships (DDG-20-24) have a stem anchor to avoid damage to the big SQS-23 bow sonar dome. DDG-2-14 have the older twin-arm Mk 11 Tartar missile launcher, while the later ships have the lighter single-arm Mk 13 launcher, which can launch Tartars at the same rate of about six per minute. It is reported that missile capacity varies slightly, being 42 with the Mk 11 and 40 with the Mk 13 launcher.

From FY 1980 the whole class will undergo an Anti-Air Warfare (AAW) mid-life modernisation which is expected to stretch their hull life by another 15 or 20 years. The modernisation will include the conversion of the magazine and launchers to handle Standard SM-1 SAMs and Harpoon SSMs (32-36 Standards and 4-8 Harpoons). The Anti-Radiation Homing (ARM) variant of the Standard will be carried as well, and Infra-Red Guided Projectiles (IRGP) will be provided for the 5in guns. The existing sonars will be replaced with twin hull-mounted SQS-23 sonars known as SQS-23 PAIR, and the radars will be updated.

The major difference in the Australian ships is the provision of a deckhouse between the funnels to house the Ikara anti-submarine missile system. The German ships, on the other hand, look quite different, sprouting curious squared-off macks. Internally they differ in having the German Satir data-handling system. Both classes are currently being modernised, but not to the same standard as the American ships. The German ships will have four Harpoon SSM launchers in place of the after 5in mounting.

◀ A *Lütjens*-class destroyer of the Federal German Navy leading two *Hamburg*-class ships. While generally similar to the original American design they have macks instead of funnels and their top-hamper differs in many respects. They differ internally as a result of the adoption of a German data-processing system.

▼ The USS *Tatnall* (DDG-19) entering Portsmouth in May 1975. Note the prominent SPS-39 3-D radar bracketed on the forward side of the second funnel, and the single Mk 13 Tartar missile launcher right aft. Note also the "E," awarded for efficiency, on the starboard bridge wing above the DesRon 14 insignia.

# *Forrest Sherman* class

| Name | Number |
|---|---|
| ***Forrest Sherman*** | DD-931 |
| ***Bigelow*** | DD-942 |
| ***Mullinnix*** | DD-944 |
| ***Hull*** | DD-945 |
| ***Edson*** | DD-946 |
| ***Turner Joy*** | DD-951 |
| ***Barry*** | DD-933 |
| ***Davis*** | DD-937 |
| ***Jonas Ingram*** | DD-938 |
| ***Manley*** | DD-940 |
| ***Du Pont*** | DD-941 |
| ***Blandy*** | DD-943 |
| ***Morton*** | DD-948 |
| ***Richard S. Edwards*** | DD-950 |
| ***Decatur*** (ex-DD-936) | DDG-31 |
| ***John Paul Jones*** (ex-DD-932) | DDG-32 |
| ***Parsons*** (ex-DD-949) | DDG-33 |
| ***Somers*** (ex-DD-947) | DDG-34 |

Note: DD-939 was allocated to an ex-German destroyer, *Z.39*.

**Displacement** 2,780-2,850 tons (standard), 4,200 tons (full load)
**Dimensions** 127.4m (oa) × 13.7m × 6.1m (418ft (oa) × 45ft × 20ft)
**Propulsion** 2 shafts, geared steam turbines, 4 boilers; 70,000 shp = 32.5 knots
**Armament** (*Forrest Sherman*) 3 single 5in (127mm) 54-cal guns, 1 twin 3in (76mm) 50-cal guns, 2 triple 12.7in (324mm) torpedo tubes
(ASW) 2 single 5in (127mm) 54-cal guns, 1 8-tube Asroc ASW launcher, 2 triple 12.7in (324mm) Mk 32 torpedo tubes
(DDG) 1 single Tartar SAM launcher, 1 single 5in (127mm) 54-cal gun, 1 8-tube Asroc ASW launcher, 2 triple 12.7in (324mm) Mk 32 torpedo tubes
**Complement** (FS) 17 officers, 275 enlisted men
(ASW) 17 officers, 287 enlisted men
(DDG) 22-25 officers, 315-339 enlisted men

18 *Forrest Sherman* built 1953-59 by Bath Iron Works, Bethlehem Steel Co, Puget Sound SB + DD Co, Ingalls SB Co. *Bigelow*, *Edson*, *Forrest Sherman*, *Hull*, *Mullinnix* and *Turner Joy* unconverted. 8 converted for ASW: *Barry*, *Blandy*, *Davis*, *Du Pont*, *Jonas Ingram*, *Manley*, *Morton* and *Richard S. Edwards*. 4 converted to DDG (*Decatur* class): *Decatur*, *John Paul Jones*, *Parsons* and *Somers*.

The first post-war destroyers built for the US Navy were the 18 *Forrest Sherman* class, ordered under FY 1953 to 1956. They reflected the general growth of destroyers, being some 400 tons heavier than the previous *Gearing*s, but embodied few new ideas. The main improvement was in armament, with three of the new single 5in/54-cal Mk 42 DP guns and two twin 3in automatic AA mountings. Though there were no

The after superstructure of the USS *Bigelow* (DD-942), showing the experimental 20mm Vulcan Phalanx Close-In Weapon System (CIWS) ahead of the 5in gun. This weapon, based on the successful Gatling gun used in aircraft, is intended to destroy sea-skimming missiles by sheer weight of metal.

The *Hull* (DD-945) firing the prototype lightweight 8in Mk 71 gun during trials. Although successful, the gun has now been removed and lack of funds may prevent its adoption. Firing laser-guided, rocket-assisted shells, it would be a comparatively cheap anti-ship weapon, as well as providing much-needed fire support.

anti-ship torpedoes, each ship had four tubes for firing Mk 35 anti-submarine torpedoes.

The class fell into three groups. The *Decatur* (DD-936-944) and *Hull* groups (DD-945-951) each had different bows from the original type. Since completion they have been further subdivided as a result of modernisation work.

Although they were a great improvement on wartime destroyers, by the mid-1950s the *Forrest Sherman*s were badly outclassed in the anti-aircraft and anti-submarine roles. Four were converted to missile ships in 1965-68 and eight were given an anti-submarine conversion in 1967-71. Rising costs ruled out the conversion of the remaining eight (DD-931, 942, 944-46 and 951).

The four DDGs were each given a single-arm Tartar SAM launcher aft in place of the two 5in guns, and massive lattice masts to carry the radar arrays, but their small size meant that they could carry only one missile fire-control director. They were intended to have Dash drone ASW helicopters, but when this system failed they were given Asroc instead. The reduced effectiveness of their missile armament was one reason for not extending the *Forrest Sherman* programme.

The ASW modernisation was more cost-effective. The after deckhouse was extended to the edge of the weather deck to form a flight deck for the Dash helicopter; this was subsequently replaced by an Asroc launcher and the hangar was not installed. All were fitted with a variable-depth sonar on the fantail, and *Barry* was given the new SQS-23 bow sonar, which necessitated repositioning of her anchors.

The unmodernised ships have been used for various trials and subsidiary duties. In 1977 *Edson* was assigned to the naval reserve for engine-room training at Newport, Rhode Island, while *Bigelow* and *Hull* have tested two new weapons, the 20mm Vulcan Phalanx Gatling gun and the lightweight 8in Mk 71. The *Hull* proved that a major-calibre gun could be fired safely from a destroyer, and it is said that "not so much as a light bulb broke" during the firing trials.

The modernised ships will continue to serve for some years but the future of the six unmodernised ships must be uncertain. In all probability they will be reduced to reserve training duties or transferred to other navies.

# FRAM I *Gearing* class

| Name | Number |
|---|---|
| ***Hamner*** | DD-718 |
| ***Southerland*** | DD-743 |
| ***William C. Lawe*** | DD-763 |
| ***McKean*** | DD-784 |
| ***Henderson*** | DD-785 |
| ***Hollister*** | DD-788 |
| ***Higbee*** | DD-806 |
| ***Corry*** | DD-817 |
| ***Johnston*** | DD-821 |
| ***Robert H. McCard*** | DD-822 |
| ***Myles C. Fox*** | DD-829 |
| ***Charles P. Cecil*** | DD-835 |
| ***Fiske*** | DD-842 |
| ***Vogelgesang*** | DD-862 |
| ***Steinaker*** | DD-863 |
| ***Harold J. Ellison*** | DD-864 |
| ***Cone*** | DD-866 |
| ***Damato*** | DD-871 |
| ***Hawkins*** | DD-873 |
| ***Rogers*** | DD-876 |
| ***Dyess*** | DD-880 |
| ***Newman K. Perry*** | DD-883 |
| ***John R. Craig*** | DD-885 |
| ***Orleck*** | DD-886 |
| ***Meredith*** | DD-890 |
| ***Marcilio Dias*** (Brazil) | D 25 |
| ***Mariz e Barros*** | D 26 |
| ***Presidente Eloy Alfaro*** (Ecuador) | |
| ***Kanaris*** (Greece) | 210 |
| ***Kontouriotis*** | 213 |
| ***Sachtouris*** | 214 |
| ***Tombazis*** | 215 |
| ***Kwang Ju*** (South Korea) | DD 90 |
| ***Taejon*** | DD 99 |
| ***Kang Won*** | ? |
| ***Tariq*** (Pakistan) | D 165 |
| ***Taimur*** | D 166 |
| ***Churruca*** (Spain) | D 61 |
| ***Gravina*** | D 62 |
| ***Mendez Nuñez*** | D 63 |
| ***Langara*** | D 64 |
| ***Blas de Lezo*** | D 65 |
| ***Chien Yang*** (Taiwan) | 921 |
| ***Han Yang*** | 978 |
| ***Lao Yang*** | ? |
| ***Liao Yang*** | 938 |
| ***Kai Yang*** | ? |
| ***Te Yang*** | 925 |
| ***Shen Yang*** | 932 |
| ***Lai Yang*** | 981 |
| ***M. Fevzi Çakmak*** (Turkey) | D 351 |
| ***Gayret*** | D 352 |
| ***Adatepe*** | D 353 |

**Displacement** 2,425 tons (standard), 3,480-3,520 tons (full load)
**Dimensions** 119.0m (oa) × 12.4m × 5.8m (390.5ft (oa) × 40.9ft × 19ft)
**Propulsion** 2 shafts, geared steam turbines, 4 boilers; 60,000 shp = 34 knots
**Aircraft** Fitted for Dash
**Armament** 2 twin 5in (127mm) 38-cal guns, 1 × 8-tube Asroc ASM launcher, 2 triple 12.7in (324mm) Mk 32 torpedo tubes
**Complement** 14 officers, 260 enlisted men

USN operates 28 *Gearing*s built 1944-51. 28 transferred from 1971 onwards. Brazil (2), Ecuador (1), Greece (4), South Korea (3), Pakistan (2), Spain (5), Taiwan (8), Turkey (3).

The Fleet Rehabilitation and Modernisation (FRAM) programme undertaken in FY 1960-64 was an ambitious attempt to arrest the march of block obsolescence in the US Navy. A series of comprehensive overhauls saved a large number of the *Fletcher*, *Allen M. Sumner* and *Gearing*-class destroyers from the scrapheap, allowing them to continue in service as anti-submarine escorts.

Three new weapon systems were at the heart of the FRAM programme: the Mk 44 acoustic homing torpedo, the Asroc long-range ASW missile and the Dash drone helicopter. The FRAM I overhaul was intended to extend the life of the 15-year-old destroyers by at least 8-10 years, and the long-hulled *Gearing*s benefited in particular.

The failure of Dash made the conversion less effective than it might have been, but still the *Gearing*s became formidable ships. An Asroc launcher was mounted amidships, triple Mk 32 torpedo tubes were mounted either forward or amidships, and the radars were modernised. Most ships lost one twin 5in gun mounting, and the positions of the remainder varied; some had guns forward and aft, others had both forward. The distinctive features of the FRAM I were the new conical funnel-caps and the massive Dash hangar aft.

Many of the class have been scrapped and they are disappearing from the US Navy, but a number survive in smaller navies. Several of those transferred have been cannibalised for spares, and the majority of those still serving in the USN will probably go the same way.

▲ The Turkish destroyer *Adatepe* is typical of the large number of *Gearing*-class destroyers given the FRAM I conversion. Note the big Asroc launcher amidships and the hangar for the Dash drone helicopter aft. Modernised US destroyers can be recognised by their distinctive funnel caps.

## FRAM II *Allen M. Sumner* class

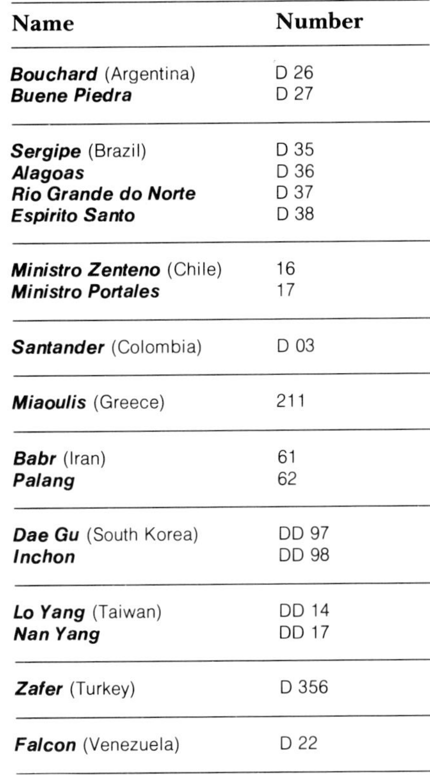

| Name | Number |
|---|---|
| ***Bouchard*** (Argentina) | D 26 |
| ***Buene Piedra*** | D 27 |
| ***Sergipe*** (Brazil) | D 35 |
| ***Alagoas*** | D 36 |
| ***Rio Grande do Norte*** | D 37 |
| ***Espirito Santo*** | D 38 |
| ***Ministro Zenteno*** (Chile) | 16 |
| ***Ministro Portales*** | 17 |
| ***Santander*** (Colombia) | D 03 |
| ***Miaoulis*** (Greece) | 211 |
| ***Babr*** (Iran) | 61 |
| ***Palang*** | 62 |
| ***Dae Gu*** (South Korea) | DD 97 |
| ***Inchon*** | DD 98 |
| ***Lo Yang*** (Taiwan) | DD 14 |
| ***Nan Yang*** | DD 17 |
| ***Zafer*** (Turkey) | D 356 |
| ***Falcon*** (Venezuela) | D 22 |

The Chilean *Ministro Zenteno* looks like a *Gearing* FRAM I but is in fact a FRAM II of the *Allen M. Sumner* class. Her funnels are closer together, leaving no space for an Asroc launcher, although she has a variable-depth sonar (VDS) aft. As in other FRAM conversions, the Dash drones are no longer operated.

**Displacement** 2,200 tons (standard), 3,320 tons (full load)
**Dimensions** 114.8m (oa) × 12.4m × 5.8m (376.5ft (oa) × 40.9ft × 19ft)
**Propulsion** 2 shafts, geared steam turbines, 4 boilers; 60,000 shp = 34 knots
**Aircraft** Fitted for Dash
**Armament** 3 twin 5in (127mm) 38-cal guns, (some ships) 1 or 2 twin 3in (76mm) 50-cal guns or 1 20mm Vulcan Gatling gun, 2 triple 12.7in (324mm) Mk 32 torpedo tubes, 2 Hedgehog A/S mortars
**Complement** Approx 275 officers and men

None in USN. Built 1943-46. 18 transferred 1969-74. Argentina (2), Brazil (4), Chile (2), Colombia (1), Greece (1), Iran (2), South Korea (2), Taiwan (2), Turkey (1), Venezuela (1).

There was not enough money to apply FRAM I conversions to all the USN destroyers, and in any case the smaller *Allen M. Sumner* and *Fletcher* hulls could not take Asroc, the primary weapon system of the FRAM I *Gearing*s. A further 16 *Gearing*s, 33 *Sumner*s and 3 *Fletcher*s were selected for a FRAM II conversion. This was less elaborate, and was only expected to add five years to the hull life.

Externally the FRAM II *Sumner*s looked very similar to the FRAM I *Gearing*s, but with the funnels closer together and no Asroc amidships. All but two had the Dash hangar and flight deck, but there were many differences of detail.

Out of the 33 converted none survives in the US Navy. *Frank E. Evans* was cut in half by the Australian carrier *Melbourne* during a night exercise in June 1969, while the *Bordelon* was scrapped after being badly damaged in a collision with the carrier *John F. Kennedy*. Several have been scrapped and the others transferred to friendly navies, in which they will continue to serve for some years, although lack of spares will become an increasing problem.

H.M.S. COVENTRY SUNK 5-25-82
H.M.S. SHEFFIELD SUNK 5-10-82

## *Sheffield* class

**Displacement** 3,150 tons (standard), 4,100 tons (full load)
**Dimensions** 125m (oa) × 14m × 4.3m (410ft (oa) × 46ft × 14ft)
**Propulsion** 2 shafts, 2 sets geared gas turbines (COGOG); 50,000 shp = 30 knots
**Aircraft** 1 Lynx A/S helicopter
**Armament** 1 twin Sea Dart SAM launcher, 1 single 4.5in (114mm) Mk 8 gun, 2 single 20mm guns, 2 triple 12.7in (324mm) STWS torpedo tubes
**Complement** 26 officers, 273 men

*Birmingham*, *Cardiff*, *Coventry*, *Exeter*, *Glasgow*, *Newcastle*, *Sheffield* and *Southampton* built or building from 1970 onwards by Vickers, Barrow; Cammell Laird, Birkenhead; Swan Hunter, Wallsend; Vosper Thornycroft, Woolston. *Nottingham* ordered from Vosper Thornycroft. *Manchester* ordered from Vickers, *Gloucester* from Vosper Thornycroft, *Edinburgh* from Cammell Laird and *York* from Swan Hunter. *Hercules*, *Santissima Trinidad* built and building 1971 onwards by Vickers, Barrow; and AFNE, Rio Santiago.

The cost of the DLG *Bristol* (about £40 million at 1966 prices) was regarded as too high, and so for the next class of missile-armed fleet escorts the Royal Navy produced a utility design known as the Type 42. The basis was simple: everything that could be salvaged from the Type 82, but at half the cost.

Allowing for this idiosyncratic approach to ship design, the result is an ingeniously compact warship. The Sea Dart area-defence missile system was kept, as was the same outfit of radars and sonar, and a light helicopter and hangar were incorporated at the expense of the Ikara long-range ASW missile system. The use of highly automated machinery controls allowed a reduction of 25 per cent on technical manpower as well.

The main criticism of the design is that it is cramped, and no additions can be made without removal of a major item of equipment. There is no short-range defence, but the Sea Dart has proved a particularly agile missile and performs well against low-level targets. Now that the politically inspired constraints on size have slackened, the opportunity has been taken to enlarge the design, and the Batch 2 ships (*Manchester* onwards) will be about 30ft longer and slightly wider. Although not much, this will provide better seakeeping by lengthening the forecastle and will

generate much-needed internal volume.

The withdrawal of the RN from its overseas role meant that long endurance was no longer of paramount importance, another factor in keeping size down.

The *Sheffield* was expected to encounter severe problems with the heat output from her gas turbines, and so she was fitted with experimental "ears" or elbow exhausts on the sides of her funnel. Their purpose is to prevent the exhaust gases from melting aerials and damaging radar arrays. But it is reported that the problem was exaggerated and her sisters have not been fitted with this feature. She will lose them at her next refit.

Two ships were ordered for Argentina, of which the first, *Hercules*, was delivered in 1976. Her sister, *Santissima Trinidad*, was badly damaged in the building yard at Rio Santiago by urban guerrillas. Her completion has been badly delayed but she was reported to be nearly ready at the beginning of 1979.

The class (apart from *Sheffield*) is fitted with the STWS automated anti-submarine torpedo system, with USN-pattern Mk 46s in a mounting based on the American Mk 32 launcher but controlled by a new British fire-control system.

The Sea Dart SAM system is almost identical to that in HMS *Bristol*, but the launcher is lighter and mounted forward. Two Type 909 radars are positioned forward and aft to give all-round coverage, and 22 missiles are carried. This disposition at either end of the ship is an improvement over the more usual aft layout in DDGs, and it controls the gun as well.

The *Sheffield* commissioned in 1975 and since then five more of the class have been delivered. Work has been held up by shortages of labour and materials in the shipyards, and *Cardiff* had to be towed from Barrow to Swan Hunter's Tyne yard for completion. Though much work went into achieving "identicality" between ships, this was carried to ludicrous extremes and contributed to some of the delays, with each set of drawings having to be altered if the slightest change was made in the lead ship.

Despite the delays these ships are proving a success, and as they come into service the Counties will be paid off. Present orders cover 10 ships, plus four enlarged versions, the *Manchester* class.

HMS *Sheffield* at the Jubilee Review in June 1977. Apart from her giant "ears" for cooling funnel gases and deflecting them from aerials, she is typical of the rest of the class. Note the big weatherproof domes for the Sea Dart missile directors, the big "bedstead" radar and the Wasp helicopter aft.

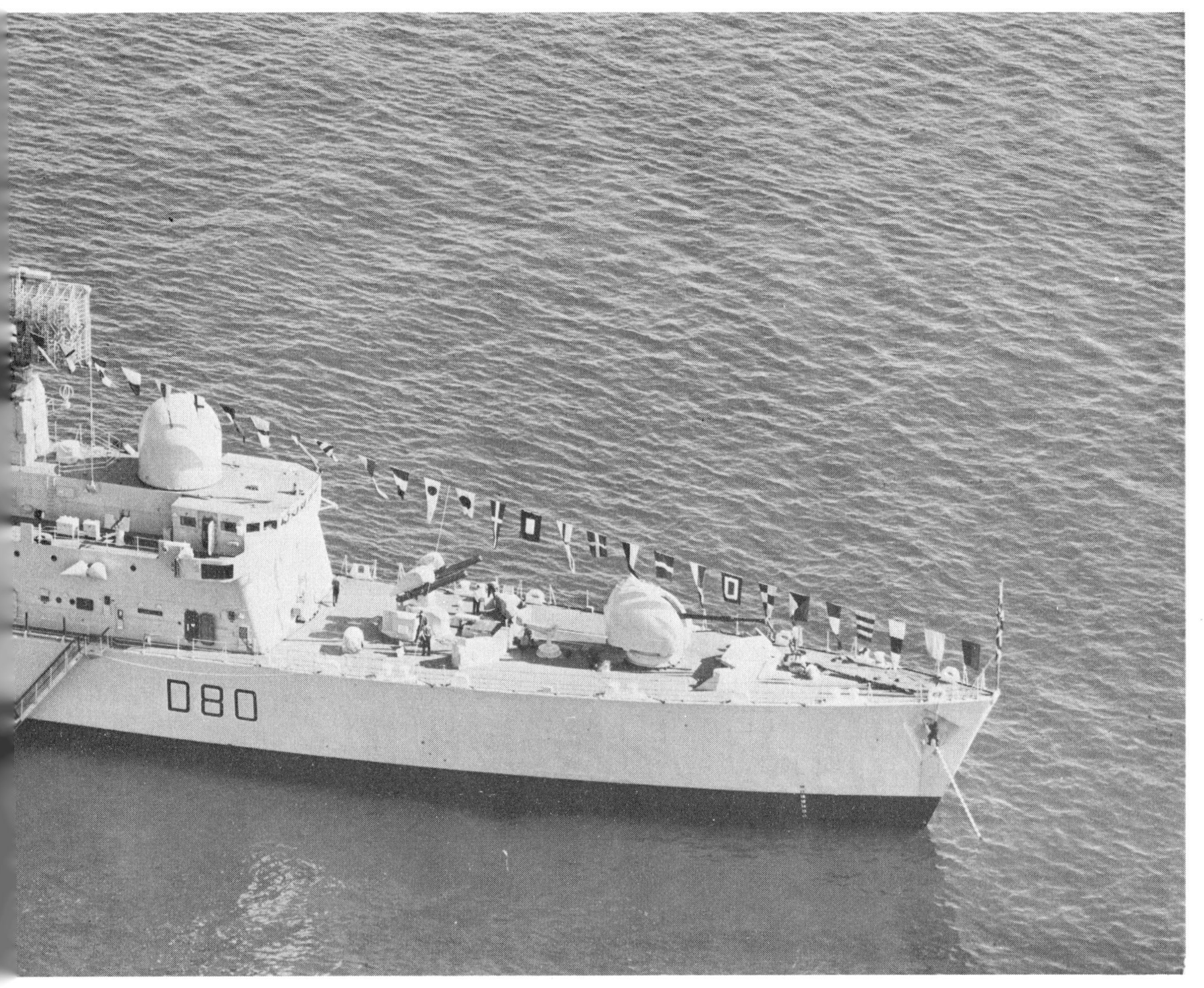

# *Georges Leygues* class

| Name | Number | Laid down | Launched | Completed | Builder |
|---|---|---|---|---|---|
| ***Georges Leygues*** | D 640 | Sep 1974 | 17 Sep 1976 | Oct 1979 | Brest Dockyard |
| ***Dupleix*** | D 641 | Oct 1975 | 2 Dec 1978 | – | Brest Dockyard |
| ***Montcalm*** | D 642 | Dec 1975 | – | – | Brest Dockyard |
| unnamed | D 643 | 1979 | – | – | Brest Dockyard |

**Displacement** 3,800 tonnes (standard), 4,170 tonnes (full load)
**Dimensions** 139.0m (oa) × 14.0m × 5.73m (455.9ft (oa) × 45.9ft × 18.7ft)
**Propulsion** 2 shafts, gas turbines or diesel drive (CODOG); 42,000 shp = 29.75 knots
**Aircraft** 2 Lynx A/S helicopters
**Armament** 1 × 8-tube Crotale SAM launcher, 4 single Exocet SSM launchers, 1 × 3.9in (100mm) gun, 2 single 20mm guns, 2× 21in (533mm) torpedo tubes
**Complement** 21 officers, 229 men

Although rated as corvettes by the French Navy, this class is equivalent to the destroyer category in other navies and even bears a strong resemblance to the big *Broadsword*-class frigates of the Royal Navy.

The C70 (C= corvette and 70 = 1970, the date of the design requirement) is intended as an ocean escort, with good anti-submarine capability, point defence against air attack and a surface strike capability. For the first she has two Lynx ASW helicopters, homing torpedoes and two big sonars. The new Crotale missile provides short-range defence, and for surface attack she carries the standard 100mm gun and four MM.38 Exocet missiles.

The class represents a new departure in being powered by the Rolls-Royce Olympus gas turbine in a Combined Diesel Or Gas Turbine (CODOG) arrangement. Gas turbines have been tried before in small escorts but this is the first time that they have been used as prime movers in a major warship.

The class is intended for quantity production, but financial problems have caused severe delays in the construction of the follow-on ships. An air-defence version is planned, with American Standard SM-1 SAMs rather than the French-made Masurca, but no order has been placed yet. The original programme allowed for 18 anti-submarine and six anti-aircraft types.

The *Georges Leygues* started her basin trials in mid-November 1977 but did not get her Crotale missile launcher until the following year. As lead ship she has undergone an extensive series of trials and did not become operational until the spring of 1979. Her first two sisters, *Dupleix* and *Montcalm*, are expected to complete in 1980.

The French destroyer *Georges Leygues* on trials at Brest in 1979, with the prototype Crotale missile launcher installed aft. The wide stern permits a full-width flight deck serving a double helicopter hangar, and four Exocet surface-to-surface missiles are mounted between the funnel and the hangar.

## *Surcouf* class

**Displacement** 2,750 tons (standard), 3,740 tons (Type T47 DDG, Type T53), 3,900 tons (Type T47ASW) (full load)
**Dimensions** (T47 ASW) 132.5m (oa), (T47 DDG, T53) 128.6m (oa) × 12.7m × 5.5m (T53); 6.3m (T47 DDG, T47 ASW) (421.3ft (oa) × 41.7ft × 18ft (T53); 21.4ft (T47 DDG, T47 ASW))
**Propulsion** 2 shafts, geared steam turbines, 4 boilers; 63,000 shp = 32 knots
**Armament** (T47 DDG) 1 single Tartar SAM launcher, 3 twin 57mm guns, 1 × 6-barrel 14.8in (375mm) Mk 54 A/S rocket launcher, 2 triple 21.7in (550mm) torpedo tubes
(T47 ASW) 2 single 3.9in (100mm) guns, 2 single 20mm guns, 1 single Malafon ASM launcher, 1 × 6-barrel 14.8in (375mm) Mk 54 A/S rocket launcher, 2 triple 21.7in (550mm) torpedo tubes
(T53) 3 twin 5in (127mm) guns, 3 twin 57mm guns, 2 single 20mm guns, 1 × 6-barrel 14.8in (375mm) Mk 54 A/S rocket launcher, 2 triple 21.7in (550mm) torpedo tubes
**Complement** (T47 DDG) 17 officers, 260 men
(T47 ASW) 15 officers, 245 men
(T53) 15 officers, 261 men

Type T47 (DDG) *Bouvet, du Chayla, Dupetit Thouars, Kersaint*
Type T47 (ASW) *Casabianca, d'Estrées, Guépratte, Maille Brézé, Vauquelin*
Type T53 *Forbin, Tartu*
Type T53 (Mod) *Duperré*
Type T56 *La Galissonnière*

Built 1951-62 by Brest Dockyard, Lorient Dockyard, F.C. Gironde, A. C. Bretagne.

As part of a massive effort to rebuild the *Marine Nationale* almost from scratch, the French ordered a class of large destroyers from 1949 to 1953. The first dozen were rated as *Escorteur Rapide Anti-aérien* (Type T47). Subsequently the designation was changed to *Escorteur de 1ère Classe*, then *Escorteur Rapide* and finally *Escorteur d'Escadre*. The last five, ordered in 1953, were intended for aircraft-direction duties and were designated Type T53R. Subsequently an extra unit, the Type T56 *La Galissonnière*, was laid down in 1957 to act as a command ship or divisional leader.

The original armament was a mixture of 5in (127mm) guns chambered to fire the standard American round, and Bofors 57mm twin guns made under licence in France. A heavy armament of torpedoes was provided, four triple banks firing both anti-ship and anti-submarine torpedoes. It is sometimes claimed that the hull was based on those of pre-war *contre-torpilleurs* or super destroyers, and certainly the dimensions are similar to those of the *Mogador* and *Volta*. But the installed power is about 50 per cent less and the shape of bow and stern is quite different. It is however possible that the characteristics of the last big destroyers built in France were taken as a starting point for calculations.

Since then the ships have undergone several transformations. Five – *d'Estrées*, *Maille Brézé*, *Vauquelin*, *Casabianca* and *Guépratte* – were converted to ASW ships in 1968-70, with variable-depth sonar on the quarterdeck, a Malafon anti-submarine missile launcher immediately ahead of it and a six-barrelled rocket launcher in "B" position. In addition, the 5in guns were replaced by two new 100mm guns and the funnels were raised.

Four ships were converted to missile destroyers, with a single-arm launcher for Tartar SAMs aft, a 3-D radar on the

ıainmast and all 5in guns removed. As n the ASW ships, the funnels were aised to keep smoke clear of the new nlarged superstructure. These ships vere the *Kersaint*, *Bouvet*, *Dupetit houars* and *du Chayla*, and they rovided valuable experience with uided weapons before the Masurca nissile was ready.

Three more ships, the *Cassard*, *Chevalier Paul* and *Surcouf*, were onverted to command ships but etained their 5in guns. The original Type '53s, the *Duperré*, *Forbin*, *auréguiberry*, *La Bourdonnais* and *artu*, were not altered in the same way, but in 1967 *Duperré* became a sonar trials ship with all of its armament removed.

Today only 13 of these handsome ships remain. The *Surcouf* was cut in two in a collision in June 1971, and the *Chevalier Paul* and *Cassard* were stricken in 1974, followed by *La Bourdonnais* in 1976 and *Jauréguiberry* in 1977. *Duperré* was refitted and rearmed for active duty in 1972-74 but ran aground at the end of 1977 in gales off Brittany. They are unlikely to be retained for many more years, and the unmodernised *Forbin* and *Tartu* will probably be the first to go.

▲ The *Duperré* in December 1968, when she was testing an experimental variable-depth sonar of immense size. Since then she has been refitted in similar fashion to her sisters, with taller funnels, Exocet missiles amidships, a 100mm gun forward and a helicopter hangar and flight deck aft.

▼ The *d'Estrées* is typical of the modernised T47 type, with 100mm guns forward and aft and a Malafon anti-submarine missile system and variable-depth sonar on the quarterdeck. During this modernisation the original short funnels were raised, completely altering their appearance.

## Krivak class

**Displacement** 3,300 tons (standard), 3,900 tons (full load)
**Dimensions** 123.4m (oa) × 14m × 5m (404.8ft (oa) × 45.9ft × 16.4ft)
**Propulsion** 2 shafts, geared gas turbines; 80,000 shp = 32 knots
**Armament** 2 twin SA-N-4 SAM launchers, 2 twin 3in (76mm) guns (later ships have 2 single 3.9in [100mm] guns instead), 1 quad SS-N-14 ASM launcher.
2 × 12-barrel MBU-2500A A/S rocket launcher, 2 quad 21in (533mm) torpedo tubes
**Complement** Approx 250 officers and men

15 + 7 Krivak IIs built from 1971 at Kaliningrad, Kerch and Leningrad. Building at about 4 per year.

This group of handsome ships provides another example of the Western tendency to exaggerate the qualities of Soviet warships. When first sighted in 1971 they were credited with a 20-mile-range surface-to-surface missile system and a speed as high as 34 knots on the power of aero-derived gas turbines. This assessment has since been revised and they are now regarded as useful ASW frigates introduced to replace the elderly *Skory* class. Estimates of their speed and installed power have been reduced, and US authorities now credit the class with a modest 29-30 knots from industrial-derived turbines.

One of the class, *Storozhevoi*, was reported to have suffered a severe breakdown of discipline in the Baltic in 1975 and to have tried to reach neutral Sweden before turning back under threat of attack from Soviet aircraft and other ships. She was shortly afterwards transferred to the Pacific.

So far 16 of the original Krivak design

▲ The Krivak-class *Storozhevoi* in April 1976, possibly in transit to the Pacific following her reported "mutiny" in 1975. The low, square-cut funnel set far aft is the most distinctive feature of the design, and the low superstructure enhances the sleek appearance.

◀ Another view of the *Storozhevoi* taken on the same occasion by a helicopter from HMS *Blake*. Note the massive SS-N-14 missile launchers forward, the "manhole cover" abaft the funnel hiding the SA-N-4 missile launcher, and the twin 76mm guns aft. The door in the stern covers the VDS well.

have been seen, followed by seven modified ships with the after guns slightly raised. Another modification is a larger type of variable-depth sonar.

These ships all bear traditional destroyer names, further confirmation of their rating. As many as four a year may be building at Kaliningrad and Leningrad in the Baltic and Kamiech-Burun in the Black Sea.

| Name |
| --- |
| **Krivak I** |
| ***Bditelny*** |
| ***Bodry*** |
| ***Dejatelny*** |
| ***Doblestny*** |
| ***Dostoiny*** |
| ***Druzhny*** |
| ***Leningradsky Komsomolets*** |
| ***Razumny*** |
| ***Razytelny*** |
| ***Razyaschy*** |
| ***Retivy*** |
| ***Silny*** |
| ***Storozhevoi*** |
| ***Svirepy*** |
| ***Zharky*** |
| **Krivak II** |
| ***Rezky*** |
| ***Rezvy*** |
| ***Razitelny*** |
| ***Grozyaschy*** |
| ***Neukrotiny*** |
| ***Bessmenny*** |
| ***Gromky*** |

# Kashin class

| Name |
|---|
| **Kashin** |
| *Obraztsovy* |
| *Odarenny* |
| *Stereguschy* |
| *Komsomolets Ukrainy* |
| *Krasny Kavkaz* |
| *Krasny Krim* |
| *Provorny* |
| *Otvazhny* |
| *Reshitelny* |
| *Skory* |
| *Smetlivy* |
| *Soobrazitelny* |
| *Sposobny* |
| *Stroyny* |
| *Strogy* |
| **Modified Kashin** |
| *Ognevoi* |
| *Slavny* |
| *Sderzhanny* |
| *Smely* |
| *Smyshlenny* |

**Displacement** (Kashin) 3,750 tons (standard), 4,500 tons (full load) (Modified Kashin) 3,950 tons (standard), 4,950 tons (full load)
**Dimensions** (K) 143.3m (oa) × 15.9m × 4.7m (470.9ft (oa) × 52.5ft × 15.4ft) (MK) 146.5m (oa) × 15.9m × 4.7m (481ft (oa) × 52.5ft × 15.4ft)
**Propulsion** 2 shafts, geared gas turbines; 96,000 shp = 35 knots
**Aircraft** (MK) Pad for helicopter
**Armament** (K) 2 twin SA-N-1 SAM launchers, 2 twin 3in (76mm) guns, 2 × 12-barrel MBU-2500A A/S rocket launchers, 2 × 6-barrel MBU-4500 A/S rocket launchers, 1 quint 21in (533mm) torpedo tubes
(MK) 2 twin SA-N-1 SAM launchers, 4 single SS-N-2 SSM launchers, 2 twin 3in (76mm) guns, 4 Gatling-type 30mm guns, 2 × 12-barrel MBU-2500A A/S rocket launchers, 1 quint 21in (533mm) torpedo tubes
**Complement** Approx 300 officers and men

15 Kashin, 5 Modified Kashin built 1962-1966 by Zhdanov (Leningrad) and Nikolaiev. More being modified.

The first class of operational warships in the world to rely on gas turbines as main propulsion, the Kashins came into service between 1962 and 1966. At first they were credited with eight gas turbines, but then it was realised that there was no room for eight normal-sized turbines delivering that sort of power. In fact Soviet sources revealed that the ships had four industrial-type turbines, the split uptakes of which had misled Western observers.

The Kashins' armament was clearly dedicated to anti-aircraft defence, with two twin-arm SA-N-1 Goa SAM launchers and two twin 76mm automatic gun mountings. The distinctive angled uptakes proved too low and had to be increased in height slightly to keep fumes away from equipment. As with other Soviet ships, virtually every square foot of deck space is covered with weapons of one sort or another.

These ships were intended to operate a helicopter, for which a control position was provided on the quarterdeck. This was clearly unusable, a weakness which, along with the lack of a surface weapon system, led in 1973 to the first modernised Kashin. Lengthened by about 10ft to allow installation of a proper helicopter landing deck (but still no hangar), she also had four SS-N-11 SSMs in single bins level with the after funnel

▲ This bow shot of an unmodified Kashin in Ethiopia in 1972 shows the mass of aerials and antennas which gives Soviet ships such an impressive appearance. It also shows how the uptakes are angled to keep exhaust gases clear of the two masts. The penalty paid in topweight and freeboard in this class is severe.

and firing aft. Another addition was a pair of 23mm Gatling gun mountings on either side amidships, presumably as a close-in defence against missiles. A variable-depth sonar was fitted under the helicopter pad.

In September 1974 the *Otvazhny* caught fire after an explosion in the Black Sea. She burned for five hours and nearly all of her 300 crew were lost in the worst peacetime disaster to befall a warship in 50 years.

Although ingenious in design the Kashins proved short of freeboard for North Atlantic operations and have been transferred to the Black Sea and Mediterranean. Modernisation presents many problems because the original hull is near its limit of weight and equipment volume.

◀ A modernised Kashin-class DDG, with Gatling guns mounted abreast of the second funnel, SS-N-2 Styx missile launchers facing aft, and a helicopter flight deck. Each of the four sets of gas turbines has its own uptake to vent the enormous amounts of heat generated; the uptakes are angled to carry the heat clear of radar arrays.

# Kanin class

**Displacement** 3,700 tons (standard), 4,700 tons (full load)
**Dimensions** 141m (oa) × 14.7m × 5.0m (465ft (oa) × 48.2ft × 16.4ft)
**Propulsion** 2 shafts, geared steam turbines, 4 boilers; 84,000 shp = 34 knots
**Aircraft** Pad for helicopter
**Armament** 1 twin SA-N-1 SAM launcher, 2 quad 57mm guns, 4 twin 30mm guns, 3 × 12-barrel MBU-2500A A/S rocket launchers, 2 quint 21in (533mm) torpedo tubes
**Complement** Approx 350 officers and men

*Boyky, Derzky, Gnevny, Gordy, Gremyashchyi, Uporny, Zhguchy* and *Zorky* built 1958-60 (as Krupny class). Converted 1967 onwards.

The eight Krupny-class destroyers completed in 1961-63 had a crude launching system for the Strela SSM, and within a short while approval was given to convert them to air-defence ships equipped with the SA-N-1 Goa SAM system.

The ships look somewhat similar to the original Krupny type, but without the massive single launchers for Strela forward and aft. The bow was also raised slightly, presumably to keep the forecastle drier in a seaway. The bridgework was enlarged and a second quadruple 57mm gun mounting was installed forward, along with a multiple ASW rocket launcher. The after quad 57mm was removed to make room for the Goa launcher and a helicopter flight deck. Subsequently four twin 30mm guns in conical "barbette" mountings were installed level with the after funnel.

These ships are getting on in years and are past what would be their mid-life in Western navies. The obsolescence of the Goa SAM makes them something of a diminishing asset, but the usual Soviet practice is to get the maximum work out of a ship before scrapping her.

▼ The Kanin-class *Boyky* shadowing HMS *Hermes* in October 1973 and making a great deal of smoke as she tries to get ahead of the carrier as fast as she can. Two of the four twin 30mm Gatlings added can be seen abreast of the after funnel on a large, boxlike deckhouse.

## Kildin class

**Displacement** 3,000 tons (standard), 4,000 tons (full load)
**Dimensions** 126.5m (oa) × 13m × 4.9m (414.9ft (oa) × 42.6ft × 16.1ft)
**Propulsion** 2 shafts, geared steam turbines, 4 boilers; 72,000 shp = 35 knots
**Armament** 4 single SS-N-2 SAM launchers, 2 twin 3in (76mm) guns, 4 quad 45mm guns, 2 × 16-barrel A/S rocket launchers, 2 twin 21in (533mm) torpedo tubes
**Complement** Approx 300 officers and men

*Bedovy*, *Neudersimy*, *Neulovimy* and *Prozorlivy* built 1958 at Zhdanov, Leningrad; and Nikolaiev. Modified 1972 onwards.

The last four Kotlin-class destroyers built in 1952-60 were completed as missile destroyers equipped with the same Strela missile as the Krupny class. Because they were smaller they had only one Strela launcher aft and carried their quadruple 57mm guns forward in "A" and "B" positions.

The conversion was completed in 1958 and they served with some success for ten years or so. But then the Strela was phased out and in 1972 the *Neulovimy* was taken in hand for modernisation. The Strela launcher and magazine were replaced by two twin 76mm gun mountings and four SS-N-2 (Mod) Styx SSMs were added abreast of the after funnel. The arrangement is identical to that of Modified Kashin, with the missile bins facing aft and inclined. The quadruple 57mm mountings were left in position forward.

The four ships are in the Black Sea Fleet, possibly because their low freeboard puts them at a disadvantage in the Arctic and Northern Atlantic. The modernised Kildins are capable ships with a reasonably balanced armament, however, and will be around for some years.

▲ A Kildin in original condition, showing the SS-N-1 Strela missile launcher aft. Since then the Strela launcher has been replaced by two twin 76mm gun mountings, and aft-facing SS-N-2 Styx missiles have been added abreast of the second funnel. The quadruple 57mm AA guns have been left in position forward and amidships.

## *Skory* class

**Name**

***Besnervny***
***Bessmertny***
***Bezuprechniy***
***Bezukoriznenny***
***Ognenny***
***Osterveniy***
***Ostorozny***
***Ostroglazy***
***Otchyanny***
***Otretovenny***
***Otvetstvenny***
***Ozhestochenny***
***Ozhivlenniy***
***Serdity***
***Seriozny***
***Smotryashchy***
***Sokrushitelny***
***Solidny***
***Sovershenny***
***Statny***
***Stepenny***
***Stoyky***
***Stremitelny***
***Surovy***
***Svobodny***
***Vazhny***
***Vdumchivy***
***Veduschy***
***Verny***
***Vidny***
***Vikhrevoy***
***Vnezapny***
***Vnimatelny***
***Volevoy***
***Vrazumitelny***

***Suez*** (Egypt)
***Al Zaffer***
***Damiette***
***8 October***

**Displacement** 2,300 tons (standard), 3,100 tons (full load)
**Dimensions** 120.5m (oa) × 11.8m × 4.6m (395.2ft (oa) × 38.9ft × 15.1ft)
**Propulsion** 2 shafts, geared steam turbines, 4 boilers; 60,000 shp = 33 knots
**Armament** 2 twin 5.1in (130mm) guns, 1 twin 3.4in (86mm) guns, 4 twin 37mm guns, 2 quint 21in (533mm) torpedo tubes, 4 depth-charge projectors (Mod) 2 twin 5.1in (130mm) guns, 5 single 57mm guns, 2 × 16-barrel A/S rocket launchers, 1 quint 21in (533mm) torpedo tubes
**Complement** Approx 280 officers and men

USSR 36 *Skory*. 6 transferred to Egypt, 4 to Indonesia, 2 to Poland. Built 1948-54 at Molotovsk and Zhdanov, Leningrad; Nikolaiev and Komsomolsk.

Large numbers of these destroyers were built in the 1950s, when Admiral Kuznetsov was labouring to rebuild the shattered Soviet Navy from the ruins of the Great Patriotic War. Greatly overrated in their day, they were in fact only an improved version of the *Ognyevoi* or *Projekt 30* type, a design which dated back to the mid-1930s. They were however built in large numbers, with 75 completed out of a planned total of 85.

The design was straightforward, with twin 130mm (5.1in) DP guns forward and aft, quintuple torpedo tubes, and turbines and boilers arranged on the unit system. The original shallow funnel caps were inadequate and many ships have since had bigger caps added to keep smoke out of the bridge. The survivors have been modified, a set of torpedo

ubes having been removed and the t of anti-aircraft armament trengthened.

The class has been much reduced by ansfers and half of them are in reserve. ney will all be scrapped before long. our were transferred to Egypt between 956 and 1962, and one was sunk or amaged beyond repair by French aircraft in 1956. Another of these ships was sunk by Israeli aircraft in retaliation for the sinking of the *Eilat* in 1967. This ship was replaced and two unmodernised ships were exchanged for sisters with more up to date AA armament. The four transferred to Indonesia were scrapped, as were the two transferred to Poland.

A *Skory*-class destroyer coming alongside, showing the strong resemblance to the pre-war *Silny* and *Ognyevoi* types. As with so many post-1950 Soviet designs, their speed was massively overestimated at 38 knots on 80,000 hp, They are now seen as a comparatively modest design.

# *Iroquois* class

| Name | Number | Laid down | Launched | Completed | Builder |
|---|---|---|---|---|---|
| ***Iroquois*** | 280 | 15 Jan 1969 | 28 Nov 1970 | 29 Jul 1972 | Marine Industries Ltd, Sorel |
| ***Huron*** | 281 | 15 Jan 1969 | 3 Apr 1971 | 16 Dec 1972 | Marine Industries Ltd, Sorel |
| ***Athabaskan*** | 282 | 1 Jun 1969 | 27 Nov 1970 | 30 Nov 1972 | Davie SB Co, Lauzon |
| ***Algonquin*** | 283 | 1 Sep 1969 | 23 Apr 1971 | 30 Sep 1973 | Davie SB Co, Lauzon |

**Displacement** 3,551 tons (standard), 4,200 tons (full load)
**Dimensions** 129.8m (oa) × 15.2m × 4.4m (426ft (oa) × 50ft × 14.5ft)
**Propulsion** 2 shafts, 2 sets geared gas turbines (COGOG); 50,000 shp = 29+ knots
**Aircraft** 2 CHSS-2 Sea King A/S helicopters
**Armament** 2 quad Sea Sparrow Mk III SAM launchers, 1 single 5in (127mm) 54-cal gun, 1 3-barrel Limbo A/S mortar, 2 triple 12.7in (324mm) Mk 32 torpedo tubes
**Complement** 27 officers, 255 men

These powerful destroyers were developed from a design for general-purpose frigates which were cancelled in 1963. The hull was retained but the armament was entirely updated to meet the rapidly changing demands of ASW.

The biggest change was to tailor the ships to operate a pair of big Sea King helicopters. This was a revolutionary step, for the Sea King was far bigger than any helicopter contemplated by other navies. By 1969, the year in which the new ships were to be laid down, the RCN had proved that it could operate a single Sea King from its *St Laurent*-class DDHs.

Apart from the problem of finding the space needed to accommodate two very large helicopters, special attention had to be paid to reducing pitch and roll to

HMCS *Iroquois* in line-ahead with the rest of the Nato STANAVFORLANT on manoeuvres in the English Channel in 1979. The DDH-280 class are instantly recognisable by the massive hangar, the twin radomes of their fire control and the Y-shaped funnels.

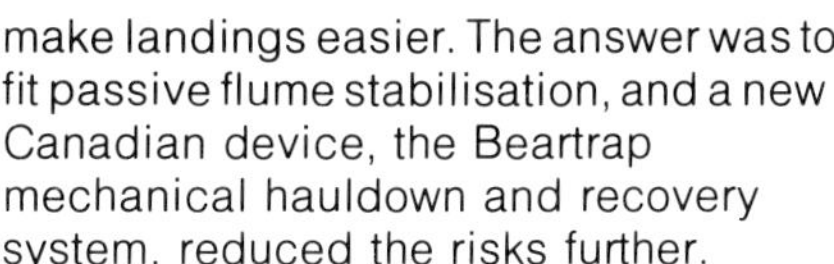

make landings easier. The answer was to fit passive flume stabilisation, and a new Canadian device, the Beartrap mechanical hauldown and recovery system, reduced the risks further.

The armament is impressive: an Italian-made 5in/54-cal gun, two quadruple Sea Sparrow close-range SAM launchers in the superstructure, triple ASW torpedo tubes and a three-barrelled Limbo depth-charge mortar. The arrangement of the Sea Sparrow SAMs is unique to this class, with four on overhead rails on either side underneath the bridge; they are normally concealed behind hinged ports.

These ships are very weatherly, with high freeboard. Although not "ice-capable" they are well suited to North Atlantic and cold-weather operations, offering maximum protection for personnel and equipment. They were the first large warships after the Soviet Kashins to be driven by gas turbines; the unusual Y-shaped funnel is needed to keep the exhaust gases clear of the radar array.

The DDH-280 class also make good flagships, and since 1978 all four have been promised to Nato as flagships for the Standing Naval Force Atlantic (STANAVFORLANT). *Iroquois* is currently (1980) serving as flagship and will be relieved by *Huron* and *Algonquin*.

These impressive ships are regarded by many as the best equipped warships for their tonnage in the world, combining a balanced armament with good electronics and command facilities.

A more conventional view of the *Huron* shows the Italian Oto-Melara 5in gun forward and the Dutch WM22 fire-control systems on either side of the bridge. The Sea Sparrow missile-launching system is unique to these ships, with quadruple launchers concealed in the forward superstructure.

## *Tromp* class

| Name | Number | Laid down | Launched | Completed | Builder |
|---|---|---|---|---|---|
| ***Tromp*** | F 801 | 4 Sep 1971 | 4 Jun 1973 | 3 Oct 1975 | K. M. de Schelde, Flushing |
| ***de Ruyter*** | F 806 | 22 Dec 1971 | 9 Mar 1974 | 3 Jun 1976 | K. M. de Schelde, Flushing |

**Displacement** 4,300 tons (standard), 5,400 tons (full load)
**Dimensions** 138.4m (oa) × 14.8m × 4.6m (454.1ft (oa) × 48.6ft × 15.1ft)
**Propulsion** 2 shafts, 2 sets geared gas turbines (COGOG); 54,000 shp = 30 knots
**Aircraft** 1 Lynx A/S helicopter
**Armament** 1 single Tartar SAM launcher, 1 8-tube Sea Sparrow BPDMS SAM launcher, 2 quad Harpoon SSM launchers, 1 twin 4.7in (120mm) guns, 2 triple 12.7in (324mm) Mk 32 torpedo tubes
**Complement** 34 officers, 267 men

Rising manpower costs in the 1960s forced the Royal Netherlands Navy to look at the cost-effectiveness of its major units, the carrier *Karel Doorman* and the cruisers *de Zeven Provincien* and *de Ruyter*, and in 1964 it was decided to replace them as flagships with two missile-armed destroyers.

Great emphasis was placed on making maximum use of the Dutch electronics industry, though not at the cost of inter-operability within Nato. Initially it was hoped to develop a new 3-D radar jointly with the British and in return to pool development costs of the Sea Dart area-defence missile. But the rising cost and space needed for Sea Dart forced the Dutch to pull out of that programme, while the British had second thoughts about buying a 3-D radar after the cancellation of their carriers in 1966. Paradoxically, the two navies came together again subsequently and collaborated with conspicuous success on a propulsion project, the Rolls-Royce Olympus and Tyne COGOG gas-turbine combination proving ideally matched to Dutch requirements.

Once Sea Dart had been abandoned there was more space for a balanced armament, and the ships were given a twin 120mm gun mounting forward and an eight-cell Nato Sea Sparrow SAM system for close-range defence; provision was also made for Harpoon SSMs on the superstructure. The guns are comparatively elderly, being the two Bofors-made mountings stripped from the old destroyer *Gelderland*. A single-arm Tartar SAM launcher is carried aft, over the helicopter hangar. The most obvious feature of this class is the massive Hollandse Signaalapparaten 3-D radar hidden under its weatherproof "golfball" dome on the forward superstructure. The low Y-shaped funnel is almost inconspicuous by comparison.

These highly automated ships are intended to provide area defence and ASW cover for convoys and task forces in the North Atlantic as well as the North Sea, and so they have ample freeboard. A noticeable feature in aerial views is their beaminess, which contributes to good seakeeping and habitability, as well as assisting in helicopter operations.

By using the best equipment available within Nato the Dutch have produced a pair of capable and battleworthy ships.

► The Royal Netherlands Navy DDG *Tromp* is one of the most advanced warships afloat, with a high degree of automation built into the weapon and ship's "housekeeping" systems. The "golfball" conceals a big 3-D radar originally intended also for the British *Bristol* class.

▼ From the beam the *Tromp* presents a compact profile, and her Y-shaped gas turbine uptakes are almost hidden. The single-arm Tartar missile launcher is further forward than in earlier DDGs, leaving room for a helicopter hangar. She operates a single Lynx for A/S duties.

F 801

## *Impavido* class

| Name | Number | Laid down | Launched | Completed | Builder |
|---|---|---|---|---|---|
| *Impavido* | D 570 | 10 Jun 1957 | 25 May 1962 | 16 Nov 1963 | Cantieri del Tirreno, Riva Trigoso |
| *Intrepido* | D 571 | 16 May 1959 | 21 Oct 1962 | 28 July 1964 | Ansaldo, Leghorn |

**Displacement** 3,201 tons (standard), 3,851 (full load)
**Dimensions** 131.3m (oa) × 13.6m × 4.5m (429.5ft (oa) × 44.7ft × 14.8ft)
**Propulsion** 2 shafts, 2 double-reduction geared turbines, 4 boilers; 70,000 shp = 33 knots
**Armament** 1 single Tartar/Standard SAM launcher, 1 twin 5in (127mm) 38-cal guns, 4 single 3in (76mm) 62-cal guns, 2 triple 12.7in (324mm) Mk 32 torpedo tubes
**Complement** 23 officers, 317 men

Two large missile destroyers were ordered under the 1956-57 and 1958-59 programmes, marking Italy's entry into this area of ship design. The missiles, fire control and main gun armament were bought from the United States but the hull was a slightly scaled-down version of the *Capitani Romani*-type light cruisers/ destroyer leaders of the Second World War. In other words, the design was an improved *Indomito*.

Like most Italian ships, the *Impavidos*

are fast and reliable steamers. On her full-power trials the *Impavido* reached 34½ knots in light condition and maintained 33 knots at her normal load.

In 1974-77 the two ships were modernised, with improvements to the missile guidance and replacement of the 5in fire control by the Argo 10/Elsag NA 10 system.

The Italian *Intrepido* and her sister *Impavido* were the first DDGs in the Italian Navy. Their twin upright funnels are distinctive because of their height. Since 1971, when this photograph was taken, both ships have been refitted with newer fire control and radars.

The *Impavido* at speed is an impressive sight. Ships designed to operate in the Mediterranean have traditionally been built with lower freeboard, but very bad weather has often hampered them. Lower endurance is also deemed acceptable in Mediterranean ships, though replenishment at sea is not always convenient.

## *Audace* class

| Name | Number | Laid down | Launched | Completed | Builder |
|---|---|---|---|---|---|
| ***Ardito*** | D 550 | 19 Jul 1968 | 27 Nov 1971 | 5 Dec 1973 | Italcantieri, Castellammare |
| ***Audace*** | D 551 | 27 Apr 1968 | 2 Oct 1971 | 16 Nov 1972 | Cantieri del Tirreno, Riva Trigoso |

**Displacement** 3,600 tons (standard), 4,400 tons (full load)
**Dimensions** 136.6m (oa) × 14.5m × 4.6m (446.4ft (oa) × 47.1ft × 15ft)
**Propulsion** 2 shafts, steam geared turbines, 4 boilers; 73,000 shp = 33 knots
**Aircraft** 2 Agusta-Bell AB.204B A/S helicopters
**Armament** 1 single Tartar SAM launcher, 2 single 5in (127mm) 54-cal guns, 2 triple 12.7in (324mm) torpedo tubes, 4 × 21in (533mm) torpedo tubes
**Complement** 30 officers, 350 men

Two new guided-missile destroyers were ordered for the Italian Navy in 1966. A development of the *Impavido* class, they are about 17ft longer and 2.4ft beamier, with about the same installed power.

Though there is less than 10 years between the designs, the new ships demonstrate vividly the great changes in

▲ This aerial view of the *Ardito* shows how the location of the helicopter hangar and flight deck takes precedence over an optimum position for the missile launcher in the latest ships. It also shows how much deck space is saved by adopting macks in place of separate masts and funnels.

◀ *Ardito* at the Royal Navy's Jubilee Review in June 1977. In addition to her Tartar SAMs aft she has four single 76mm Compact guns admidships for close-range defence; these weapons are controlled by one fire-control system on either beam. The 5in guns are primarily for surface action, with a secondary AA role.

naval technology in that time, both within Italy and elsewhere. The missile armament is the same Tartar/Standard but instead of the elderly ex-US twin 5in/38-cal the *Audace* class has two single 5in/54-cal. These are Italian-designed lightweight guns, based on the US Navy's Mk 45 but much improved. The secondary armament consists of four of the outstandingly successful Oto-Melara 76mm/62-cal Compact gun. It has basically the same barrel as the gun of the *Impavido* class but in a much improved mounting with automatic feed.

A determined weight-saving effort, with two macks in place of the tall funnels and lattice masts, enabled the designers to give the *Audace* more freeboard. The forecastle deck is carried aft to the stern to provide a flight deck for the two light helicopters carried in a hangar abaft the SAM launcher.

The *Audace* and *Ardito* have a certain elegance, with a graceful sheerline, but the conical macks and the gap between them make them look uglier than most contemporary Italian ships. Two Improved *Audace*s with gas turbines are to be built in the 1980s.

## *Indomito* class

| Name | Number | Laid down | Launched | Completed | Builder |
|---|---|---|---|---|---|
| ***Impetuoso*** | D 558 | 7 May 1952 | 16 Sep 1956 | 25 Jan 1958 | Cantieri del Tirreno, Riva Trigoso |
| ***Indomito*** | D 559 | 24 Apr 1952 | 7 Aug 1955 | 23 Feb 1958 | Ansaldo, Leghorn |

**Displacement** 2,755 tons (standard), 3,800 tons (full load)
**Dimensions** 127.6m (oa) × 13.3m × 4.5m (418.7ft (oa) × 43.5ft × 17.5ft)
**Propulsion** 2 shafts, geared steam turbines, 4 boilers; 65,000 shp = 34 knots
**Armament** 2 twin 5in (127mm) 38-cal guns, 8 twin 40mm guns, 1 × 3-barrel Menon A/S mortar, 2 triple 12.7in (324mm) Mk 32 torpedo tubes
**Complement** 15 officers, 300 men

This pair of destroyers, along with the two succeeding classes, provides an insight into the development of modern weapons and the policy of Italian ship designers. The *Indomito* class was ordered when the Italian Navy was rebuilt as part of Nato, and were that force's first new destroyers since 1945.

The model was the *Capitani Romani* large flotilla leader or "sports model cruiser," which had produced such spectacular speeds when built. But the obsession with speed was curbed, and a relatively modest 34 knots was asked for. This allowed tonnage to be much reduced, and the result was a balanced design.

The armament was almost entirely American in origin: twin 5in/38-cal DP guns forward and aft, quadruple and twin 40mm Bofors AA guns, and Mk 25 ASW torpedo tubes amidships. The only Italian equipment was a triple Menon depth-charge mortar in "B" position. Since then the armament has remained unchanged, and the ships are no longer suited to front-line service. They are to be replaced in the next few years by the Improved *Audace* class, and are presumably only retained for training and escort duties.

The *Impetuoso*, the first post-war Italian destroyer, was an adaptation of a pre-war small cruiser hull, armed largely with standard American equipment. The triple Menon depth-charge mortar can be seen trained to port abaft the forward twin 5in/38-cal mounting.

# *Haruna* class

| Name | Number | Laid down | Launched | Completed | Builder |
|---|---|---|---|---|---|
| ***Haruna*** | DD 141 | 9 Mar 1970 | 1 Feb 1972 | 22 Feb 1973 | Mitsubishi, Nagasaki |
| ***Hiei*** | DD 142 | 8 Mar 1972 | 13 Aug 1973 | 27 Nov 1974 | Ishikawajima, Tokyo |

**Displacement** 4,700 tons (standard)
**Dimensions** 153m (oa) × 17.5m × 5.1m (502ft (oa) × 57.4ft × 16.7ft)
**Propulsion** 2 shafts, geared steam turbines, 4 boilers; 70,000 shp = 32 knots
**Aircraft** 3 Sea King A/S helicopters
**Armament** 2 single 5in (127mm) 54-cal guns, 1 × 8-tube Asroc ASM launcher, 2 triple 12.7in (324mm) Mk 32 torpedo tubes
**Complement** 36 officers, 304 men

Under its third five-year defence programme the Japan Maritime Self-Defence Force ordered two large anti-submarine destroyers, the *Haruna* and *Hiei*. They are unusual in that their armament is almost entirely anti-submarine, apart from a pair of dual-purpose 5in guns. This means that they are intended to operate in company with other ships or else must be restricted to mid-ocean, away from shore-based aircraft.

Their appearance is unusual, reflecting their specialised role. The two guns are mounted forward in traditional destroyer style, in "A" and "B" positions, with an Asroc "pepperbox" abaft them. The superstructure is a single block of bridgework and a large hangar, surmounted by a massive mack and latticework extension. The hangar accommodates three Sea King ASW helicopters, giving the class a powerful anti-submarine capability and a possible option of surface strike if the Sea Kings were equipped with air-to-surface missiles.

The two ships came into service in 1973-74, and two more (DD 143 and DD 144) have been ordered under the 1975 and 1976 programmes. The basic design is the same but an eight-cell Sea Sparrow missile system will provide close-range defence against aircraft, and there is mention of two 35mm guns, presumably for close-in defence. The two new ships will be completed in 1980-81.

The Japanese DDH *Hiei* at speed. The single block of superstructure and mack are unique among large warships and reflect the basic simplicity of the design. She is nothing more than a platform for three Sea King helicopters, a big sonar and an Asroc A/S missile system, lacking even a point-defence SAM.

The long flight deck needed to operate a Sea King helicopter is noticeable in this view of the *Haruna*. Although the Japan Maritime Self-Defence Force (MSDF) buys such items as the 5in/54-cal guns and the Asroc missile systems from the United States, radars are being developed by Japanese industry.

# *Tachikaze* class

| Name | Number | Laid down | Launched | Completed | Builder |
|---|---|---|---|---|---|
| *Tachikaze* | DD 168 | 19 Jun 1973 | 7 Dec 1974 | 26 Mar 1976 | Mitsubishi, Nagasaki |
| *Asakase* | DD 169 | 27 May 1976 | 15 Oct 1977 | 1979 | Mitsubishi, Nagasaki |
| – | DD 170 | Sep 1979 | Apr 1981 | 1983 | Mitsubishi, Nagasaki |

**Displacement** 3,900 tons (standard)
**Dimensions** 143m (oa) × 14.3m × 4.6m (443ft (oa) × 47ft × 15ft)
**Propulsion** 2 shafts, geared steam turbines, 4 boilers; 60,000 shp = 33 knots
**Aircraft** Pad for helicopter
**Armament** 1 single Tartar-D SAM launcher, 2 single 5in (127mm) 54-cal guns, 1 × 8-tube Asroc ASM launcher, 2 triple 12.7in (324mm) Mk 32 torpedo tubes
**Complement** 260 officers and men

The first Japanese missile-armed destroyer, the *Amatsukaze*, was not built until 1962-65. Eleven years later an improved version, the *Tachikaze*, was ordered. She is slightly longer and beamier, but retains the main armament of the earlier design, an aft-mounted single-arm Tartar SAM launcher.

As in other navies, JMSDF ideas on ship design have changed since the 1960s. The twin 3in/50-cal automatic guns then considered adequate have been replaced by two single 5in Mk 42, one forward and one aft, and the Asroc ASW missile launcher has been moved forward from between the funnels, where it had a restricted arc of fire. Macks have replaced the tall, graceful funnels of the *Amatsukaze* but the basic radar outfit is the same.

The second ship of the class, *Asakaze*, was completed in 1979, and a third, DD 170, was laid down in September 1979. *Tachikaze* and *Asakaze* may shortly be armed with Harpoon SSMs to improve their anti-ship capability, but even without them they are impressive vessels with good freeboard and armament. The Japanese stress weatherliness in their designs, as the North-west Pacific can produce very bad weather conditions.

The *Tachikaze* is the first of a new class of missile-armed fleet escorts. As in other navies, the mack has been adopted to conserve deck space, though in this instance there has been no attempt to provide accommodation for a helicopter apart from a landing pad on the stern.

## *Niteroi* class

| Name | Number | Laid down | Lanched | Completed | Builder |
|---|---|---|---|---|---|
| ***Niteroi*** (AS) | F 40 | 8 Jun 1972 | 8 Feb 1974 | 20 Nov 1976 | Vosper Thornycroft, Woolston |
| ***Defensora*** (AS) | F 41 | 14 Dec 1972 | 27 Mar 1975 | 5 Mar 1977 | Vosper Thornycroft, Woolston |
| ***Constituicao*** (GP) | F 42 | 13 Mar 1974 | 15 Apr 1976 | 31 Mar 1978 | Vosper Thornycroft, Woolston |
| ***Liberal*** (GP) | F 43 | 2 May 1975 | 7 Feb 1977 | 9 Nov 1978 | Vosper Thornycroft, Woolston |
| ***Independencia*** (GP) | F 44 | 11 Jun 1972 | 2 Sep 1974 | Mar 1978 | Arsenal de Marinho, Rio de Janeiro |
| ***Uniao*** (GP) | F 45 | 11 Jun 1972 | 14 Mar 1975 | Oct 1978 | Arsenal de Marinho, Rio de Janeiro |

**Displacement** 3,200 tons (standard), 3,800 tons (full load)
**Dimensions** 129.2m (oa) × 13.5m × 5.9m (424ft (oa) × 44.2ft × 19.4ft)
**Propulsion** 2 shafts, geared steam turbines or diesel drive (CODOG); 56,000 shp = 30 knots
**Aircraft** 1 Lynx A/S helicopter
**Armament** (General-purpose) 2 triple Seacat SAM launchers, 2 twin Exocet SSM launchers, 2 single 4.5in (114mm) Mk 8 guns, 2 single 40mm guns, 1 × 2-barrel 14.8in (375mm) Bofors A/S mortar, 2 triple 12.7in (324mm) torpedo tubes
(Anti-submarine) 2 triple Seacat SAM launchers, 1 single 4.5in (114mm) Mk 8 gun, 2 single 40mm guns, 1 single Ikara ASM launcher, 1 × 2-barrel 14.8in (375mm) Bofors A/S mortar, 2 triple 12.7in (324mm) torpedo tubes
**Complement** 21 officers, 180 men

▼ The Brazilian frigate *Niteroi* on builders' trials in January 1976. The use of aluminium alloy in the superstructure allowed the AIO to be sited higher, resulting in a very high silhouette. One of two anti-submarine variants, she has her Ikara missile launcher abaft the helicopter deck.

The third of the class, *Constituicao*, has an extra 4.5in Mk 8 gun aft in place of the Ikara, and Exocet surface-to-surface missiles between the two masts. The remainder of the class are similar in configuration. A seventh ship modified for training may be built in Brazil.

The completion of the destroyer *Liberal* in November 1978 marked the successful conclusion of a nine-year programme. This was an outstanding achievement for British shipbuilding, for Vosper Thornycroft had to design and build four of its own Mk 10 destroyers or fast frigates and supervise the building of two more in Brazil. The contract called for all six ships to be ready for service by the beginning of 1979. This deadline was met, an event all too rare in shipbuilding.

In layout and basic design the Mk 10 draws a lot on the Royal Navy's Type 42 DDG, but with a number of changes made by the builders. With no requirement for the Sea Dart SAM, it was possible to find room for the Ikara ASW missile system in the four ASW variants or a second 4.5in gun in the general-purpose variants. Four diesels were chosen instead of the Tyne gas turbine for cruising, but the prime mover is still the Olympus.

The ships are distinctive in appearance, with a big funnel, a massive bridge and high freeboard amidships. The general-purpose ships have been fitted with four MM.38 Exocet SSMs between the bridge and the funnel, a significant addition to their fighting power.

There was talk of a follow-on order for ships armed with the Sea Dart SAM but now a training ship version is planned. The Brazilians have acquired a homogeneous squadron of useful ships to replace their somewhat ramshackle collection of ex-American Second World War destroyers.

# *Halland* class

| Name | Number | Laid down | Launched | Completed | Builder |
|---|---|---|---|---|---|
| ***Halland*** | J 18 | 1949 | 16 Jul 1952 | 8 Jun 1955 | Götaverken, Göteborg |
| ***Småland*** | J 19 | 1949 | 23 Oct 1952 | 12 Jan 1956 | Eriksberg, Göteborg |
| ***20 de Julio*** (Colombia) | D 05 | Oct 1955 | 26 Jun 1956 | 15 Jun 1958 | Kockums, Malmö |
| ***6 de Agosto*** (Colombia) | D 06 | Nov 1955 | 19 Jun 1956 | 31 Oct 1958 | Götaverken, Göteborg |

**Displacement** 2,800 tons (standard), 3,400 tons (full load)
**Dimensions** 121m (oa) × 12.6m × 4.5m (397.2ft (oa) × 41.3ft × 14.8ft)
**Propulsion** 2 shafts, geared steam turbines, 2 boilers; 58,000 shp = 35 knots
**Armament** 1 twin Rb08A SSM launcher, 2 twin 4.7in (120mm) guns, 1 twin 57mm guns, 6 single 40mm guns, 2 × 4-barrel Bofors A/S rocket launchers, 2 quad 21in (533mm) torpedo tubes. Can carry mines
**Complement** 18 officers, 272 men

In 1948 the Swedish Navy ordered two large destroyers incorporating all the lessons of the Second World War. They differed from previous Swedish destroyers in having a raised forecastle, and were significantly larger than the preceding *Öland* class. Four ships were originally projected but the *Lappland* and *Värmland* were cancelled in 1958; in 1955-58 two more, the *6 de Agosto* and *20 de Julio*, were built for Colombia.

In 1958 the Swedish ships were fitted to launch the Rb08A SSM from a ramp mounted on the after torpedo tubes. But this missile never proved totally successful, and although they were the first ships with such a weapon system it did not mark any great advance in naval technology. In 1962 they were modernised and fitted with new fire control.

The Colombian ships differed in having a uniform armament of 120mm twin guns, two forward and one aft, with 40mm guns as secondary armament. They also had one 375mm ASW rocket launcher on the forecastle instead of two. These ships have not been very well maintained, and it was reported that *20 de Julio* was due for disposal in 1978; *6 de Agosto* was given an extensive machinery overhaul in the United States in 1975, but is rated for no more than 25 knots.

The *Halland* and *Småland* are in good condition, thanks to the Royal Swedish Navy's policy of rotating ships into the reserve fleet for a year after every two years' front-line service. However, under the current policy of devoting more money to fast strike craft they are now up for sale and could well replace their sisters in the Colombian Navy.

The Swedish *Halland* reflects the Royal Swedish Navy's attention to seakeeping, with good freeboard and fully enclosed gun mountings. When fitted with the Rb08A missile in 1958 they were the first missile-armed destroyers in the world. The two quadruple A/S rocket launchers can be seen on the forecastle.

# *Hamburg* class

| Name | Number | Laid down | Launched | Completed | Builder |
|---|---|---|---|---|---|
| ***Hamburg*** | D 181 | 1959 | 26 Mar 1960 | 23 May 1964 | Stülcken, Hamburg |
| ***Schleswig-Holstein*** | D 182 | 1959 | 20 Aug 1960 | 12 Oct 1064 | Stülcken, Hamburg |
| ***Bayern*** | D 183 | 1961 | 14 Aug 1962 | 6 Jul 1965 | Stülcken, Hamburg |
| ***Hessen*** | D 184 | 1962 | 4 May 1963 | 8 Oct 1968 | Stülcken, Hamburg |

**Displacement** 3,400 tons (standard), 4,400 tons (full load)
**Dimensions** 134m (oa) × 13.4m × 5.2m (439.7ft (oa) × 44ft × 17ft)
**Propulsion** 2 shafts, geared steam turbines, 4 boilers, 68,000 shp = 35.8 knots
**Armament** 4 single Exocet SSM launchers, 3 single 3.9in (100mm) guns, 4 twin 40mm guns, 2 × 4-barrel Bofors 12in (305mm) A/S mortars, 6 × 12.7in (324mm) torpedo tubes, 60-80 mines
**Complement** 17 officers, 263 men

The first large warships built in Germany after the Second World War, the *Hamburg* class met the standards then being set by the largest of their kind. There were originally to have been 12 of this class, but a rapid increase in cost meant that only four were completed.

The design emphasised defence against air attack, incorporating four of a new type of French 100mm (3.9in) DP gun, each with its own fire-control director, and four twin 40mm Bofors. The intended torpedo armament, a quintuple bank of 21in tubes between the funnels, was replaced before completion with ASW torpedo tubes disposed in singles on the beam and a pair firing aft through the stern.

► The *Hessen* (right) and *Hamburg* docked at the Blohm & Voss yard in Hamburg. When this photograph was taken all four ships still had both their after 100mm guns; after 1975 they were given four Exocet surface-to-surface missiles in "X" position. Note the port for A/S torpedoes in *Hessen*'s transom stern.

▼ *Bayern* in 1969, showing the massive superstructure of these German destroyers. Note the twin 40mm Breda Bofors guns abreast of the forward superstructure and aft, and the single A/S torpedo tubes below the starboard seaboat. Another pair of tubes, firing aft, is mounted below the quarterdeck.

The armament reflected the fact that West Germany had no indigenous armaments industry at the time. The radar was Dutch, the guns were French and Italian/Swedish, the torpedoes Swedish and the fire control and the anti-submarine rocket launchers Dutch.

In 1975-77 all four were modernised, with new Hollandse Signaalapparaten radar and four MM.38 Exocet SSMs in place of one of the after 100mm guns. They have a unique silhouette, with massive funnels and lofty superstructure, but the low freeboard betrays their limitations outside the Baltic Approaches. The design was developed from a late wartime project for a flush-deck destroyer.

# Escorts

The modern frigate bears little resemblance to its ancestors in a line dating back to the 17th century, having gone through several transformations over the last 35 years alone. Originally a frigate was a single-deck man-o'-war classed as 5th or 6th Rate, and so unfit to take her place in the line of battle. Towards the end of the Napoleonic Wars the frigate grew very big, a tendency which continued when steam power was introduced in the 1840s. The frigate's function remained the same, however: to scout for the fleet, protect convoys and harry enemy shipping. In short the frigate was the ideal "cruizer", big enough to operate independently for lengthy periods and so well armed as to make her a dangerous opponent for all but the biggest warships.

Although gradually displaced by the hybrid two-decked corvette in the 19th century, frigates continued to be built, and the first seagoing ironclads, the French *Gloire* and the British *Warrior* and *Black Prince*, were first rated as frigates on account of their single gun decks. Big commerce-raiding frigates continued to be built during the 1860s and the finest of these, HMS *Raleigh*, has the distinction of being the last to figure on the Navy List as such. She was listed as a frigate until 1889, after which her designation was changed to "3rd Class Cruiser."

Thereafter the term went into limbo for nearly 60 years, being replaced entirely by "cruiser". Then in 1943, when the Royal Navy and Royal Canadian Navy introduced the new twin-screw, high-endurance escorts known as the "River" class, there was some debate over what to call them. At first they were known as twin-screw corvettes, a cumbersome and completely misleading term, for they bore no relation to the "Flower" class. Then the Canadians took to calling them frigates, and eventually the Admiralty recognised the term officially despite its lack of any historical basis.

It was in retrospect an unfortunate decision, creating untold confusion and incidentally driving out the time-honoured and completely appropriate term "sloop". Into the frigate category were gathered ex-American destroyer escorts, sloops, and eventually even corvettes and "Hunt"-class destroyers. In the 1950s a change of armament in a destroyer was deemed sufficient to make her a frigate, and for the Royal Navy the term came to cover any seagoing ship intended for escort or anti-submarine duties.

This would have been reasonable enough if other navies had followed the same policy. But the Americans dubbed their big destroyers frigates for a while, and built three enormous nuclear-powered ships and a series of missile-armed escorts, otherwise known as guided missile destroyer leaders or DLGs. Other navies applied the term to 600-ton coastal escorts, and by the end of the 1960s confusion reigned supreme. Since then matters have been somewhat simplified. The Americans have re-rated the bigger DLGs as cruisers and have put the latest destroyer escorts (DEs) into the frigate category. In other navies the term "corvette" has been resurrected to cover the smaller escorts which are clearly not capable of deep-water operations.

It is therefore not easy to trace the development of the frigate, although since the Royal Navy's "River" class it is possible to discern a pattern of priorities. The "Rivers" emphasised habitability and seaworthiness, with a relatively light armament which could be used in all weathers. They proved ideal for the North Atlantic, with a length of hull which matched the wave period and so reduced discomfort for the crew. The succeeding "Loch" and "Bay" classes were anti-submarine and anti-aircraft variants on a common hull, which was itself no more than a "River" hull redesigned for welding and mass production. The armament was more sophisticated but still subordinated to the main role of North Atlantic convoy escort.

In 1944 work started on new designs to match the fast U-Boats known to be building in Germany, but the end of hostilities slowed down this programme and its results were not seen until 1955. The advent of the Cold War and the rapid build-up of the Soviet submarine fleet forced the Nato navies to strengthen their anti-submarine forces, and as a stopgap the Royal Navy converted a number of wartime destroyers into frigates: the Type 15 "full" conversion and the Type 16 "interim" conversion. At the same time four new classes of frigates were ordered for the RN, while the USN also embarked on a new DE programme.

The 1944 frigate concept envisaged a standard hull with a good turn of speed and high endurance, to be armed for the ASW, anti-aircraft or air-direction roles. Endurance was to be provided by diesels, but this meant that speed could not be more than 25 knots. In order to provide high pursuit speed for use against the latest Soviet submarines the designers were forced to go back to steam turbines. But as this pushed up cost alarmingly it was decided to divide production between a twin-screw "quality" type and a single-screw "utility" type.

Eight diesel frigates were built but proved only a qualified success, the engines proving to be less easy to maintain than had been hoped. The dozen utility frigates were too small to be really effective, but the quality frigates, known as Type 12, proved an outstanding success. Not only was the armament powerful but the hull form was first-class, turning out to be weatherly and highly manoeuvrable. The first six, the *Whitby* class, were followed by nine *Rothesay*-class ships of a slightly modified type, and more were planned. But by the early 1960s there was a turn away from the idea of single-purpose escorts, and to meet a staff requirement for a general-purpose ship the *Rothesay* hull was radically redesigned to increase its effectiveness. What emerged was much more than a revamp of the existing design; it was a totally new ship.

The *Leander* design achieved a remarkable increase in the amount of equipment carried by extending the forecastle deck aft to the stern, by providing a much bigger superstructure and by a clever redistribution of weights. The additions included a long-range air-warning radar and a Wasp A/S helicopter. The *Leander*s were built in large numbers: 26 for the RN, two each for New Zealand, Australia and Chile, six in the Netherlands and another six in India. The older *Rothesays* and *Whitbys* in various navies were rebuilt to accommodate many of the *Leanders*' features.

Faced in the late 1950s with the mass obsolescence of its wartime destroyers, the US Navy revived the concept of the DE. The first DEs, started at the time of the Korean War, had not been an outstanding success, but in 1961 the *Bronstein* class marked a new departure in being as big as conventional destroyers and faster than their predecessors. After a series of short runs quantity production began with the *Knox* class in 1965, and by 1974 a total of 46 had been built. Then came the gas turbine-powered *Oliver Hazard Perry* class, intended to run to some 90 units by the end of the next decade.

All these frigates have been built primarily for the traditional role of convoy escort, but there are other ships which emphasise the vagueness of the category. The new British *Broadsword* and French *Georges Leygues* classes exemplify this, displacing nearly 4,000 tons and carrying surface-to-surface missiles, helicopters and long-range sonar. Tasked with the location and destruction of nuclear submarines, neither type has to protect other ships and is therefore armed with a short-range anti-aircraft missile system.

The term "corvette" is more usually reserved for ships at the other end of the scale. They fall into two distinct categories, one intended for escort duties in coastal waters, such as the French *d'Estienne d'Orves* class, and the other intended to provide a spearhead for coastal forces, such as the Danish *Niels Juel* class.

The *d'Estienne d'Orves* class, actually rated as *avisos* or sloops, are versatile ships capable of long-range operations. The weapon load is impressive: a 100mm (3.9in) gun, two surface-to-surface missiles, and A/S rocket launchers and torpedoes. The later ships of the class are to carry a new light helicopter, further evidence of the flexibility of the design.

The operation of helicopters from frigates is now a well established practice. These aircraft still serve primarily as delivery systems for anti-submarine weapons such as homing torpedoes or anti-ship missiles, but the new generation of lightweight radars also allows them to extend the parent ship's radar coverage, and so reconnaissance is now becoming as important as the strike role. Another logical development is the provision of over-the-horizon guidance for long-range missiles. There are drawbacks, however: helicopters need constant maintenance to keep them flying, and the hangar, workshop and extra personnel make big demands on space and money. The bigger escorts like the *Broadsword* class are being equipped with two helicopters to ensure that one machine is available for longer. Current thinking in some quarters is that helicopters would be better used in larger numbers from special helicopter carriers, leaving the escorts to carry the maximum payload of weapons and sensors. But for the moment the helicopter-equipped escort is still the most potent anti-submarine unit.

## *Knox* class

| Name | Number |
|---|---|
| ***Knox*** | FF-1052 |
| ***Roark*** | FF-1053 |
| ***Gray*** | FF-1054 |
| ***Hepburn*** | FF-1055 |
| ***Connole*** | FF-1056 |
| ***Rathburne*** | FF-1057 |
| ***Meyerkord*** | FF-1058 |
| ***W. S. Sims*** | FF-1059 |
| ***Lang*** | FF-1060 |
| ***Patterson*** | FF-1061 |
| ***Whipple*** | FF-1062 |
| ***Reasoner*** | FF-1063 |
| ***Lockwood*** | FF-1064 |
| ***Stein*** | FF-1065 |
| ***Marvin Shields*** | FF-1066 |
| ***Francis Hammond*** | FF-1067 |
| ***Vreeland*** | FF-1068 |
| ***Bagley*** | FF-1069 |
| ***Downes*** | FF-1070 |
| ***Badger*** | FF-1071 |
| ***Blakely*** | FF-1072 |
| ***Robert E. Peary*** | FF-1073 |
| ***Harold E. Holt*** | FF-1074 |
| ***Trippe*** | FF-1075 |
| ***Fanning*** | FF-1076 |
| ***Quellet*** | FF-1077 |
| ***Joseph Hewes*** | FF-1078 |
| ***Bowen*** | FF-1079 |
| ***Paul*** | FF-1080 |
| ***Aylwin*** | FF-1081 |
| ***Elmer Montgomery*** | FF-1082 |
| ***Cook*** | FF-1083 |
| ***McCandless*** | FF-1084 |
| ***Donald B. Beary*** | FF-1085 |
| ***Brewton*** | FF-1086 |
| ***Kirk*** | FF-1087 |
| ***Barbey*** | FF-1088 |
| ***Jesse L. Brown*** | FF-1089 |
| ***Ainsworth*** | FF-1090 |
| ***Miller*** | FF-1091 |
| ***Thomas C. Hart*** | FF-1092 |
| ***Capodanno*** | FF-1093 |
| ***Pharris*** | FF-1094 |
| ***Truett*** | FF-1095 |
| ***Valdez*** | FF-1096 |
| ***Moinester*** | FF-1097 |
| ***Baleares*** (Spain) | F-71 |
| ***Andaluçia*** | F-72 |
| ***Cataluña*** | F-73 |
| ***Asturias*** | F-74 |
| ***Extremadura*** | F-75 |

**Displacement** 3,011 tons (standard), 4,100 tons (full load)
**Dimensions** 126.5m (oa) × 14.25m × 7.6m (415ft (oa) × 46.75ft × 24.75ft)
**Propulsion** 1 shaft, geared steam turbine; 35,000 shp = 27 knots
**Aircraft** 1 SH-2 Lamps helicopter
**Armament** 1 × 8-cell Asroc Mk 16 ASM launcher, 1 × 8-cell Sea Sparrow SAM launcher, 1 × 5in (127mm) 54-cal gun, 4 × 12.7in (324mm) ASW torpedo tubes
**Complement** 16 officers, 201 enlisted men

FF-1052-4, 1062, 1064, 1066, 1070-71 built by Todd, Seattle; FF-1055, 1058, 1060, 1067, 1074, 1076 by Todd, San Pedro; FF-1056, 1059, 1061, 1068, 1072, 1075, 1077-1097 by Avondale, Louisiana; FF-1057, 1063, 1065, 1069, 1073 by Lockheed Shipbuilding; Spanish ships all by Empresa Nacional Bazán, El Ferrol.

The US Navy was badly hit by block obsolescence in the 1960s, when most of the wartime destroyers and DEs completed in 1943-45 had reached the end of their hull lives. The FRAM programme saved many destroyers for a few more years but at best it could only be a palliative. On the other hand, the enormous cost of the DDGs and DLGs made a one-for-one replacement programme impossible.

The answer was to design a utility destroyer/destroyer escort with as few complexities as possible and build it in large numbers. This was apparently a simple matter, but in the context of a big peacetime navy it proved much harder to achieve than anyone had expected. Designing for utility is easy enough, but such solutions immediately attract criticism for being weak in certain directions. The *Knox* class was bitterly assailed from all sides by critics who compared her unfavourably on various grounds with DDGs of greater size (and cost). The strongest criticism was directed at the lack of an area-defence missile, although the ships have since been fitted with the Sea Sparrow Basic Point Defence Missile System (BPDMS) for close-range defence. More valid criticism is directed at the single screw, the result of political intervention. Though this arrangement is cheaper, a single-shaft ship is harder to manoeuvre

The USS *Pharris* (FF-1094) replenishing under way during a STANAVFORLANT exercise in 1978. The hangar was fitted to allow this class to operate the Dash drone, but the flight deck had to be strengthened and the hangar modified to permit operations with the heavier Seasprite Lamps manned machine.

The Spanish *Baleares* and her sisters have the same handsome mack of the *Knox* class but have a single Tartar SAM launcher aft in place of the helicopter hangar and flight deck. The forward Asroc launcher and big bow sonar are retained, however, giving the Spanish ships a good ASW armament.

and a minor machinery breakdown can leave it helpless. Like other escorts, the *Knox* class was also hit by the failure of the Dash helicopter, which robbed them of a potent ASW system.

In other respects, however, the ships show up better than is generally realised. The hull is based on the *Brooke* and *Garcia* classes (SCB 199C and SCB 200) but is larger because the more complex pressure-fired boilers were not adopted. The funnel was incorporated into a big cylindrical mack unique to this class, leaving the decks clear. The Asroc launcher is immediately abaft the 5in Mk 42 gun and the Sea Sparrow launcher is right aft.

Part of the dissatisfaction with these ships stems from their rising cost. To remedy the lack of an ASW helicopter they were modified to take the Interim Lamps Seasprite helicopter, which meant that the flight deck had to be strengthened and the hangar altered. However, this modification, combined with the big SQS-26 bow sonar, turns the class into very capable ASW ships, which is what they were meant to be.

An additional 10 ships, DE-1098-1107, were authorised in FY 1968, but DE-1102-1107 were deferred in 1968; later that year three more, DE-1099-1101, were deferred because of financial problems, and the following year DE-1098 was deferred. A modified version was built under licence in Spain, armed with a single-arm Tartar SAM launcher aft in place of the helicopter hangar. DE-1101 was to have been propelled by gas turbines.

In June 1975 these ships were re-rated as frigates and given FF numbers. They form the largest single group of warships in the world.

## *Brooke* and *Garcia* classes

| Name | Number |
|---|---|
| ***Garcia*** | FF-1040 |
| ***Bradley*** | FF-1041 |
| ***Edward McDonnell*** | FF-1043 |
| ***Brumby*** | FF-1044 |
| ***Davidson*** | FF-1045 |
| ***Voge*** | FF-1047 |
| ***Sample*** | FF-1048 |
| ***Koelsch*** | FF-1049 |
| ***Albert David*** | FF-1050 |
| ***O'Callahan*** | FF-1051 |
| ***Brooke*** | FFG-1 |
| ***Ramsey*** | FFG-2 |
| ***Schofield*** | FFG-3 |
| ***Talbot*** | FFG-4 |
| ***Richard L. Page*** | FFG-5 |
| ***Julius A. Furer*** | FFG-6 |

DE-1039, DE-1042 and DE-1046 were numbers assigned to Portuguese DEs for accounting purposes.

**Displacement** 2,620/2,640 tons (standard), 3,245/3,400 tons (full load)

**Dimensions** 126.3m (oa) × 13.5m × 7.3m (414.5ft (oa) × 44.15ft × 24ft)
**Propulsion** 1 shaft, geared steam turbine; 35,000 shp = 27 knots
**Aircraft** 1 SH-2 Lamps
**Armament** (*Garcia*) 2 × 5in (127mm) 38-cal DP guns, 1 Asroc Mk 16 ASM launcher, 6 × 12.7in (324mm) Mk 32 ASW torpedo tubes
(*Brooke*) 1 × 5in (127mm) 38-cal DP gun, 1 Tartar/Standard SAM launcher, 1 Asroc Mk 16 ASM launcher, 6 × 12.7in (324mm) ASW torpedo tubes
**Complement** 17 officers, 219/230 enlisted men

16 ships built by Bethlehem Steel, San Francisco; Avondale Shipyards; Defoe Shipbuilding Company; Lockheed Shipbuilding & Construction Company; Bath Iron Works.

These two classes are ASW and AAW variants based on a common hull. The 10 *Garcia* class (design SCB 199A) were authorised as DEs in FY 1961 (two ships), FY 1962 (three ships) and FY 1963 (five ships); the six *Brooke*s (design SCB 199B) were divided between FY 1962 and FY 1963.

The *Garcia*s are armed with two single 5in/38-cal DP guns but their main weapon system is the Asroc ASM launcher and the SQS-26 sonar. The Dash helicopter was never fitted, except briefly in the *Bradley*, and until recently they carried no helicopter in the hangar. The addition of the SH-2 Seasprite has restored much of their ASW capability.

The *Brooke*s carry a single-arm Tartar SAM launcher in place of the second 5in gun, and the radar fit differs accordingly. They have the same sonar outfit as the gun-armed ships, and like them have only recently regained a helicopter. Both classes have high-performance pressure-fired boilers, but these units caused so many maintenance problems that they have not been fitted to the succeeding class.

The *Talbot* was used to evaluate systems for the *Oliver Hazard Perry* class. She was given a 76mm Oto-Melara DP gun in place of the forward 5in, a Hollandse Signaalapparaten Mk 92 fire-control radar, and a STIR radar on the fantail. She has since been refitted to her original state.

These ships are capable escorts but proved too complex to be built in any numbers. They paved the way for the *Knox* and *Perry* classes, and will be in service for some years. In June 1975 they were reclassified, the *Garcia*s becoming frigates FF-1040-1051 (ex-DE-1040-1051) and the *Brooke*s becoming FFG-1-6 (ex-DEG-1-6) respectively.

The *Voge* and her sister frigates of the *Garcia* class foreshadow the *Knox* class in general conception and layout. The hangar aft was intended for the Dash drone helicopter, but this system was cancelled before the class entered service and served in only one *Garcia* for a short while.

# *Oliver Hazard Perry* class

| Name | Number | Laid down | Launched | Completed |
|---|---|---|---|---|
| ***Oliver Hazard Perry*** | FFG-7 | 12 Jan 1975 | 25 Sep 1976 | 17 Dec 1977 |
| ***McInerney*** | FFG-8 | 16 Jan 1978 | 4 Nov 1978 | 1980 |
| ***Wadsworth*** | FFG-9 | 13 Jul 1977 | 29 Jul 1978 | 1980 |
| ***Duncan*** | FFG-10 | 29 Apr 1977 | 1 Mar 1978 | 1980 |
| ***Clark*** | FFG-11 | 17 Jul 1978 | – | 1980 |
| ***George Philip*** | FFG-12 | 14 Dec 1977 | – | 1980 |
| ***Samuel Eliot Morison*** | FFG-13 | 4 Dec 1978 | 14 Jul 1979 | 1980 |
| ***Sides*** | FFG-14 | 7 Aug 1978 | 19 May 1979 | 1980 |
| ***Estocin*** | FFG-15 | – | 3 Nov 1979 | – |
| ***Clifton Sprague*** | FFG-16 | – | – | – |
| ***John A. Moore*** | FFG-19 | 19 Dec 1978 | – | – |
| ***Antrim*** | FFG-20 | 21 Jan 1978 | 27 Mar 1979 | – |
| unnamed | FFG-21 | – | – | – |
| ***Fahrion*** | FFG-22 | 1 Dec 1978 | – | – |
| ***Lewis B. Puller*** | FFG-23 | 23 May 1979 | – | – |
| unnamed | FFG-24 | – | – | – |
| unnamed | FFG-25 | 24 Oct 1979 | – | – |
| unnamed | FFG-26 | – | – | – |
| unnamed | FFG-27 | – | – | – |
| ***Boone*** | FFG-28 | 27 Mar 1979 | – | – |
| unnamed | FFG-29 | – | – | – |
| unnamed | FFG-30 | – | – | – |
| ***Stark*** | FFG-31 | – | – | – |
| ***Adelaide*** (Australia) | F 01 (ex-FFG-17) | 29 Jul 1977 | – | – |
| ***Canberra*** | F 02 (ex-FFG-18) | 1 Mar 1978 | – | – |
| ***Sydney*** | F 03 (ex-FFG-35) | 21 Jan 1980 | – | – |
| unnamed (Spain) | – | ordered 1977 | – | – |
| unnamed | – | – | – | – |
| unnamed | – | – | – | – |

**Displacement** 3,605 tons (full load)
**Dimensions** 135.6m (oa) × 13.7m × 7.5m (445ft (oa) × 45ft × 24.5ft)
**Propulsion** 1 shaft, gas turbines; 40,000 shp = 28 knots
**Aircraft** 2 Lamps helicopters
**Armament** 1 Standard/Harpoon SAM/SSM launcher, 1 × 76mm/62-cal DP gun, 1 × 20mm Phalanx CIWS, 6 × 12.7in (324mm) Mk 32 ASW torpedo tubes
**Complement** 14 officers, 162 enlisted men

10 laid down by Bath Iron Works, Maine; Todd Shipyard, Seattle and San Pedro; 8 authorised FY 1977, 8 FY 1978, 8 FY 1979; 24 projected for FY 1980, 1981 and 1982. 3 building by E. N. Bazán at El Ferrol.

Logical successors to the *Knox* class, these ships are utility escorts capable of providing area defence at the cost of some ASW capability. Known originally as the Patrol Frigate (SCB 261), the design is, like the *Knox*, in reality a utility destroyer.

As before, political pressure resulted

in these ships having only one shaft, though the powerplant comprises two gas turbines. This choice of powerplant has reduced the complement to 176 from the 236 of the *Knox* class, leading to a much more significant saving on cost in the long term. Being simpler to maintain and repair by removal, gas turbines are also cheaper to run.

Because it is intended to build 72 ships, the design of the hull is meant to assist prefabrication as much as possible. The superstructure is a series of boxes, giving the ship a slab-sided appearance. The diminutive funnel is so low as to be almost unnoticeable, and may yet have to be raised to keep exhaust gases clear of deck fittings.

The armament marks a change in policy. Instead of the traditional 5in gun there is a single Oto-Melara 76mm/62-cal Compact gun (made under licence in the US as the Mk 75) between the mast and the funnel. A Phalanx Gatling gun is to be mounted at the after end of the hangar. The two missile-armed helicopters represent a strike capability and can provide targeting data for the Standard missile if it is to be used against surface targets.

As with the *Knox* class, the *Perry* class

◀ The *Oliver Hazard Perry* (FFG-7) on builders' trials out of Bath Iron Works, Maine. The modern tendency towards boxlike structures is exemplified by this design, which offers a compact layout with minimum waste of deck space. The funnel is kept deliberately short to allow the 76mm gun to fire aft.

▲ The first missile-armed warships had their launchers aft, but it is now recognised that the limitations of guided weapons make it necessary to "point" the ship roughly in the direction of the target to assist in fire control. Thus the *Oliver Hazard Perry* and her sisters have the single Mk 13 launcher on the forecastle.

has attracted harsh criticism, much of it unjustified. Between the two classes there will be over 100 "platforms" at sea, all with ASW capability of one sort of another, and it is hard to see how this could have been improved on at the price.

The lead ship, *Oliver Hazard Perry*, was commissioned in December 1977 and the next seven are afloat. Funds have been allocated for hulls up to FFG-42, and three ships are building under licence in Spain. It is proposed to fit the later ships with Harpoon SSMs; this will not involve external alterations, as they will be fired from the Standard launcher.

*Oliver Hazard Perry* was classified as PF-109 when laid down, but in June 1975 she was re-rated as a guided missile frigate and given the hull number FFG-7.

## *Broadsword* class

| Name | Number | Laid down | Launched | Completed | Builder |
|---|---|---|---|---|---|
| ***Broadsword*** | F 88 | 7 Feb 1975 | 12 May 1976 | 21 Feb 1979 | Yarrow, Glasgow |
| ***Battleaxe*** | F 89 | 4 Feb 1976 | 12 May 1977 | – | Yarrow, Glasgow |
| ***Brilliant*** | F 90 | 24 Mar 1977 | 15 Dec 1978 | – | Yarrow, Glasgow |
| ***Brazen*** (ex-***Boxer*** | F 91 | 19 Aug 1978 | – | – | Yarrow, Glasgow |
| ***Beaver*** | – | – | – | – | Yarrow, Glasgow |
| (unnamed) | – | – | – | – | Yarrow, Glasgow |

**Displacement**, 4,250 tons (standard), 4,750 tons (full load)
**Dimensions** 131.2m (oa) × 14.8m × 4.3m (430ft (oa) × 48.5ft × 14ft)
**Propulsion** 2 shafts, 2 sets gas turbines (COGOG); 56,000 shp = 30+ knots
**Aircraft** 2 Lynx A/S helicopters
**Armament** 2 × 6-tube Seawolf SAM launchers, 1 quad Exocet SSM launcher, 2 single 40mm L/70 guns, 2 triple 12.7in (324mm) STWS torpedo tubes
**Complement** Approx 250 officers and men

In the late 1950s the Royal Navy drew up staff requirements for a frigate to follow the *Leander*, which was then in the final phase of design. But rapid advances in submarine and ASW technology meant that the requirements had to be repeatedly altered to keep pace. This led to an unusually protracted development, during which the concept of the new frigate (known as the Type 22) changed completely from a general-purpose escort to a big mid-ocean submarine-hunter.

The new design was built around two systems: a big, new panoramic multiple-frequency sonar developed from the bow sonars installed experimentally in HMS *Matapan*, and Seawolf, a guided weapon which could counter the most pressing threat, long-range anti-ship missiles. The latter were expected to come from Soviet cruisers such as the Kresta and Kynda classes, but what was feared even more was the SS-N-7 "pop-up" missile carried by the Charlie submarines. It was envisaged that these weapons could be fired from *within* the normal radar horizon, allowing the defences even less time to react.

The ASW role of the ship was affected by a long-term Nato plan to counter the Soviet submarine threat. This was based on a chain of sensors laid in crucial transit areas or choke points such as the Iceland-Faeroes passage, through which Soviet nuclear submarines would have to pass to attack shipping carrying reinforcements to Europe, for example. Known as the Sound Underwater Surveillance System (SOSUS), it comprises a large number of passive underwater sensors reporting positions, tracks and noise signatures of individual submarines to shore stations. Thus a SOSUS station can report by data link to a patrolling frigate in the Iceland-Faeroes Passage the position, track and even the class or type of a hostile submarine long before it comes within sonar range of the ship.

Size and ruggedness are prerequisites for patrols in such distant waters, and a stable platform for helicopter operations is also necessary. The light helicopter had proved itself so vital to ASW that the new ships were designed with a hangar for the new Lynx light ASW and strike helicopter. Experience was to show that maintenance was the biggest problem, however, and so at a late stage in the design the Type 22 was given two Lynxes. Fortunately the size of the ship permitted the change.

Seawolf proved fully capable of performing its task, and has even tracked and destroyed a 4.5in shell, a target smaller than any anti-ship missile and travelling at twice the speed. The system is backed up by no fewer than five computers to process the information from the radars.

The defensive armament, if it can be called that, is the MM.38 Exocet SSM, designed to keep hostile surface ships at a distance; two 40mm Bofors guns are also carried.

The *Broadsword* class which resulted from these complex requirements is unique. By far the largest escorts to be built for the RN, they are also the first British warships to carry missiles as both main and secondary armament. They are also uncompromisingly rugged in appearance, almost to the point of ugliness, although from some angles they have a certain symmetry. The machinery is the standard Olympus/Tyne gas turbine combination, but with improved access and removal

routes and a higher degree of automation. The funnel incorporates certain improvements suggested by the *Sheffield* class.

There is talk of a dozen ships, but only six had been ordered by mid-1979. The last two are to be 30ft longer to allow an unidentified weapon system to be installed. Despite bitter criticism, mainly from people unaware of the new role envisaged for the ships, there is no doubt that they are extremely capable and are a powerful addition to the RN's strength.

Even ugly warships have their good angles, as proved by this view of HMS *Broadsword* on trials in Kilbrandon Sound. Note the six-cell Seawolf missile launcher above the four Exocet launchers. The compact aerial at the head of the foremast houses antennas for the Types 967 and 968 radars back-to-back.

HMS ARDENT SUNK 5-21-82
H.M.S. ANTELOPE SUNK 5-24-82

# *Amazon* class

| Name | Number | Laid down | Launched | Completed | Builder |
|---|---|---|---|---|---|
| ***Amazon*** | F 169 | 16 Nov 1969 | 26 Apr 1971 | 11 May 1974 | Vosper Thornycroft, Woolston |
| ***Antelope*** | F 170 | 23 Mar 1971 | 16 Mar 1972 | 19 July 1975 | Vosper Thornycroft, Woolston |
| ***Active*** | F 171 | 23 Jul 1971 | 23 Nov 1972 | 17 Jun 1977 | Vosper Thornycroft, Woolston |
| ***Ambuscade*** | F 172 | 1 Sep 1971 | 18 Jan 1973 | 5 Sep 1975 | Yarrow, Glasgow |
| ***Arrow*** | F 173 | 28 Sep 1972 | 5 Feb 1974 | 29 Jul 1976 | Yarrow, Glasgow |
| ***Alacrity*** | F 174 | 5 Mar 1973 | 18 Sep 1974 | 2 Jul 1977 | Yarrow, Glasgow |
| ***Ardent*** | F 184 | 26 Feb 1974 | 9 May 1975 | 14 Oct 1977 | Yarrow, Glasgow |
| ***Avenger*** | F 185 | 30 Oct 1974 | 20 Nov 1975 | 15 Apr 1978 | Yarrow, Glasgow |

**Displacement** 2,750 tons (standard), 3,250 tons (full load)
**Dimensions** 117.0m (oa) × 12.7m ×4.4m (384ft (oa) × 41.8ft × 14.5ft)
**Propulsion** 2 shafts, 2 sets geared gas turbines (COGOG); 56,000 shp = 32 knots
**Aircraft** 1 Lynx A/S helicopter
**Armament** 1 quad Seacat SAM launcher, 4 single Exocet SSM launchers (*Active* onwards), 1 single 4.5in (114mm) Mk 8 gun, 2 single 20mm guns, 2 triple 12.7in (324mm) STWS torpedo tubes
**Complement** 13 officers, 164 ratings

During the 1960s, while work on a *Leander* replacement was in full swing, it became apparent that there would be a need for a general-purpose escort to replace the *Leopard* and *Salisbury*-class diesel-engined frigates built in 1953-60. Because the Ship Department was fully occupied with the Type 22 and other major projects, it was decided to enlist the help of private shipbuilders in designing a patrol frigate for the RN, the first time this had been done since the

building of the first destroyers 70 years before.

Two companies provided the expertise: small-ship specialists Vosper Thornycroft, and Yarrow. In fact the design was a three-way affair, with the Director-General Ship Department working closely with the two firms to ensure that the design met the RN's needs. For example, the propulsion plant of the *Sheffield*-class (Type 42) DDGs was adapted for the new ships, making the frigates the first all-gas turbine warships designed for the Royal Navy.

The layout and appearance of the *Amazons* owe much to a long series of designs produced by Vosper Thornycroft and the original Thornycroft company, going back to the innovative escort destroyers *Brecon* and *Brissenden* of the Second World War. The use of aluminium in the superstructure kept dimensions down to the length and beam of the *Leanders*, while the installed power was nearly doubled. This involved no sacrifice of armament, and the new Type 21 frigates have a single 4.5in Mk 8 gun forward, Seacat close-range SAMs aft, and a hangar and flight deck for a Lynx helicopter. The subsequent addition of four MM.38 Exocet SSMs ahead of the bridge provides even greater firepower.

Although lightly built, these ships have proved popular. They are well laid-out internally, and need fewer men to run them than comparable earlier vessels. They lack a long-range air-warning and surveillance radar, which limits their usefulness on independent missions, but have a good sonar, the hull-mounted Type 184M, the STWS close-range ASW torpedo system and the Lynx helicopter. Despite their popularity they are too cramped to permit any worthwhile additions, and the class will not receive a major mid-life refit. Instead they will be scrapped or sold.

The *Amazon* entered service in November 1969 and the *Avenger*, the eighth ship, came into service early in 1978. Discussions with Greece and Argentina about possible export sales proved abortive because the financial credits could not be arranged.

The previous *Amazon* and *Ambuscade* were experimental prototype destroyers built to their own designs by Thornycroft and Yarrow in the 1920s. To honour this previous association the same names were given to the lead ships from the two yards.

The *Avenger* is the last of the *Amazon*-class (Type 21) frigates. Her profile is typical of a "Thornycroft look" going back to the *Brecon* and *Brissenden* of 1942, though the design was worked out in conjunction with Yarrow and the Ministry of Defence.

## *Leander* class

| Name | Number |
|---|---|
| ***Aurora*** (Ikara-armed) | F 10 |
| ***Euryalus*** | F 15 |
| ***Galatea*** | F 18 |
| ***Arethusa*** | F 38 |
| ***Naiad*** | F 39 |
| ***Dido*** | F 104 |
| ***Leander*** | F 109 |
| ***Ajax*** | F 114 |
| ***Cleopatra*** (Exocet-armed) | F 28 |
| ***Sirius*** | F 40 |
| ***Phoebe*** | F 42 |
| ***Minerva*** | F 45 |
| ***Danae*** | F 47 |
| ***Juno*** | F 52 |
| ***Argonaut*** | F 56 |
| ***Penelope*** | F 127 |
| ***Achilles*** (Seawolf conversion in hand) | F 12 |
| ***Diomede*** | F 16 |
| ***Andromeda*** | F 57 |
| ***Hermione*** | F 58 |
| ***Jupiter*** | F 60 |
| ***Bacchante*** | F 69 |
| ***Apollo*** | F 70 |
| ***Scylla*** | F 71 |
| ***Ariadne*** | F 72 |
| ***Charybdis*** | F 75 |
| ***Swan*** (Australia) | 50 |
| ***Torrens*** | 53 |
| ***Condell*** (Chile) | 06 |
| ***Almirante Lynch*** | 07 |
| ***Nilgiri*** (India) | F 32 |
| ***Himgiri*** | F 33 |
| ***Dunagiri*** | F 34 |
| ***Udaygiri*** | F 35 |
| ***Taragiri*** (completing) | F 36 |
| ***Vindhyagiri*** (building) | F 37 |
| ***Van Speijk*** (Netherlands) | F 802 |
| ***Van Galen*** | F 803 |
| ***Tjerk Hiddes*** | F 804 |
| ***Van Nes*** | F 805 |
| ***Isaac Sweers*** | F 814 |
| ***Evertsen*** | F 815 |
| ***Waikato*** (New Zealand) | F 56 |
| ***Canterbury*** | F 421 |

**Displacement** 2,450 tons (standard), 2,860 tons (full load) (Broad-beamed) 2,500 tons (standard), 2,962 tons (full load)
**Dimensions** 113.4m (oa) × 12.5m (BB 13.1m) × 5.5m (372ft (oa) × 41ft (BB 43ft) × 18ft)
**Propulsion** 2 shafts, geared steam turbines, 2 boilers; 30,000 shp = 30 knots
**Aircraft** 1 Wasp A/S helicopter
**Armament** 1 quad Seacat SAM launcher (some ships), 1 twin 4.5in (114mm) guns, 2 single 40mm guns (some ships), 2 single 20mm guns, 1 × 3-barrel Limbo A/S mortar (Ikara) 2 quad Seacat SAM launchers, 2 single 40mm guns, 1 single Ikara ASM launcher, 1 × 3-barrel Limbo A/S mortar (Exocet) 2 quad Seacat SAM launchers, 4 single Exocet SSM launchers, 2 single 40mm guns, 2 triple 12.7in (324mm) STWS torpedo tubes
**Complement** 251-260 officers and men

26 *Leanders* built 1959-71. Most now converted to ASW or SSM vessels: 8 narrow-beam and the 10 broad-beam *Leanders* to SSM, and 8 narrow-beam to ASW. 2 Modified *Leanders* built 1965-71 for Australia by Cockatoo Dockyard; Williamstown Dockyard. 2 *Leanders* built 1971-74 for Chile by Yarrow, Glasgow. 6 Modified *Leanders* built and building 1970 onwards for India by Mazagon Docks Ltd, Bombay. 2 *Leanders* built 1964-71 for New Zealand by Yarrow, Glasgow; Harland &

Wolff, Belfast. 6 Modified *Leanders* built 1963-68 by KM de Schelde, Flushing; Nederlandse D & S M, Amsterdam.

This class still forms the backbone of the Royal Navy's escort force, being the largest single group of major British ships built since 1945. The design stems from a project known as the 1944 Frigate, a scheme to produce anti-submarine, anti-aircraft and aircraft-direction ships based on a common hull. They were to be diesel-driven for high endurance, but after 1945 the overriding requirement was for a high pursuit speed to enable them to catch fast submarines such as the German Type XXI and its derivatives.

The hull which emerged from this requirement was remarkable, with a raised, flared forecastle to throw spray aside, a narrow V-section forward to prevent slamming in a seaway, and a deep mid-section for a good sustained speed in bad weather. Known as the Type 12 hull, it proved very manoeuvrable and outstandingly seaworthy. The steam machinery was not capable of producing high smooth-water speeds, but on only 75 per cent of the power of a wartime destroyer it could enable a steady 27-28 knots to be maintained in all but the worst weather, something a destroyer could never guarantee.

The first ships with this new hull were the six-strong *Whitby* class, built 1954-58 and now reduced to only two ships retained for training. They were followed by nine *Rothesays*, basically similar but with improved internal layout and minor modifications to the armament. They were built in 1957-61 and were intended to form a class of 12 ships. They were refitted in 1966-72 to incorporate as many features of the *Leander* class as possible, and are still in service.

Experience with the Type 81 or *Ashanti* class suggested that it was time to re-introduce the concept of the general-purpose frigate, with good all-round anti-submarine, anti-aircraft and aircraft-direction capabilities. Accordingly, the last three *Rothesay* hulls were completed to an entirely new design. To accommodate a significant increase in the weights carried in the hull the designers had to re-arrange the ship entirely, moving heavy weights lower down, extending the forecastle deck right aft to the stern and replacing the water ballast tanks with self-compensating fuel tanks. The result was a transformation, and although the ships are still loosely referred to as Type 12s, all that remains of the original design is the shape.

The *Leander* class formed three groups: the original *Leander* class of 10 ships, built 1959-66 with Y-100 steam plant; the six *Phoebe* class, built 1963-67 with Y-136 machinery; and the 10 "broad-beamed" *Andromeda* class, built 1966-73 with Y-160 machinery. The broad-beamed ships have 2ft added to their beam to offset the extra topweight. As a result, they do not have to carry the same permanent ballast as the earlier ships and so offer slightly more space internally.

All 10 of the original *Leanders* were intended to have the Ikara long-range anti-submarine missile system, starting

HMAS *Swan* has many features of the RN *Leander*, itself derived from the *Whitby/Rothesay* design, but lacks a helicopter. Note the dome housing the director for the Ikara A/S missile (mounted aft on the starboard side) and the Dutch radar arrays. The masting is also unique to this ship and her sister *Torrens*.

in 1970 with the *Leander*. Only eight ships were finally converted, however, and the other two *Leanders* and the six *Phoebes* were given the Exocet surface-to-surface missile. The *Andromeda* group are now being converted to operate the Seawolf SAM system and the big Type 2016 panoramic search sonar.

In place of the 4.5in twin gun mounting the Ikara *Leanders* have a "zareba" housing the Ikara missile launcher. The cumbersome arrangement of Seacat launcher and director aft was improved, with the director placed on the centreline and two quadruple launchers winged out. The Ikara guidance system replaced the MRS-3 director above the bridge, and the Type 965 long-range air-warning radar was removed from the mainmast. Two 40mm Bofors guns were added abreast of the foremast.

The Exocet group also lost the 4.5in gun mounting, and had the Seacat system over the hangar improved and were given an extra Seacat launcher forward of the four Exocets. To improve the ASW armament the hangar has been enlarged to take the Lynx helicopter, and triple STWS ASW torpedo tubes have been added on the after superstructure. The Type 965 radar has been retained on the mainmast to give the ships the ability to track aircraft, and the opportunity has been taken to increase the fuel stowage by 50 per cent, resulting in a valuable range increment.

The "Batch 3" *Leanders* will have four Exocets forward and the diminutive Seawolf launcher forward and aft. The major problem is the topweight resulting from mounting the back-to-back Types 967/968 tracking radars and the Type 910 fire control. To compensate for this, every scrap of excess topweight has been cut out, including the funnel cap; even the torpedo tubes have been lowered one deck level.

The *Leander* has proved very popular, being built to a modified design by the Royal Netherlands Navy and for the Chilean, Indian and New Zealand navies. The Australian Navy has modified two of its *Rothesay* class (known locally as the "River" class), the *Swan* and *Torrens*, to the same standard, but without a helicopter hangar. The most interesting series is the class built in India: the first two are like the Dutch *Leanders* in having Hollandse Signaalapparaten M4 directors for their Seacat SAMs, but standard RN radars for fire control and air warning. The next two have an Indian-built LW02 HSA air-warning radar on the mainmast and DA05 on the foremast. The first four have an enlarged hangar to take an Alouette III helicopter, but the last two are to have an enlarged hull to allow a Sea King helicopter to be embarked.

Although HMS *Diomede* is one of the third batch of "broad-beamed" *Leanders*, she will still exemplify the original configuration of the class until she receives Seawolf. The only changes apparent in this June 1977 view are the addition of Corvus chaff rockets abreast of the mainmast and minor additions to the aerials and ECM arrays.

▲ HMS *Euryalus*, an Ikara conversion also pictured in June 1977. Note the Ikara launcher hidden in its "zareba" at the former 4.5in gun turret position, the extra Seacat missile launcher above the hangar roof, and the variable-depth sonar on the stern. Many *Leanders* have had their VDS removed.

▼ *Cleopatra*, an Exocet conversion, resembles the Ikara *Leanders* but with four MM.38 launchers forward and a third Seacat close-range SAM launcher ahead of them. They also differ from the first batch in having triple STWS torpedo tubes abreast of the mainmast and an enlarged hangar for the Lynx helicopter.

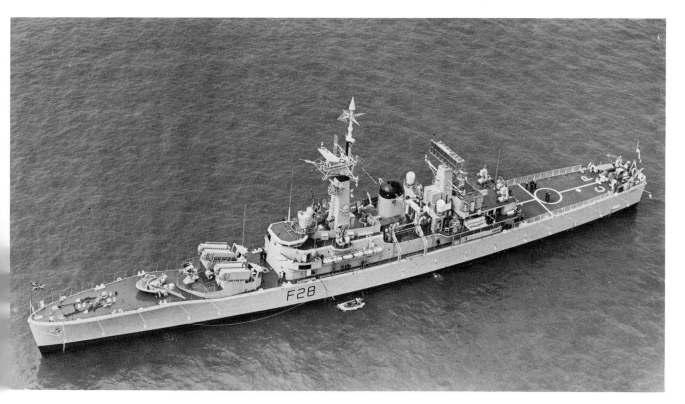

## *Ashanti*/"Tribal" class

| Name | Number | Laid down | Launched | Completed | Builder |
|---|---|---|---|---|---|
| ***Ashanti*** | F 117 | 15 Jan 1958 | 9 Mar 1959 | 23 Nov 1961 | Yarrow, Glasgow |
| ***Eskimo*** | F 119 | 22 Oct 1958 | 20 Mar 1960 | 21 Feb 1963 | J. S. White, Cowes |
| ***Gurkha*** | F 122 | 3 Nov 1958 | 11 Jul 1960 | 13 Feb 1963 | Thornycroft, Woolston |
| ***Mohawk*** | F 125 | 23 Dec 1960 | 5 Apr 1962 | 29 Nov 1963 | Vickers-Armstrong, Barrow |
| ***Nubian*** | F 131 | 7 Sep 1959 | 6 Sep 1960 | 9 Oct 1962 | Portsmouth Dockyard |
| ***Tartar*** | F 133 | 22 Oct 1959 | 19 Sep 1960 | 26 Feb 1962 | Devonport Dockyard |
| ***Zulu*** | F 124 | 13 Dec 1960 | 3 Jul 1962 | 17Apr 1964 | Alexander Stephen, Glasgow |

**Displacement** 2,300 tons (standard), 2,700 tons (full load)
**Dimensions** 109.7m (oa) × 12.9m × 5.3m (360ft (oa) × 42.3ft × 17.5ft)
**Propulsion** 1 shaft, geared steam turbine and gas turbine (COSAG), 1 boiler; 20,000 shp = 25 knots
**Aircraft** 1 Wasp A/S helicopter
**Armament** 2 quad Seacat SAM launchers, 2 single 4.5in (114mm) guns, 2 single 20mm guns, 1 × 3-barrel Limbo A/S mortar
**Complement** 13 officers, 240 men

The first British frigates built after 1945 were a specialised series of anti-submarine (*Whitby* and *Blackwood* classes), anti-aircraft (*Leopard* class) and aircraft-direction (*Salisbury* class) types, a result of the belief that equipment had become too complex for it all to be accommodated in one hull. But by 1954 electronic technology was advancing so rapidly that it would soon be possible to house items such as long-range radar and data-processing

equipment in a much smaller volume than before. Nor was this the only area in which space was being saved; the gas turbine promised a great deal of power for a smaller volume than the traditional steam boilers and turbines.

The new Type 81 frigate was to be given an experimental steam-and-gas turbine combination, with a steam turbine for main drive and a gas turbine for "cold" starting and high-speed boost. This would give a sea speed of only 25 knots, not enough to pursue a high-speed submarine, but for that purpose the ship would be given a Wasp light helicopter. This would act as a weapon-carrier, dropping an acoustic torpedo in an area indicated by the sonar plot. Long-range air warning would be provided by a single Type 965 "bedstead" radar, allowing the ship to function as part of a radar picket, and for self-defence she would have the Seacat short-range SAM system.

These ships were intended to replace the nine ageing *Loch*-class frigates in the Persian Gulf, and so habitability and good all-round capability were prime requirements. The main armament, two single Mk 4 4.5in guns, was relatively unsophisticated but adequate for the job. It earned the unkind nickname of "guided flagpoles".

In the event only seven of the Tribal class were built, and for some years all but *Zulu* carried 40mm Bofors guns in place of the Seacat system. Despite some initial problems the machinery proved successful, paving the way for the COGOG systems now in service. The most successful aspect of the design was the ingenious helicopter hangar. The hangar roof also functions as the lift, and when the Wasp is struck down the roof is closed by separate sections.

The Tribals are now showing their age, and are not worth any major modernisation. It is possible that they could be paid off or even sold to another navy within the next few years. They remain useful escort vessels, however, and with their flush decks and two raked funnels are among the best-looking ships in the RN.

HMS *Mohawk* and her sisters were unusual in having the first flush deck seen in a British light warship for nearly 60 years. Note the elderly Mk 4 4.5in single gun forward, the single mast and twin funnels. The Wasp helicopter is on the hangar roof, which also serves as the lift.

## *Commandant Rivière* class

**Displacement** 1,750 tons (standard), 2,250 tons (full load)
**Dimensions** 103.7m (oa) × 11.7m × 4.8m (340.3ft (oa) × 38.2ft × 15.7ft)
**Propulsion** 2 shafts, diesel drive; 16,000 bhp = 25 knots
**Armament** 4 single Exocet SSM launchers, 2 single 3.9in (100mm) guns, 2 single 30mm guns, 1 quad 12in (305mm) A/S mortar, 2 triple 21in (533mm) torpedo tubes
**Complement** 10 officers, 157 men

*Amiral Charner, Balny, Commandant*

*Bory, Commandant Bourdais, Commandant Rivière, Doudart de Lagrée, Enseigne de Vaisseau Henry, Protet* and *Victor Schoelcher* built 1957-65 by Lorient Dockyard. *Comandante Hermenegildo Capelo, Comandante Joao Belo, Comandante Roberto Ivens* and *Comandante Sacadura Cabral* built 1965-69 for Portugal by A & C de Nantes.

These handsome little ships were designed as *avisos* or colonial sloops, with the dual role of escort and patrol vessel for overseas stations. They have a relatively modest armament but good habitability and endurance.

For the colonial role the ships can embark 80 troops and two 9-metre landing craft. Since 1973 two ships, the *Enseigne de Vaisseau Henry* and *Commandant Bory*, have had MM.38 Exocet SSMs in place of one of the after 100mm guns, and others, with the exception of the *Balny*, are being converted. The *Amiral Charner* has a helicopter platform.

Two ships were used as testbeds for experimental machinery. The *Balny* spent nine years trying out a new Combined Diesel and Gas Turbine (CODAG) system, before being accepted by the French Navy. The *Commandant Bory* had Sigma free-piston generators and gas turbines, replaced in 1974-75 by the standard diesels fitted in the rest of the class.

Four ships with a slightly beamier hull were built for Portugal in 1965-69.

Although these ships are useful coastal escorts they do not have enough space for sophisticated ASW armament. They will serve for a few years longer but are too small to warrant any degree of modernisation to improve their armament, other than the fitting of Exocet SSMs.

The *Protet* under way, showing the original appearance of the class. She and most of her sisters now have two MM.38 Exocet surface-to-surface missiles in place of "X" 100mm gun, but one or two have platforms for a light helicopter. Note the low freeboard forward and the triple A/S torpedo tubes amidships.

## *d'Estienne d'Orves* class

**Displacement** 950 tons (standard), 1,170 tons (full load)
**Dimensions** 80.0m (oa) × 10.3m × 3.0m (262.5ft (oa) × 33.8ft × 9.8ft)
**Propulsion** 2 shafts, diesel drive; 11,000 bhp = 24 knots
**Armament** 2 single Exocet SSM launchers (on ships on foreign service), 1 single 3.9in (100mm) gun, 2 single 20mm guns, 1 × 6-barrel 14.8in (375mm) A/S rocket launcher, 4 torpedo tubes
**Complement** 5 officers, 70 men

*Amyot d'Inville, Commandant Blaison, Commandant de Pimodan, d'Estienne d'Orves, Détroyat, Drogou, Enseigne de Vaisseau Jacoubet, Jean Moulin, Lieutenant de Vaisseau Lavallée, Premier Maître l'Her, Second Maître le Bihan* and *Quartier Maître Anquetil* built and building 1972 onwards at Lorient Dockyard. *Lieutenant de Vaisseau le Henaff* and *Commandant l'Herminier* sold to South Africa in 1976 but resold to Argentina in 1978, renamed *Drummond* and *Guerrico*; one more to be built.

A further class of *avisos*, smaller than the *Commandant Rivière* class but also capable of coastal ASW as well as colonial service, was ordered for the French Navy. The A69 design is remarkably compact, with a 100mm DP gun forward, a single mack amidships and a six-barrelled ASW rocket launcher on the after superstructure. Four single tubes firing ASW torpedoes are also mounted in the after superstructure. Ships earmarked for the Mediterranean have been fitted with two MM.38 Exocet SSMs abaft the mack, and the rest are fitted for rapid conversion if needed.

The last two ships, *Commandant Blaison* and *Enseigne de Vaisseau Jacoubet*, are to be fitted with a helicopter hangar and flight deck capable of accommodating the new lightweight Dauphin helicopter. They will also be fitted with stabilisers to compensate for the extra topweight.

Two ships out of the programme, *Lieutenant de Vaisseau le Henaff* and *Commandant l'Herminier*, were sold to South Africa as the *Good Hope* and *Transvaal*, and it was intended to lay down two replacements with the same names. But the French Government announced that it would not allow the ships to be handed over, in response to the UN embargo on arms sales to South Africa, and the current status of the two ships is uncertain. Late in 1978 they were sold to the Argentinian Navy, with a third to be built in France.

It was originally intended to build 14 A69-type *avisos*, followed by the similar A70 armed with MM.38 Exocets. But this plan has now been shelved, hence the fitting of Exocet to some ships. An additional A69 may however be added to the programme. Progress has been much slower than planned as a result of the financial crisis in France; the last ship was not laid down until 1979 and will not enter service until the end of 1981.

▶ The *Jean Moulin* and two sisters under construction in the covered building berth at Lorient. Note the construction of the mack, the ramps for two Exocet missiles immediately abaft it, and the six-barrelled A/S rocket launcher on the deckhouse. When this photograph was taken the ship had been under construction for only 284 days.

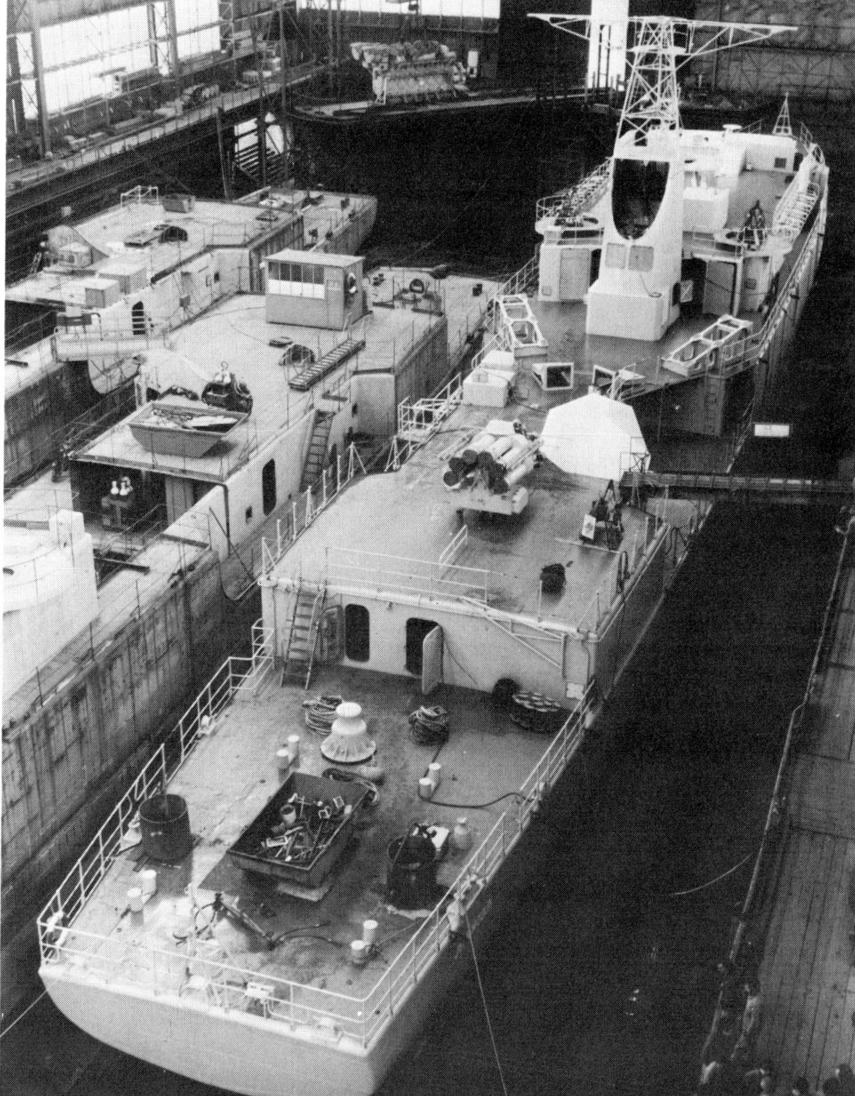

▼ The *d'Estienne d'Orves* at sea soon after completion. Note how the 100mm gun forward seems to dwarf the hull, an indication of how small these ships are. The Exocet missiles have not yet been installed and the A/S torpedo tubes are hidden behind doors beneath the A/S rocket launcher in the after superstructure.

## Riga class

| Name | Number |
|---|---|
| ***Barsuk*** | |
| ***Buyvol*** | |
| ***Byk*** | |
| ***Gepard*** | |
| ***Giena*** | |
| ***Kobchik*** | |
| ***Lisa*** | |
| ***Medved*** | |
| ***Pantera*** | |
| ***Shakal*** | |
| ***Turman*** | |
| ***Volk*** | |
| + 25 other units, whose names are unknown | |
| ***Druzki*** (Bulgaria) | 31 |
| ***Smeli*** | 32 |
| ***Kuei Lin*** (China) | 204 |
| ***Kuei Yang*** | 205 |
| ***K'un Ming*** | 206 |
| ***Ch'Eng Tu*** | 207 |
| ***Ernst Thälmann*** (German Democractic Republic) | 141 |
| ***Hämeenmaa*** (Finland) | – |
| ***Uusimaa*** | – |
| ***Jos Sudarso*** (Indonesia) | 351 |
| ***Lambung Mangkurat*** | 357 |
| ***Nuku*** | 360 |

**Displacement** 1,200 tons (standard), 1,600 tons (deep load)
**Dimensions** 91.0m (oa) × 9.5m × 3.4m (298.6ft (oa) × 31.5ft × 11ft)
**Propulsion** 2 shafts, geared steam turbines; 20,000 shp = 28 knots
**Armament** 3 single 100mm guns, 2 twin 37mm guns, 3 × 533mm torpedo tubes, 4 depth-charge throwers (replaced by 2 × 5 or 16-barrelled MBU rocket launchers)
**Complement** 150

Builders: various Baltic, Black Sea and Siberian yards, and the Watun yard, Shanghai.

Between 1952 and 1959 the Soviet Navy built some 50 1,200-ton escorts based on the Kola class. They bore a basic resemblance to pre-war torpedo boats of the *Yastreb* class, and it is no coincidence that both the Rigas and Kolas had a triple set of torpedo tubes amidships.

The Riga class (the Nato practice at the time was to allocate a code name according to the area of the first sighting) were virtually escort destroyers, with a heavy surface armament of guns and torpedo tubes, and only light ASW armament. This equipment is now quite obsolete for anything but coastal patrol and the ships must be showing signs of old age. Some have been modernised, with the torpedo tubes removed and more extensive radar arrays fitted.

Four of this class were assembled in Chinese shipyards with Soviet technical assistance in 1958-59. East Germany received five, of which only the *Ernst Thälmann* survives. Indonesia has only three out of six left, but Bulgaria and Finland retain their two ships apiece. It is believed that only about 37 Rigas survive, and their age makes it certain that they will either be reduced to auxiliary duties or scrapped in the next few years. In their day, however, they were cheap and simple coastal escorts which could free bigger warships for more important tasks.

A Riga-class escort in original condition, with three single 100mm hand-worked guns and three torpedo tubes amidships. The sharply raked bow and pronounced sheer offset the low freeboard to some extent, but the Rigas are not suitable for ocean work.

# Petya and Mirka classes

**Displacement** (Petya) 950-1,000 tons (standard), 1,100 tons (full load) (Mirka) 1,050 tons (standard), 1,100 tons (full load)
**Dimensions** 82m (oa) × 9.1m × 3.0-3.2m (268.75ft (oa) × 29.75ft × 9.6-10.4ft)
**Propulsion** (P) 2 shafts, diesels (M) 2 shafts, gas turbines and diesels; 12,000 shp + 4,000 bhp = 28 knots
**Armament** (PI, MI) 2 twin 76mm DP guns, 5 single 406mm ASW torpedo tubes, 4 × 16-barrelled MBU ASW rocket launchers
(PII, PI Mod, MII) 4 × 76mm DP guns, 2 quint 406mm ASW torpedo tubes, 2 MBU rocket launchers
**Complement** 100

13 Petya Is, 9 Petya I Mods and 26 Petya IIs built 1960-64, plus 10 Petya IIs built for India; 20 Mirka Is and Mirka IIs. Indian ships: *Arnala* (P 68), *Androth* (P 69), *Anjadip* (P 73), *Andaman* (P 74), *Amini* (P 75), *Kamorta* (P 77), *Kadmath* (P 78), *Kiltan* (P 79), *Kavarathi* (P 80), *Katchal* (P 81), *Kanjar* (P 82) and *Amindivi* (P 83).

In 1960 the Soviet Navy started work on a class of smaller diesel-engined corvettes or small frigates to follow the Rigas. These are code-named the Petya class by Nato, and by Western standards carry a heavy armament on a small hull.

There appear to have been problems with these ships, probably because too much was attempted on a limited displacement. The two rapid-fire 76mm DP gun mountings and fire control could only be accommodated by keeping the freeboard low, and this in turn must make for poor seakeeping. This would explain the subsequent addition of a bulwark on the forecastle. Indian sources also speak of mechanical unreliability.

The later ships, code-named Petya II, were given a second set of quintuple 16in ASW torpedo-tubes aft in place of the MBU rocket launchers. Eight of the original type were refitted with a deck-house and variable-depth sonar aft in place of the MBUs, and this variant is known in the West as the Petya I Mod (formerly thought to be Petya III).

Construction stopped in about 1964, with about 22 Petya Is and 26 Petya IIs built at Nikolaiev and Kaliningrad. These ships are very useful as coastal escorts, and have been followed by the 20 Mirka class. These have the same hull but, because they have gas turbines as well as diesels, the low diesel exhaust has been done away with in favour of side exhausts. They all have the deckhouse aft for the VDS, as in the Petya I Mod, but the Mirka I differs from the Mirka II in having only one set of 16in ASW torpedo tubes.

Construction was divided between Leningrad and Kaliningrad in 1964-69. Names have been reported for only a few of these classes: *Protivnika* (Petya) and *Gangutets* and *Tuman* (Mirka). Twelve Petya IIs were transferred to India between 1969 and 1974, two to Syria in 1975-76 and two to Vietnam in 1978.

This Mirka-class small escort, in company with a Kynda-class cruiser, is armed with two twin 76mm gun mountings and five 16in A/S torpedo tubes. Note the big, poop-mounted exhausts for her gas turbines. The Mirka II differs in having the after MBU rocket launchers (between the ventilators and gun) replaced with an extra set of tubes.

## *Annapolis* class

| Name | Number | Laid down | Launched | Completed | Builder |
|---|---|---|---|---|---|
| ***Annapolis*** | 265 | Jul 1960 | 27 Apr 1963 | 19 Dec 1964 | Halifax Shipyard |
| ***Nipigon*** | 266 | Apr 1960 | 10 Dec 1961 | 30 May 1964 | Maritime Industries, Sorel |

**Displacement** 2,400 tons (standard), 3,000 tons (full load)
**Dimensions** 113.1m (oa) × 12.8m × 4.4m (371.0ft (oa) × 42.0ft × 14.4ft)
**Propulsion** 2 shafts, geared steam turbines, 2 boilers; 30,000 shp = 28 knots
**Aircraft** 1 CHSS-2 Sea King A/S helicopter
**Armament** 1 twin 3in (76mm) 50-cal guns, 1 × 3-barrel Limbo A/S mortar, 2 triple 12.7in (324mm) Mk 32 torpedo tubes
**Complement** 11 officers, 199 men

In 1951 the Royal Canadian Navy embarked on an ambitious anti-submarine escort project of its own. With technical assistance from the Royal Navy and US Navy the *St Laurent* class were built in 1950-57. They proved successful and 7 more *Restigouche* class followed in 1952-59.

The major threat in the 1950s was from a huge Soviet submarine fleet, and so the RCN devoted most of its efforts to improving ASW. In 1956 a series of trials of the HO-45 helicopter in the old River class frigate HMCS *Buckingham* showed that it would be feasible to operate a new ASW helicopter from frigates. This was the Sikorsky SH-3A Sea King, a much

larger machine than anything previously operated from a small warship. A new handling device had to be designed to enable the flight deck crew to handle such a large helicopter without undue risk.

The three programmes came together in 1964, when the *St Laurent*-class destroyer escort *Assiniboine* began flight deck and hangar compatibility trials. After three years of intensive trials with a new device known as the Beartrap, it was possible to take the first ships in hand for conversion from DDE to DDH (helicopter-carrying destroyer) standard. The first to embark an operational Sea King flight was HMCS *Saguenay* in 1967.

In the meantime, a further two improved *Mackenzie*-class DDEs had been laid down in 1960, and the opportunity was taken to complete these ships as DDHs. They therefore represent the ultimate development of the original concept. The funnel was split to allow maximum room for the helicopter, and one Limbo Mk 10 mortar was dropped to make room for a Variable-Depth Sonar (VDS) aft. The weight was already well over that of the original design and so the British Mk 6 3in gun mounting had to be dropped in favour of the lighter US-pattern Mk 33.

The machinery was identical to that of the original class but the hull was slightly longer; the stern was cut away to facilitate handling of the VDS, and earlier ships were similarly modified.

The *Annapolis* and *Nipigon* underwent mid-life modernisation in 1977-79, but apart from electronics, communications and accommodation overhauls they were not radically altered. Until the first of the new patrol frigates is built they will remain the most modern Canadian escorts after the four *Iroquois*-class DDHs.

HMCS *Annapolis* and her sister *Nipigon* were altered during construction to permit operation of the Sea King helicopter. The funnel was divided into two uptakes to give maximum width to the hangar, and the stern was modified to improve handling of the variable-depth sonar. Excess weight forced a return to the light Mk 33 3in twin gun mounting, however.

# *Peder Skram* class

| Name | Number | Laid down | Launched | Completed | Builder |
|---|---|---|---|---|---|
| ***Peder Skram*** | F 352 | 25 Sep 1964 | 20 May 1965 | 30 Jun 1966 | Helsingörs J & M |
| ***Herluf Trolle*** | F 353 | 18 Dec 1964 | 8 Sep 1965 | 16 Apr 1967 | Helsingörs J & M |

**Displacement** 2,030 tons (standard), 2,720 tons (full load)
**Dimensions** 112.6m (oa) × 12m × 3.6m (396.5ft (oa) × 39.5ft × 11.8ft)
**Propulsion** 2 shafts, geared gas turbine or diesel drive (CODOG); 44,000 shp = 30 knots
**Armament** (*Herluf Trolle*) 1 quad Sea Sparrow SAM launcher, 8 Harpoon SSM launchers, 1 twin 5in (127mm) 38-cal guns, 2 twin 40mm guns, 4 × 21in (533mm) torpedo tubes, depth-charge throwers
**Complement** 190 officers and men

Two fast frigates were laid down in 1964 for the Royal Danish Navy. The design was Danish but financial support was provided under the offshore procurement provisions of the Mutual Defence Aid Programme (MDAP). Thus the plans had to be submitted to the US Bureau of Ships before financial support was forthcoming.

The ships which resulted were good-looking, with large twin funnels and a flush deck. The main armament of American twin 5in/38-cal DP guns was mounted forward, with two twin 40mm Bofors guns at the after end of the shelter deck for close-range AA defence. The original design provided for a set of triple 21in torpedo tubes amidships and the Norwegian Terne anti-submarine rocket launcher, but these weapons were subsequently dropped. The AA armament was noticeably feeble, but the design allowed for the eventual installation of the Sea Sparrow close-range SAM system, and this was done in 1976-77 in the *Herluf Trolle*. The eight-cell launcher was put on the quarterdeck, and a new deckhouse was built on the after superstructure to house the fire control. At the same time "B" gun mounting was replaced with eight Harpoon SSMs. The *Peder Skram* paid off in 1977 and recommissioned towards the end of 1979.

This modernisation has turned what were once rather large but under-armed ships into useful command ships with a good surface strike capability.

The Danish *Peder Skram*, originally designed with torpedo tubes amidships, shows her destroyer origins. Since this photograph was taken both she and her sister have had the "B" twin 5in gun mounting replaced by Harpoon missiles, and the after superstructure has been built up to accommodate the Nato Sea Sparrow SAM system.

## *Köln* class

| Name | Number | Laid down | Launched | Completed | Builder |
|---|---|---|---|---|---|
| ***Köln*** | F 220 | 21 Dec 1957 | 6 Dec 1958 | 15 Apr 1961 | Stülcken, Hamburg |
| ***Emden*** | F 221 | 15 Apr 1958 | 21 Mar 1959 | 24 Oct 1961 | Stülcken, Hamburg |
| ***Augsburg*** | F 222 | 29 Oct 1958 | 15 Aug 1959 | 7 Apr 1972 | Stülcken, Hamburg |
| ***Karlsruhe*** | F 223 | 15 Dec 1958 | 24 Oct 1959 | 15 Dec 1962 | Stülcken, Hamburg |
| ***Lübeck*** | F 224 | 28 Oct 1959 | 23 Jul 1960 | 6 Jul 1963 | Stülcken, Hamburg |
| ***Braunschweig*** | F 225 | 28 Jul 1960 | 3 Feb 1962 | 16 Jun 1964 | Stülcken, Hamburg |

**Displacement** 2,100 tons (standard), 2,550 tons (full load)
**Dimensions** 110m (oa) × 11.0m (oa) × 3.4m (360.9ft (oa) × 36.1ft × 11.2ft)
**Propulsion** 2 shafts, geared gas turbines and diesel drive (CODAG); 36,000 bhp = 32 knots
**Armament** 2 single 3.9in (100mm) guns, 2 twin + 2 single 40mm guns, 2 × 4-barrel Bofors A/S mortars, 2 twin 21in (533mm) torpedo tubes, 80 mines
**Complement** Approx 200 officers and men

As soon as permission was given for the Federal Republic of Germany to re-arm in the early 1950s, work started on designs for new ships. The pressing need was for a class of escorts well armed with AA guns and ASW weapons, but there was a political problem faced by no other navy. Only nine years after the Second World War, with many French, British and American commentators voicing misgivings about the decision to allow German re-armament, it would have been impossible for the Federal German Navy to buy complete designs abroad. Yet there was little or no indigenous design experience, and the rapid building of ships would stretch that experience to the limit.

The answer was to buy as much equipment as possible "off the shelf," and to adapt a late 1944-vintage design for a fleet torpedo boat. The French were willing to supply their excellent Creusot-Loire 100mm DP gun, Sweden provided torpedoes and anti-submarine rocket launchers, and Holland contributed radar and fire control. A CODAG powerplant was contrived by combining an industrial Brown-Boveri gas turbine with MAN diesels.

The result was a class of six ships built in 1957-64. They are unusual in appearance, with a reverse rake to the funnel top to deflect smoke. Some problems with topweight were

encountered, and after completion one of the forward M45 directors was removed. In fact these ships proved none too robust for the North Sea, and all six were taken in for stiffening and modification in 1966-68.

The machinery has not been an outstanding success either. The gas turbine is big and heavy, being designed for a shore power station, and the ships are short on endurance. Internally they are cramped, the result of trying to do rather too much on a limited displacement.

The six *Köln*s form the 2nd Frigate Squadron. They are to be replaced by the *Bremen* class in the early 1980s.

▲ The *Emden* presents a well-armed profile, with the forward 100mm gun, a twin Breda Bofors and one of the two quadruple Bofors A/S rocket launchers visible. Intended for the Baltic Approaches, this class is inevitably fitted with a heavy air-defence armament but is also well equipped for ASW.

◀ The Federal German Navy's frigate *Karlsruhe* has an unusual profile, with low freeboard but a piled-up superstructure and a reverse rake to the funnel. Note the French-pattern 100mm guns and the single A/S torpedo tubes amidships. The radars are Dutch and the 40mm guns are Italian, as in the *Hamburg* class.

# *Lupo* and *Maestrale* classes

| Name | Number |
|---|---|
| ***Lupo*** | F 564 |
| ***Sagittario*** | F 565 |
| ***Perseo*** | F 566 |
| ***Orsa*** | F 567 |
| ***Meliton Carvajal*** (Peru) | 51 |
| ***Manuel Villavicencio*** | 52 |
| (unnamed) | – |
| (unnamed) | – |
| ***Mariscal Sucre*** (Venezuela) | F 21 |
| ***Almirante Luis Brion*** | F 22 |
| ***General Rafael Urdaneta*** | F 23 |
| ***General Soublette*** | F 24 |
| ***General Salom*** | F 25 |
| ***General José Felix Ribas*** | F 26 |
| ***Maestrale*** | F 570 |
| ***Grecale*** | F 571 |
| ***Libeccio*** | F 572 |
| ***Scirocco*** | F 573 |
| ***Aliseo*** | F 574 |
| ***Euro*** | F 575 |

***Lupo***
**Displacement** 2,208 tons (standard), 2,500 tons (full load)
**Dimensions** 108.4m (oa) × 11.3m × 3.7m (355.4ft × 37.1ft × 12.1ft)
**Propulsion** 2 shafts, gas turbine or diesel drive (CODOG); 50,000 shp = 35 knots
**Aircraft** 2 Agusta-Bell AB.204B A/S helicopters
**Armament** 1 × 8-tube Albatros SAM launcher (Sea Sparrow/Aspide), 8 single Otomat SSM launchers, 1 single 5in (127mm) gun, 2 twin 40mm L/70 Compact guns, 2 triple 12.7in (324mm) Mk 32 torpedo tubes
**Complement** 16 officers, 169 men

***Maestrale***
**Displacement** 2,500 tons (standard), 2,800 tons (full load)
**Dimensions** 122.7m (oa) × 13.4m × 12.9m (405ft (oa) × 42.5ft × 13.4ft)
**Propulsion** As *Lupo*, but speed = 30 knots
**Armament** 4 Otomat SSM launchers, 1 × 8-cell Albatros SAM system, 1 × 5in/54-cal gun, 2 twin 40mm L/70 Compact guns, 2 triple 12.7in (324mm) ASW torpedo tubes
**Complement** 23 officers, 190 ratings

In 1970 the Italian Navy decided to embark on a new building programme, partly to replace elderly tonnage and partly to remedy serious unemployment in the shipyards. In a bold bid to capture export markets the old Cantieri del Tirreno yard at Riva Trigoso near La Spezia was modernised and redesigned for the mass production of frigates.

The design chosen was an updated version of the 2,700-ton *Alpino* class built in 1963-68. But instead of the original Tosi-Metrovick gas turbine and Tosi diesel CODOG powerplant the new ships were to have the General Electric LM-2500, built under licence by Fiat, and diesels designed by Grandi Motori Trieste. The weight saved on this

installation would go towards a greater weapon load, always a good selling point for export customers.

The Italian armaments industry was also producing new weapons, notably the Otomat surface-to-surface missile, the Oto-Melara 127mm/54-cal gun, a development of the US Navy's Mk 45 lightweight gun, and the Breda 40mm L/70 Compact point-defence gun mounting.

Two important overseas customers had already placed orders by the time the first ship, the *Lupo*, ran her first trials in mid-1977: Venezuela ordered six in October 1975, while the year before Peru had ordered four, two of them to be built at Callao.

The *Lupo*'s heavy weapon load and good high-speed performance made a great impression when she first appeared, and short delivery times and comparative cheapness made her even more attractive to overseas customers. But a closer look at the design shows that it is overloaded and short on habitability and endurance. The proof of this can be

◀ The Italian frigate *Lupo* on builders' trials. She is armed with an Oto-Melara 5in gun forward, an eight-cell Nato Sea Sparrow SAM above the hangar and twin Breda 40mm Compact guns on either beam aft. The Otomat surface-to-surface missiles had not yet been installed when this photograph was taken.

▲ The launch of the Venezuelan *Almirante Luis Brion* in February 1979. Note the bulbous bow, a common feature of modern warships and intended to improve high-speed performance. Both these vessels and the Peruvian *Lupo* class are very similar to the Italian ships in all but minor details.

seen in the following *Maestrale* class, which have virtually the same payload, exchanging four Otomat missiles for an extra helicopter; they are 50ft longer and over 4ft beamier.

The four *Lupo* class for the Italian Navy were delivered between 1977 and 1979. The first Peruvian ship, the *Meliton Carvajal*, was commissioned in 1978, with her sister following in 1979. The first Venezuelan unit, the *Mariscal Sucre*, commissioned in 1978 and the second, the *Almirante Luis Brion*, was launched in February 1979.

Work is proceeding in parallel on the six *Maestrale* class, with the lead ship laid down in 1978 and due to be launched in February 1980. They will be very similar in appearance to the *Lupo* class, but with the Sea Sparrow/Aspide SAM launcher moved forward to "B" position and the Breda Compact twin gun mounting moved to the forecastle deck; the four Otomat SSMs will be on the helicopter hangar roof instead of the shelter deck.

There has been talk of further sales of *Lupo*s to Egypt and other countries, but so far nothing has come of the negotiations, officially at least. Two more *Maestrale*s, the *Espero* and *Zeffiro*, have been postponed.

## *Albatros* class

| Name | Number |
|---|---|
| ***Aquila*** (ex-*Lynx*) | F 542 |
| ***Albatros*** | F 543 |
| ***Alcione*** | F 544 |
| ***Airone*** | F 545 |
| ***Bellona*** (Danish) | F 344 |
| ***Flora*** | F 346 |
| ***Triton*** | F 347 |
| ***Pattimura*** (Indonesia) | 801 |
| ***Sultan Hasanudin*** | 802 |

**Displacement** 800 tons (standard), 950 tons (full load)
**Dimensions** 76.3m (oa) × 9.6m × 2.8m (250.3ft (oa) × 31.5ft × 9.2ft)
**Propulsion** 2 shafts, diesel drive; 5,200 bhp = 19 knots
**Armament** 4 single 40mm guns, 2 triple 12.7in (324mm) Mk 32 torpedo tubes, 2 Hedgehog A/S mortars, 2 depth-charge throwers
**Complement** 7 officers, 111 men

*Airone, Albatros, Alcione* and *Aquila* (ex-*Lynx*) built in 1953-56 by Castellammare and Breda Marghera. *Bellona, Diana, Flora* and *Triton* built 1953-57 by Castellammare; Tirreno, Riva Trigoso; and CN di Taranto for Denmark. *Pattimura* and *Sultan Hasanudin* built by Ansaldo, Livorno, 1956-58.

Eight small corvettes were ordered in 1953 from Italian yards, with funds supplied through the United States' Mutual Defence Aid Programme (MDAP). Three were retained by the Italian Navy, four went to Denmark and one went to the Netherlands. Two slightly larger versions were laid down for Indonesia three years later. The design was compact and cheap, but too small for any worthwhile armament or for anything but coastal escort work.

The Italian Navy now has four of the class, the *Lynx* having been transferred from the Netherlands Navy at Den Helder in October 1961. They were due to be rearmed with 76mm Oto-Melara guns but this was never carried out. They are due for replacement, being a quarter of a century old, but no announcement has been made about their future. The Danish trio (*Diana* was scrapped in 1974) will be replaced as soon as the *Niels Juel*-class corvettes are ready, but the Indonesian pair will probably last much longer. Only one of these ships is in commission, and if previous experience is anything to go by, she will not be in first-class condition.

The Danish corvette *Flora* and her sisters differ from their Italian sisters in being armed with two single 3in guns and having a British Plessey AWS-1 surveillance radar at the masthead. Two Hedgehog A/S spigot mortars can be seen forward of the bridge, and there is a single 40mm AA gun aft.

## *Chikugo* class

| Name | Number |
|---|---|
| ***Chikugo*** | DE 215 |
| ***Ayase*** | DE 216 |
| ***Mikuma*** | DE 217 |
| ***Tokachi*** | DE 218 |
| ***Iwase*** | DE 219 |
| ***Chitose*** | DE 220 |
| ***Niyodo*** | DE 221 |
| ***Teshio*** | DE 222 |
| ***Yoshino*** | DE 223 |
| ***Kumano*** | DE 224 |
| ***Noshiro*** | DE 225 |

**Displacement** 1,470-1,500 tons (standard), 1,700 tons (full load)
**Dimensions** 93m (oa) × 10.8m × 3.5m (305.5ft (oa) × 35.5ft × 11.5ft)
**Propulsion** 2 shafts, diesel; 16,000 bhp = 25 knots
**Armament** 1 twin 3in (76mm) 50-cal guns, 1 twin 40mm guns, 1 × 8-tube Asroc ASM launcher, 2 triple 12.7in (324mm) Mk 32 torpedo tubes
**Complement** 165 officers and men

*Ayase, Chikugo, Chitose, Iwase, Kumano, Mikuma, Niyodo, Noshiro, Teshio, Tokachi* and *Yoshino* built 1968 onwards by Ishikawjima, Tokyo; Mitsui, Tamano; and Hitachi, Maizuru.

Between 1968 and 1977 the Japanese Maritime Self-Defence Force built 11 small anti-submarine frigates. They are the smallest escorts in the world to carry a major ASW system, in this case Asroc. In fact they could be described as floating Asroc platforms, and they must be compared with the Soviet Petya and Mirka types. There is however little point in fitting an expensive and sophisticated missile system in a ship too small to take advantage of its full capabilities.

The *Chikugo* class also have a heavy AA armament for their size: a twin 3in Mk 33 AA gun mounting forward and a twin 40mm AA Bofors aft, to say nothing of two sonars and a full radar outfit. One can only wonder if the ship has room for the processors needed to handle the data generated by no fewer than five sensors. By comparison, the Royal Navy found that the *Blackwood*-class frigates, with almost identical dimensions, could only mount three 40mm Bofors guns with local tachymetric sights and two Mk 10 depth-charge mortars.

The first ship to enter service was the name ship, in July 1970, and the last was the *Noshiro* in August 1977. The machinery comprises twin-shaft Burmeister & Wain diesels made under licence by Mitsui.

The Japanese escort *Ayase* (DE-216) is just over 300ft long and yet carries a twin Mk 33 3in AA gun mounting forward, a twin 40mm aft, and an eight-cell Asroc A/S missile launcher. Note the stem anchor, necessary to prevent damage to the bow sonar. The radars are produced in Japan.

## *Kortenaer* class

| Name | Number | Laid down | Launched | Completed |
|---|---|---|---|---|
| **Kortenaer** | F 807 | Apr 1975 | 18 Dec 1976 | Oct 1978 |
| **Callenburgh** | F 808 | Jun 1976 | 26 Mar 1977 | Jul 1979 |
| **Van Kinsbergen** | F 809 | Sep 1975 | 16 Apr 1977 | 1980 |
| **Banckert** | F 810 | Feb 1976 | 1 Jul 1978 | 1980 |
| **Piet Heyn** | F 811 | Apr 1977 | 1 Jun 1978 | 1981 |
| **Pieter Florisz** | F 812 | Jul 1977 | 1979 | 1982 |
| **Witte de With** | F 813 | Jun 1978 | 1979 | 1982 |
| **Abraham Crijnssen** | F 816 | Oct 1978 | – | 1983 |
| **Philips van Almonde** | F 823 | Oct 1977 | 11 Aug 1979 | 1982 |
| **Blois van Treslong** | F 824 | Apr 1978 | – | 1983 |
| **Jan van Brakel** | F 825 | Nov 1979 | – | 1983 |
| **Willem van der Zaan** | F 826 | Jan 1980 | – | 1983 |
| unnamed | – | – | – | 1984 |
| **Bremen** (West Germany) | F 226 | Jul 1979 | building | – |
| unnamed | F 227 | – | building | – |
| unnamed | F 228 | – | building | – |
| unnamed | F 229 | – | building | – |
| unnamed | F 230 | – | building | – |
| unnamed | F 231 | – | building | – |
| +6 ships | – | – | projected | – |

**Displacement** 3,500 tons (mean load)
**Dimensions** 128m (oa) × 14.4m × 4.4m (419.8ft (oa) × 47.2ft × 14.3ft)
**Propulsion** 2 shafts, 2 sets geared gas turbines (COGOG); 58,000 shp = 30 knots
**Aircraft** 2 Lynx A/S helicopters
**Armament** 1 × 8-tube Sea Sparrow SAM launcher, 2 quad Harpoon SSM launchers, 2 single 3in (76mm) gun, 2 triple × 12.7in (324mm) Mk 32 torpedo tubes
**Complement** 185 officers and men

Ten ordered from Koninklijke Maatschappij de Schelde, Flushing, and building 1975 onwards; *Philips van Almonde* and *Blois van Treslong* building by Dok en Werfmaatschappij Wilton, Fijenoord, from 1978. Six of modified design, the *Bremen* class, ordered from Bremer Vulkan (1), AG Weser (1), Howaldtswerke (1), Nordseewerke (1) and Blohm & Voss (2), in 1976 for completion in 1981. No 13 of *Kortenaer* class deferred.

In the late 1960s the Royal Netherlands Navy was planning its replacements for the dozen destroyers of the *Holland* and *Friesland* classes. Nato, which at that time had a Brussels-based study group looking into ideas for a "Nato Frigate", a standard hull which could be built in European shipyards to a common specification, showed great interest in the Dutch designs. The Nato Frigate became the Nato Frigate Project, based in Koblenz, but in the meantime the Dutch Materiel Directorate promised to plan its own frigates with an eye on possible collaboration with other countries in the alliance. For this reason the resulting Dutch design became the *Standaard* (Standard) or "S" type.

The first contracts were signed in August 1974, when four ships were ordered; another four were ordered three months later, and the last four in December 1976. The ship in question was still a purely Dutch design, but it matched the Nato Frigate requirements in so many respects that the Federal German Navy decided to adopt it, and in 1974 work began on project definition of the German Fregatte 122, now known as the *Bremen* class.

The design drew heavily on experience with the *Tromp*-class DDGs. The propulsion system was the same – Rolls-Royce Olympus and Tyne gas turbines in a COGOG arrangement – and the same Nato Sea Sparrow and Harpoon missiles were fitted. But the Oto-Melara 76mm Compact replaced the 4.7in guns, and a second helicopter was added.

There were few problems until the Germans started to adapt the design to their own requirements. Some of the differences were understandable; for example, it proved too expensive to try to adapt the Dutch DAISY command and control system to match the German SATIR, and so the German system was used in the F-122. But other changes caused nothing but trouble. Under intense American commercial pressure the Germans decided to replace the Olympus gas turbines with General Electric LM-2500s, and to compensate for the LM-2500's high fuel consumption they turned for cruise power to their own MTU diesel in place of the British Tyne gas turbine. It was not merely a matter of converting from COGOG to CODOG, for the MTU diesels could not fit into the same space as the Tynes; this meant shifting bulkheads and altering the gearing system and fuel stowage. All this was done in the face of Dutch advice, for the RNIN was very satisfied with the propulsion system that they had put in the Standard and maintained that the balance of the design was being destroyed for no good reason.

But the Germans went even further, trying to squeeze two Lamps helicopters into a space designed for the compact Lynx. The Lamps III Seahawk is as big as a Sea King, and this would have meant redesigning the whole after portion of the ship. At this point the Germans gave up and accepted the Lynx.

The *Kortenaer* started her sea trials early in 1978 and the *Callenburgh* completed in the autumn of 1979. A 13th ship, with a Standard SAM system, was to have been laid down but has been deferred. She was ordered at the end of 1979 and will act as a squadron flagship; her name will probably be *Jacob van Heemskerck*. The German ships are to be commissioned in 1981-84. In January 1978 it was reported that Iran would be buying 12 F-122s, half to be built in Holland and half in Germany, but the revolution in Iran put paid to that. This deal was in fact an attempt by US industry to evade President Carter's ceiling on foreign military sales, there being a large amount of US equipment – including 5in guns, Mk 86 fire control and LM-2500 gas turbines – aboard these ships.

One item of armament – a Close-In Weapon System (CIWS) for use against sea-skimming missiles – remains in dispute. The Dutch favour the Goalkeeper quadruple 30mm gun mounting whereas the Germans want the American ASMD, an adaptation of the Stinger missile. In the Dutch ships the 30mm mounting would replace the after 76mm gun; the later ships are initially being fitted with a 40mm Bofors instead of the 76mm weapon.

The *Kortenaer*, first of the "Standard" frigates, on builders' trials. She still has scaffolding around the foremast but the armament is complete. The second 76mm gun on the hangar roof is ultimately to be replaced by the SEM-30 quadruple 30mm gun mounting, designed as a close-in weapon system for use against missiles.

# *Oslo* and *da Silva* classes

| Name | Number | Laid down | Launched | Completed |
|---|---|---|---|---|
| ***Oslo*** | F 300 | 1963 | 17 Jan 1964 | Jan 1966 |
| ***Bergen*** | F 301 | 1964 | 23 Aug 1965 | Jun 1967 |
| ***Trondheim*** | F 302 | 1963 | 4 Sep 1964 | Jun 1966 |
| ***Stavanger*** | F 303 | 1965 | 4 Feb 1966 | Dec 1967 |
| ***Narvik*** | F 304 | 1964 | 8 Jan 1965 | Nov 1966 |
| ***Almirante Pereira da Silva*** (Portugal) | F 472 | 1962 | 2 Dec 1963 | Dec 1966 |
| ***Almirante Gago Coutinho*** | F 473 | 1963 | 13 Aug 1965 | Nov 1967 |
| ***Almirante Magalhaes Correa*** | F 474 | 1965 | 26 Apr 1965 | Nov 1968 |

**Displacement** 1,450 tons (standard), 1,745 tons (full load)
**Dimensions** 96.6m (oa) × 11.2m × 5.3m (317ft (oa) × 36.7ft × 17.4ft)
**Propulsion** 1 shaft, geared steam turbines, 2 boilers; 20,000 shp = 25 knots
**Armament** (*Oslo*) 1 × 8-tube Sea Sparrow SAM launcher, 6 single Penguin SSM launchers, 2 twin 3in (76mm) 50-cal guns, 1 × 6-tube Terne A/S rocket launcher, 2 triple 12.7in (324mm) Mk 32 torpedo tubes
(*Almirante Pereira*) 2 twin 3in AA guns, 2 × 375mm ASW rocket launchers, 2 triple 12.7in (324mm) ASW torpedo tubes
**Complement** 11/12 officers, 140/154 men

▶ Comparison between the *Oslo* class and the *Correa* (below) shows how far the Norwegians adapted the *Dealey* design to meet their own needs and to make great improvements. Note the Nato Sea Sparrow SAM launcher and the diminutive Penguin surface-to-surface missiles on the quarterdeck. A Terne A/S rocket launcher is mounted forward.

▼ The Portuguese *Almirante Magalhaes Correa* follows the original American *Dealey* design very closely, apart from the quadruple 375mm A/S rocket launchers immediately abaft the forward 3in guns. Note also the variable-depth sonar on the stern and the triple Mk 32 A/S torpedo tubes on the shelter deck abaft the bridge.

At the end of the 1950s the Norwegian Navy's motley collection of pre-war torpedo boats and ex-British "Hunt"-class destroyers was ageing rapidly, and so it was decided to build five new ships. MDAP aid was forthcoming from the United States and approval was given late in 1960 to lay five keels at Horten Naval Dockyard.

The design was based on the US Navy's *Dealey* class, but with modified topsides and a new armament. The original gun armament of the *Dealey* class, two twin 3in Mk 33, was retained, but the Terne ASW rocket launcher was mounted immediately abaft the forward guns. The Norwegian-made Penguin short-range SSM, with six launchers aft, was added later. The radar was supplied by Hollandse Signaalapparaten, and the Nato Sea Sparrow SAM was installed for close-range AA defence. The machinery was made in Norway under licence.

Compared with the original design (of which none remain in the USN) and the three built in Portugal under MDAP in 1962-68, the *Oslo* class is a big improvement. The Portuguese ships have no SAM system, no SSMs and only the elderly four-barrelled Bofors rocket launchers and triple Mk 32 torpedo tubes as ASW armament.

## *João Coutinho* class

| Name | Number | Laid down | Launched | Completed |
|---|---|---|---|---|
| ***Antonio Enes*** | F 471 | Apr 1968 | 16 Aug 1969 | Jun 1971 |
| ***João Coutinho*** | F 475 | Sep 1968 | 2 May 1969 | Mar 1970 |
| ***Jacinto Candido*** | F 476 | Apr 1968 | 16 Jun 1969 | Jun 1970 |
| ***General Pereira d'Eca*** | F 477 | Oct 1968 | 26 Jul 1969 | Oct 1970 |
| ***Augusto de Castilho*** | F 484 | Aug 1968 | 4 Jul 1969 | Nov 1970 |
| ***Honorio Barreto*** | F 485 | Jul 1968 | 11 Apr 1970 | Apr 1971 |
| ***Baptista de Andrade*** | F 486 | 1972 | 2 Mar 1973 | Nov 1974 |
| ***João Roby*** | F 487 | 1972 | 3 Jun 1973 | Mar 1975 |
| ***Alfonso Cerqueira*** | F 488 | 1973 | 6 Oct 1973 | Jun 1975 |
| ***Oliveira E. Carmo*** | F 489 | 1972 | Feb 1974 | Feb 1975 |

**Displacement** 1,203 tons (standard), 1,380 tons (full load)
**Dimensions** 84.6m (oa) × 10.3m × 3.6m (227.5ft (oa) × 33.8ft × 11.8ft)
**Propulsion** 2 shafts, diesels; 10,560 bhp = 24.4 knots
**Armament** (Portugal) 1 twin 3in (76mm 50-cal guns, 2 single 40mm guns, 1 Hedgehog A/S mortar, 2 depth-charge throwers
(Colombia) 2 single Exocet SSM launchers, 1 single 3.9in (100mm) DP gun, 2 single 40mm guns, 2 triple 12.7in

324mm) Mk 32 torpedo tubes
**Complement** 9 officers, 91 men

*Alfonso Cerqueira*, *Antonio Enes*, *Augusto de Castilho*, *Baptista de Andrade*, *General Pereira d'Eca*, *Honorio Barreto*, *Jacinto Candido*, *João Coutinho*, *João Roby* and *Oliveira E. Carmo* built 1968-75 by Empresa Naçional, Bazán; Blohm & Voss AG, Hamburg.

In 1968 the Portuguese Navy ordered three frigates from Germany, and later the same year another three were laid down at the Spanish Bazán yard at El Ferrol. The design was utilitarian: a light frigate for general patrol and escort, with twin Mk 33 3in guns forward and two Bofors 40mm mountings aft. The ASW armament was confined to depth charges and no sonar was fitted.

In 1972-73 a further four with a more up-to-date armament were laid down. A French 100mm DP gun was mounted forward, two MM.38 Exocet SSMs aft and triple Mk 32 ASW torpedo tubes amidships. The sensors were also improved, with a Thomson-CSF Diodon sonar and a Plessey AWS-2 air-warning and surveillance radar; the French Pollux fire control was also fitted.

When completed in 1974-75 the new ships proved too much for the impoverished Portuguese Navy to run, and in 1977 they were reported to have been sold to Colombia. The deal fell through, however, and they have reverted to Portuguese ownership.

The Portuguese *Baptista de Andrade* shows what could be done with a relatively unsophisticated design. The 100mm gun replaces an obsolescent US 3in/50-cal twin mounting, the French Pollux fire-control system is mounted over the bridge, and there is a Plessey AWS-2 radar at the masthead.

# Fast Strike Craft

The ancestor of the fast strike craft of today is the steam torpedo boat of the 1870s, a fast steel-hulled launch originally intended to use the spar torpedo but quickly adapted to fire the Whitehead or "fish" torpedo. Such was the slow rate of firing for all guns of the period, the fast and nimble torpedo boat would have been a difficult target to hit, but this was counterbalanced by the short range and inaccuracy of the torpedo.

As its name implied, the "torpedo boat destroyer" eclipsed the torpedo boat and took over its attacking function. Undeterred, in the First World War the British produced their Coastal Motor Boat (CMB), a 40ft skimming craft designed to launch torpedoes from a stern trough. The Italians were also attracted by the concept and produced large numbers of *Motobarca Armata Silurante* (MAS, or torpedo-armed motor boats). Great things were hoped for but, as with the original torpedo boats, their frailty and lack of endurance severely limited their effectiveness. In practice the MAS only managed to sink one old Austrian warship in Trieste harbour in 1917 and the dreadnought *Szent Istvan* at sea in 1918, and the CMBs sank an old Russian light cruiser and damaged a depot ship in Kronstadt in 1919 during the War of Intervention.

Despite this unimpressive record the building of "mosquito craft" flourished between the two World Wars, particularly in Italy and Germany. The *schnellboot*, powered by a superb Daimler-Benz high-speed diesel, was developed by Lürssenwerft into the formidable wartime craft known to the British as the E-Boat. The British responded with Motor Torpedo Boats (MTBs), then Motor Gun Boats (MGBs), and finally they expanded the designs so that they could function interchangeably. The US Navy developed its PT Boats to exploit conditions in the Solomons.

Considering the effort put into their development, the various fast strike craft of the Second World War were something of a disappointment. Their lack of seaworthiness was a limiting factor, and the command problems of fighting an action from so low down were very great. Despite their numbers, the Italian and Japanese forces achieved virtually nothing, while the Americans, British and Germans fought many bloody close-range encounters but did not sink anything like the tonnage of ships that they claimed. Their most significant victim was the British cruiser *Manchester*, sunk by *schnellboote* off Tunisia in 1942.

After the Second World War the gas turbine promised much higher speeds and it was only a matter of time before the guided missile became simple enough to install in a small hull. The appeal of the guided missile lay in its lack of recoil; unlike the gun, it exerted minimal downward thrust on the deck. The Soviet Navy led the way in the early 1960s by converting a large number of P-6 MTB hulls into missile boats, with two SS-N-2 Styx (Nato designation) 25km-range surface-to-surface missiles. The conversion, known in the West as the Komar, may have been adequate for inshore work but was clearly overloaded and was soon superseded by the larger Osa design, with four Styx missiles. The sinking of the old Israeli destroyer *Eilat* by three Styx hits in 1967 lent the idea vastly increased respectability, and as soon as the first Western SSMs, the French Exocet and the Italian Otomat, were available, designs for strike craft built around them began to proliferate.

The gun, on the other hand, has come back into fashion. Several designs incorporate the Italian Oto-Melara 76mm Compact and the Breda 40mm Compact twin, and the larger designs carry a combination. In theory such vessels exceed some larger warships in hitting power, and many smaller navies have invested heavily in them as an alternative to the big, expensive frigate. But no matter how much electronics and miniaturisation can achieve, the problem for strike craft remains what it was a century ago: crews cannot take prolonged buffeting in rough weather and so strike craft cannot maintain lengthy patrols in open water. This limits them to coastal waters and specific sea states. Nor are they cheap, as every cubic foot is crammed with equipment needing expensive maintenance. The cost of a strike craft armed with four SSMs and ready for sea can easily equal that of a 3,000-ton frigate, and all operators of strike craft have found them very costly to maintain.

To offset the strike craft's chronic lack of line-of-sight information, designers have had to incorporate lightweight, fully stabilised surveillance radars, and recent designs have even included a small helicopter. Although in theory it is possible to fly a helicopter from a small, lively platform, such operations are very dangerous and nobody has yet produced a very small and fully helicopter capable warship.

The need to reduce drag has led to the hovercraft and the hydrofoil, but the former has not proved an unqualified success as a warship while the latter has only just begun to develop its potential. The hovercraft seems likely to demonstrate its true value in the mine countermeasures and ship-to-shore logistics roles, but it is far too noisy for raiding and very expensive on fuel. The hydrofoil suffers from lack of endurance but has proved surprisingly capable of rough-weather operation.

## *Pegasus* class

| Name | Number | Laid down | Launched | Commissioned |
|---|---|---|---|---|
| ***Pegasus*** | PHM-1 | May 1973 | 9 Nov 1974 | Jul 1977 |
| ***Hercules*** | PHM-2 | May 1974 | – | 1982 |
| ***Taurus*** | PHM-3 | Jan 1979 | – | 1981 |
| ***Aquila*** | PHM-4 | – | – | 1981 |
| ***Aries*** | PHM-5 | – | – | 1981 |
| ***Gemini*** | PHM-6 | – | – | 1982 |

**Displacement** 241.3 tonnes (full load)
**Dimensions** 40.0m (oa) × 8.6m × 7.1m (foils extended) (131.2ft (oa) × 28.2ft × 6.2ft)
**Propulsion** Twin gas turbines driving waterjets; 18,000 shp = 48 knots
**Armament** 8 Harpoon SSM launchers, 1 × 76mm DP gun
**Complement** 4 officers, 17 enlisted men

In an attempt to produce a standard Nato hydrofoil the US Navy embarked on a collaborative programme with West Germany and Italy in the early 1970s. The Germans backed out, however, and the Italians chose to develop their own smaller *Sparviero*, based on the Boeing *Tucumcari*.

The class has had a troubled history as a result of inflation and political indecision. Two ships were authorised under the Fiscal Year 1973 research and development programme, followed by four more in the FY 1975 shipbuilding programme. The *Pegasus* was laid down in 1973 and made her first foilborne journey in February 1975. The *Hercules* (formerly named *Delphinus*) was laid down in May 1974 but work was stopped when she was 40 per cent complete. The reason was rising costs, and in April 1977 she and her sisters PHM-3-6 were cancelled. The White House then asked for money to complete the class, but this was withheld until August 1977, when the Secretary of Defence finally released the funds.

The names have been re-allocated, with the result that *Taurus* (PHM-3) will be the first to complete, in February 1981. The others are to be completed by March 1982.

The armament is most impressive for a small warship: eight Harpoon SSMs and an Oto-Melara 76mm gun. Experience with the *Pegasus* in the Pacific Fleet shows that she is reliable and seaworthy. However, in the late summer of 1979 she ran aground in shallow water and damaged herself severely.

The fully armed hydrofoil warship is taking much longer to perfect than anyone expected. This is not so much a result of any weakness of hydrofoils as such, as of the fact that in times of financial stringency the high unit cost of specialised craft is hard to justify. Such ships are opposed on the grounds that the funding for them will have to be subtracted from money devoted to other less glamorous but essential equipment.

The Boeing-built hydrofoil *Pegasus* (PHM-1) running foilborne. On her 40m hull she has an Oto-Melara 76mm gun and five Harpoon surface-to-surface missiles, a heavy armament by any standards. Although she herself recently ran aground, the concept has proved successful and five more PHMs are building.

## Osa class

**Displacement** 160/165 tons (standard), 200/210 tons (full load)
**Dimensions** 39.3m (oa) × 7.7m × 1.8m (128.7ft (oa) × 25.1ft × 5.9ft)
**Propulsion** 3 shafts, diesels; 12,000 bhp = 32 knots
**Armament** 4 SS-N-2 Styx SSM launchers, 2 twin 30mm AA guns (a few ships are reported with SA-7 Grail SAM launchers)
**Complement** 30

70 Osa I (Soviet Navy)
50 Osa II (Soviet Navy)

3 Osa I and Osa II (Algeria)

4 Osa I (Bulgaria)

80 (?) Osa (China, many locally built)

8 Osa I and Osa II (Cuba)

6 Osa I (Egypt)

15 Osa I and Osa II (East Germany)

16 Osa I and Osa II (India)

14 Osa I and Osa II (Iraq)

8 Osa I (North Korea)

12 Osa I (Poland)

5 Osa I (Romania)

3 Osa II (Somalia)

6 Osa I (Syria)

10 Osa I (Yugoslavia)

Between 1959 and 1971 the Soviet Navy built some 40 strike craft armed with a new 25-mile-range surface-to-surface missile. Code-named Komar in the West, the new type was a modification of the standard P-6 torpedo boat with two SS-N-2 Styx SSMs mounted aft.

The Komar was clearly an interim design, probably intended to strengthen coastal defences quickly and cheaply, but it lacked seaworthiness and, above all, deck and interior space. Work was however proceeding in parallel on a boat of twice the tonnage and 50ft longer, to carry four Styx missiles. This appeared in 1961 and was immediately code-named Osa. A large number must have been built, for even after numerous transfers to other countries the latest count shows 120 Osa Is and Osa IIs in the Soviet Navy.

A few names, including *Brestskii Komsomolets*, *Tambovskii Komsomolets* and *Kirovskii Komsomolets*, have been reported. The Osa I boats have slab-sided Styx launchers, whereas the Osa IIs have cylindrical containers, giving rise to suspicions that there may be a modified Styx.

As the first surface-to-surface missile used successfully in combat, the Styx has commanded a lot of respect. On 21 October 1967 two Komars sank the Israeli destroyer *Eilat* off Port Said, and in December 1971 Indian Osas sank the Pakistani destroyer *Khaibar* and several

merchant ships. But this reputation was dealt a sharp blow in October 1973 when a force of Israeli missile boats, using the much shorter-ranged Gabriel, slaughtered a force of Syrian Osas and Komars without loss to themselves. Gradually it dawned on Western observers that the Styx had been credited with much greater effectiveness than it actually possessed. It is in fact a relatively crude weapon which achieved its successes against virtually no opposition, the victims being either merchantmen or very obsolete warships with no ECM or weapons capable of dealing with it.

Soviet Osa II missile patrol boats in line-ahead. The bulk of the SS-N-2 Styx can be gauged by the comparative size of the men on the bridge and by the fact that the Osa is hardly 25ft in the beam. The large "searchlight" is the antenna of the fire-control system for the two twin 30mm gun mountings.

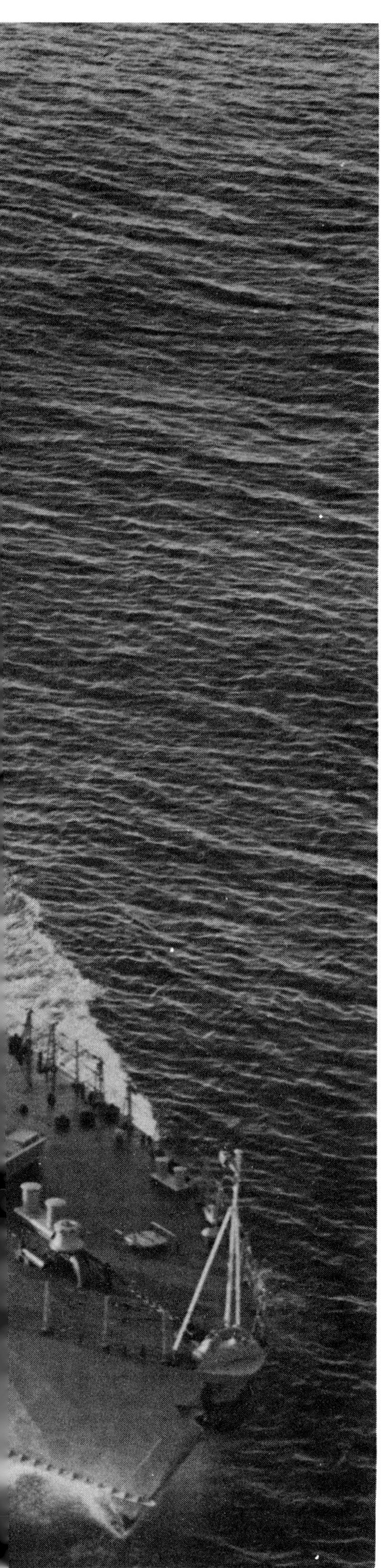

## Nanuchka class

**Displacement** 800 tons (standard), 950 tons (full load)
**Dimensions** 59m (oa) × 12.0m × 3.0m (193ft (oa) × 39ft × 9ft)
**Propulsion** 3 shafts, diesels; 28,000 bhp = 32 knots
**Armament** 6 SS-N-9 SSM launchers (6 SS-N-2 Mod SSMs in Indian ships), 1 twin SA-N-4 SAM launcher, 1 twin 57mm DP guns
**Complement** 70

17 built at Leningrad since 1969. 6 delivered or building for India; *Vijay Durg*, *Sinhu Durg* and *Hos Durg* delivered since March 1977.

A new Soviet missile-armed corvette first sighted in 1969 was code-named Nanuchka. It was armed with a new surface-to-surface missile, the SS-N-9, and a close-range SAM system designated SA-N-4.

Good-looking and robust ships, the Nanuchkas have a flared forecastle flanked by triple launch tubes for the SS-N-9. The SA-N-4 is housed in a "pop-up" position on the forecastle, with its launcher normally covered by folding hatches.

Although their size suggests largely coastal duties, Nanuchkas have been sighted in the North Sea and the Mediterranean. Two have been given to India, but with the modified SS-N-2 Styx instead of the SS-N-9. A new type of twin 57mm DP gun mounting is positioned aft, acting as a useful back-up to the SA-N-4 missile.

Some 17 Nanuchkas have been reported, and a further six are being supplied to India.

▲ A rare view of a Nanuchka in a Soviet dockyard. Note the lattice-work rail used for loading the SS-N-9 missile and inspecting it during maintenance. Even more interesting is the twin-arm SA-N-4 short-range SAM launcher, just visible forward of the rail.

◀ A Soviet Nanuchka-type corvette in the North Sea in 1976. What appears to be an empty seating for a gun is in fact a weatherproof lid concealing the SA-N-4 "pop-up" missile launcher. Despite their chunky appearance the Nanuchkas are comparatively large: 59m in length and displacing some 950 tons full load.

## *Reshef* class

| Name | Commissioned |
|---|---|
| ***Reshef*** | Apr 1973 |
| ***Keshet*** | Oct 1973 |
| ***Romah*** | Mar 1974 |
| ***Kidon*** | Sep 1974 |
| ***Tarshish*** | Mar 1975 |
| ***Yaffo*** | Apr 1975 |
| ***Mitzahon*** (*Reshef II*) | Dec 1978 |
| + 5 *Reshef IIs* | |

**Displacement** (*Reshef I*) 415 tons (standard)
**Dimensions** (RI) 58m (oa) × 7.8m × 2.4m (190.5ft (oa) × 25ft × 8ft)
(*Reshef II*) 61m (oa) × ? × ? (202.5ft (oa) × ? × ?)
**Propulsion** (RI) 2 shafts, diesels; 10,680 bhp = 32 knots
(RII) probably similar, but more power to raise speed to 36 knots
**Armament** 6 Gabriel SSM launchers, 4 Harpoon SSM launchers, 2 × 76mm/62-cal DP guns, 2 × 20mm Oerlikon guns
**Complement** 45

Profiting by their experience in the Six-Day War of 1967, the Israelis designed an enlarged version of their 45-metre *Saar* and *Mivtach* classes, originally designed by Lürssenwerft but built by Constructions Mécaniques de Normandie at Cherbourg. By increasing the length to 58m and beam to 7.8m they were able to mount an extra 76mm gun without sacrificing any of the Gabriel missile launchers.

Along with the smaller Israeli missile boats, the *Reshef*s are unique in being the only Western warships to have fought (and won) a surface engagement with guided weapons. This makes them of more than passing interest to naval commentators, for the Gabriel 1 missile apparently has half the range of the SS-N-2 Styx missile used by the Syrian and Egyptian strike craft. It is believed that this disadvantage was more than offset by skilful use of chaff and electronic countermeasures.

The first two boats, *Reshef* and *Keshet*, were completed in time to take part in the Yom Kippur War of October 1973, and are believed to have fought in an action which accounted for 14 Syrian Osas off Lattakieh. Since then they have been joined by four more, and six more of the enlarged *Reshef II* type were ordered in January 1975. Six of the standard type were built in South Africa, three at Haifa and three at Durban. These boats are believed to carry numbers only, and no Gabriel missiles are evident in the only photograph so far released.

An indication of the high endurance and weatherliness of these patrol boats was given when *Reshef*, *Keshet*, *Romah* and *Kidon* were transferred to the Red Sea. They went via the Cape of Good Hope in pairs and refuelled at sea without calling on shore facilities in South Africa. In July 1976 two crossed the Atlantic and called at New York.

At present the class is armed with a mix of the 12.5-mile-range Gabriel 1 and the new 22-mile-range Gabriel 2, as well as four long-range Harpoon SSMs; it is intended to phase out Gabriel 1 eventually. The Red Sea boats are fitted with sonar for ASW duties.

The three South African boats sailed from Haifa in March 1978, freeing the Haifa Shipyard for work on the Israeli Navy's *Reshef IIs*.

The *Jim Fouche*, first of the South African *Reshef*-type fast strike craft. Although there is no sign of Gabriel missiles the seatings for these weapons can be seen. Above the bridge there is what appears to be an optronic fire-control director of unknown origin.

## Speedy

**Displacement** 117 tonnes (standard)
**Dimensions** 27.4m (oa) × 9.5m × 1.5m (foils up) (90ft (oa) × 31ft × 4.8ft)
**Propulsion** Twin gas-turbine waterjets; 6,000 shp = 42-45 knots (cruising speed)
**Armament** Nil
**Complement** 18

In 1978 the Royal Navy placed a contract with Boeing Marine Systems for a military hydrofoil fishery-protection vessel. Based on the commercial Jetfoil, it is intended to carry out high-speed interceptions of poaching trawlers or other lawbreakers after they have been detected by conventional offshore patrol vessels and maritime patrol aircraft.

The principal changes to the Jetfoil to fit it for its new task were the omission of the passenger accommodation, provision of diesel engines for hullborne running, and a doubling of the fuel capacity by the addition of wing tanks.

The craft was christened HMS *Speedy* when she was launched on 9 July 1979; she was then shipped to the United Kingdom for a period of intensive trials and evaluation. It was originally intended to ship an armament of two single 20mm Oerlikon guns, but single machine guns currently seem more likely. In any case, an offshore patrol vessel achieves her purposes by making the interception, and weaponry is almost irrelevant. It has been suggested that the *Speedy* may not be able to cope with North Sea conditions, but the Jetfoil and the Boeing-built *Tucumcari* have coped with Sea State Lower 6. Moreover, it is almost impossible to fish in rougher weather.

If the *Speedy* proves a success Boeing proposes a force of five hydrofoils to police the North Sea fishing grounds and oilfields.

HMS *Speedy*, the Royal Navy's first hydrofoil in nearly 40 years, running trials off Seattle in 1979. To be fitted with two rigid inflatable dinghies on the cabin roof and possibly two 7.62mm machine guns in the bridge wings, she will act as a fast strike craft target and perform fishery protection duties.

## *Snögg* class

| Name | Number | Commissioned |
|---|---|---|
| ***Snögg*** | P 980 | 1970 |
| ***Rapp*** | P 981 | 1970 |
| ***Snar*** | P 982 | 1970 |
| ***Rask*** | P 983 | 1971 |
| ***Kvikk*** | P 984 | 1971 |
| ***Kjapp*** | P 985 | 1971 |

**Displacement** 100 tons (standard), 125 tons (full load)

**Dimensions** 36.5ft (oa) × 6.2m × 1.3m (120ft (oa) × 20.5in × 5ft)

**Propulsion** 2 shafts, diesels; 7,200 bhp = 32 knots

**Armament** 4 Penguin SSM launchers, 4 single 21in (533mm) torpedo tubes, 1 × 40mm L/70 Bofors AA gun

**Complement** 18

The Royal Norwegian Navy maintains a mixed force of light craft armed with torpedoes, guns and Penguin surface-to-surface missiles. The *Snögg*

class were based on the missile-armed *Storm* class of 1962-68, but carry heavy torpedo armament at the expense of missiles.

The hull has a round-bilge form designed for good seakeeping and endurance, rather than the high smooth-water speed of the hard-chine *Tjeld* class, which are being phased out as new construction comes forward. The *Snögg* (originally to be named *Lyr*) was commissioned in 1970 and, like her sisters, was built by Bätservice, Mandal.

The armament comprises four Penguin SSMs in their distinctive containers on the quarterdeck, four single torpedo tubes on the beam, and a single 40mm Bofors AA gun forward. MTU diesels driving two shafts provide a top speed of 32 knots.

The Norwegian fast strike craft *Rapp* at sea on builders' trials in 1970. Her torpedo tubes are apparent in this view, and Penguin missiles were fitted later. The deeply indented Norwegian coastline makes missile and torpedo attack by small craft an extremely effective form of coastal defence.

# Spica class

| Name | Number | Commissioned |
|---|---|---|
| ***Spica*** | T 121 | Aug 1966 |
| ***Sirius*** | T 122 | Dec 1966 |
| ***Capella*** | T 123 | Mar 1967 |
| ***Castor*** | T 124 | Jul 1967 |
| ***Vega*** | T 125 | Dec 1967 |
| ***Virgo*** | T 126 | Mar 1968 |
| ***Nörrkoping*** | T 131 | Mar 1973 |
| ***Nynäsham*** | T 132 | Sep 1973 |
| ***Norrtälje*** | T 133 | Feb 1974 |
| ***Varberg*** | T 134 | Jun 1974 |
| ***Västeräs*** | T 135 | Oct 1974 |
| ***Västervik*** | T 136 | Jan 1975 |
| ***Umeä*** | T 137 | May 1975 |
| ***Pitea*** | T 138 | Sep 1975 |
| ***Lulea*** | T 139 | Nov 1975 |
| ***Halmstad*** | T 140 | Apr 1975 |
| ***Strömstad*** | T 141 | Sep 1975 |
| ***Ystad*** | T 142 | Jan 1976 |

**Displacement** 200/230 tons (standard), 230/260 tons (full load)
**Dimensions** 41m (oa) × 7.1m × 1.6m (134.5ft (oa) × 23.25ft × 5.1ft)
**Propulsion** 3 shafts, gas turbines; 12,720 shp = 40 knots
**Armament** 6 single 21in torpedo tubes, 1 × 57mm Bofors gun
**Complement** 7 officers, 21 ratings

When these big 41-metre torpedo boats first appeared they set new powerplant standards. Propelled by three Bristol Siddeley Proteus gas turbines, they could make 40 knots in smooth water and were armed with six wire-guided torpedoes for surface attack and a 57mm gun for anti-aircraft defence.

The first group, known as the T 121

type, were built in 1964-68, the first three by Götaverken, Gothenburg, and the other three by Karlskronavarvet. Plans for four more, numbered T 127-130, were cancelled in favour of a modified T 131 type. These had the same hull and engines and the same wire-guided torpedoes but an improved 57mm gun and Swedish Philips 9LV200 fire control in place of the Hollandse Signaal-apparaten M22.

The 12 improved *Spica*s were all built at Karlskronavarvet in 1970-76, the first being the *Norrköping* and the last the *Ystad*.

The purchase of the Norwegian Penguin SSM has led to discussions about refitting the *Spica*s. The two after torpedo tubes will be replaced by launchers for the Saab/Bofors RBS 15 missile system.

Ships like these are ideal for hit-and-run tactics in the Swedish Archipelago. Over the years the Swedish Navy has brought such operations to a fine art, and the long-range, fast-running Tp61 torpedo poses a major threat to any Soviet ships trying to force a way out of the Baltic.

The *Spica* at sea, showing her clean lines. The wheelhouse is set deliberately far back to reduce pitching and to give the 57mm gun a 360° field of fire. She differs from the Improved *Spica* or *Nörrköping* class in having the Signaal M22 fire-control radar in place of the PEAB 9LV200 type, and an earlier mark of 57mm gun.

# *Constitucion* class

| Name | Number | Commissioned |
|---|---|---|
| ***Constitucion*** | P 11 | Aug 1974 |
| ***Federacion*** | P 12 | Mar 1975 |
| ***Independencia*** | P 13 | Sep 1974 |
| ***Libertad*** | P 14 | Jun 1975 |
| ***Patria*** | P 15 | Jan 1975 |
| ***Victoria*** | P 16 | Sep 1975 |

**Displacement** 150 tons (standard)
**Dimensions** 36.88m (oa) × 7.16m × 1.73m (121ft (oa) × 23.4ft × 5.7ft)
**Propulsion** 2 shafts, diesels; 7,000 bhp = 27 knots
**Armament** *Constitucion, Independencia* and *Patria*, 1 × 76mm/62-cal DP gun; *Federacion, Libertad* and *Victoria,* 2 Otomat SSM launchers, 1 × 40mm L/70 AA gun
**Complement** 18

In 1972 the Venezuelan Navy placed an order with Vosper Thornycroft for six 37-metre fast patrol boats, three with Otomat surface missiles and three with the Oto-Melara 76mm DP gun. Observers seeking a reason for this order did not have far to look: the Venezuelan Navy was small and elderly, but the nearby Cuban Navy had 20 Komar and Osa missile patrol boats. Such was the growing prestige of fast strike craft at the time, it was inevitable that the first new construction should remedy that deficiency first.

The hull is the standard Vosper Thornycroft 37-metre type used in previous designs, with a prominent knuckle forward to deflect the spray without sacrificing buoyancy. The machinery chosen was a two-shaft diesel arrangement, with German MTU 16-cylinder engines. Unlike British diesels of equal power, the MTUs have an underwater exhaust to muffle noise; there was in any case no room for a funnel on such a compact hull.

Although the boats are divided into gun and missile-armed versions, they are designed to be interchangeable if the need should arise; the gunboats have deck chocks to permit a conversion to missiles. The gunboats received their armament at the builders' yard but the missile boats went to La Spezia to receive and test-fire their Otomats.

The first boat, *Constitucion*, was laid down in January 1973 and the last, *Victoria*, was delivered in September 1975.

The *Constitucion* on builders' trials in 1974. Note how the knuckle deflects spray despite the high speed. The three gun-armed versions have a forward-mounted Oto-Melara 76mm Compact dual-purpose gun capable of firing 80 rounds per minute, and Selenia and SMA electronics.

*Federacion*, first of the missile-armed trio. They are identical apart from having two Otomat surface-to-surface missiles aft, a Bofors 40mm L/70 gun forward and no gunnery director above the bridge. If necessary the three gunboats could be rearmed as missile craft.

## *Combattante* type

### Combattante II

| Name | Number | Completed |
|---|---|---|
| ***S 41-60*** (West Germany) | P 6141-6160 | Oct 1972-Aug 1975 |
| ***Ipoplioarhos Batsis*** class (Greece) | P 54-57 | Dec 1971-Jul 1972 |
| ***Kaman*** class (Iran) | P 221-232 | Aug 1977-1978 |
| ***Beir Grassa*** class (Libya) | – | building |
| ***Perdana*** class (Malaysia) | P 3501-04 | Dec 1972-Mar 1973 |

### Combattante III

| Name | Number | Completed |
|---|---|---|
| ***Antiploiarhos Laskos*** class (Greece) | P 50-53 | Apr 1977-Nov 1977 |
| 3 unnamed (Nigeria) | – | fitting-out 1979 |

**Displacement** (*Combattante II*) 234 tonnes (standard) (*Combattante III*) 385 tonnes (standard)
**Dimensions** (CII) 47m (oa) × 7.1m × 2.5m (154.1ft (oa) × 23.25ft × 8.1ft) (CIII) 56.2m (oa) × 8m × 2.1m (184ft (oa) × 26ft × 7ft)
**Propulsion** 4 shafts, diesels; 12,000-18,000 bhp = 35½-36½ knots
**Armament** (CII) (typical) 4 MM.38 Exocet SSMs, 2 twin 35mm AA guns (CIII) 4 MM.38 Exocet SSMs, 2 single 76mm DP guns, 2 twin 30mm AA guns, 2 × 21in torpedo tubes
**Complement** 4/5 officers, 36/40 enlisted men

The original French patrol craft *la Combattante*, which was used to test missile systems at sea. When this photograph was taken she was armed with a rocket launcher aft and a quadruple launcher for SS-12 wire-guided missiles. She was subsequently refitted for the first firings of the MM.38 Exocet.

The firing of the MM.38 Exocet surface-to-surface missile from the wooden-hulled 23-knot patrol craft *la Combattante* proved the feasibility of fitting big SSMs to fast strike craft. But the transition from there to the big steel-hulled boats known as the *Combattante* type needs some explanation.

In 1970 the Federal Germany Navy wished to buy the Exocet missile to create a new force of missile-armed strike craft in the Baltic. But the French were reluctant to sell the missile unless the Germans would agree to build half the hulls in French shipyards. Unfortunately for the Germans, they had already parted with a licence to a French yard to allow a 35-knot, 45-metre steel-hulled design to be built for Israel (the Germans did not wish to anger the Arabs). The French soon produced a 47-metre version of their own, misleadingly termed *Combattante II* but very similar to the original Lürssenwerft design. Thus the Germans had to agree to buy their own design back, and to accept that all the fitting-out of the boats would be done in France.

As a result, France shot to the forefront of the fast strike craft market, and since 1970 has won contracts from several countries. The usual armament is an Oto-Melara 76mm gun forward and four MM.38 Exocets angled out amidships, but the Iranian boats, for example, have Harpoon.

The next development was the *Combattante III*, a 56-metre design. The increase in size permits a second Oto-Melara gun and other weapons, either torpedoes or light guns.

Although many navies have pinned their faith in *Combattante*s or their Lürssen equivalent, these craft have their limitations. Their command and control capability is bound to be rudimentary, however micro-miniaturised the weapons systems may be, for the radar horizon of a small craft is limited. Seakeeping is another problem, and the missile strike craft is in much the same position as the torpedo boat a hundred years ago: superb on paper but in practice good only in specific conditions. In calm weather and given air cover, the missile strike craft can prove highly effective in the coastal defence role and can even undertake offensive missions, but the human factor alone limits its radius of action from base. Nor are they as cheap as claimed. Ton for ton, a *Combattante* is no cheaper than a frigate and requires constant maintenance from a highly trained crew if she is to remain effective.

# Weapon Systems

The term "weapon system" is not merely jargon: the big difference between the armaments of 30 years ago and those of today is the fact that they must now be considered as single complexes comprising projectile launcher, fire control, external sensors and data-processing equipment. This is without doubt the most important single change in warship design since the Second World War, and it accounts for the staggering cost of modern warships.

Naval weapon systems fall into four main categories: strategic, anti-air, anti-ship and anti-submarine. Until now, strategic weapons have included only submarine-launched intermediate-range ballistic missiles (IRBMs) such as Polaris and Trident, and nuclear-armed bombers operating from US carriers. The big carriers are currently used for striking at tactical targets – hostile ships, submarines or shore installations in support of amphibious operations – but the cruise missile will provide a new strategic capability. One of the advantages of the cruise missile is the fact that it can be fired easily from a surface ship or from a submarine's torpedo tubes. It can thus be used by hunter-killer submarines as well as the specialised SSBNs.

Air-defence systems include both guns and missiles, while guns play a bigger role in anti-ship systems. Anti-submarine systems include rocket launchers of various types, homing torpedoes and even guided weapons, but the payload is always a depth charge (sometimes nuclear) or a homing torpedo. Depending on their role, submarines are armed with anti-submarine or anti-ship torpedoes, in addition to the strategic systems already mentioned.

The gun appeared to be in decline after reaching its peak of performance in 1945, but since then the world's navies have become less infatuated with missiles. At first this was only because they needed a "Cold War" weapon which could be used in limited action. But designers realised that a fire-control system capable of guiding a missile onto a fast target can just as easily provide data for a rapid-firing gun, and anti-missile and anti-aircraft gun systems are now under development.

There is no doubt that electronically guided weapons have a greater killing potential than unguided rockets and guns, but the massive increase in complexity makes missile systems less trustworthy and infinitely more costly. The biggest headaches for weapons designers are, first, the fact that only a fraction of the missiles in service since 1945 have been tried in action, and, second, the virtual impossibility of testing defences realistically. The missiles themselves are too expensive to be fired frequently, but ships are even more expensive and no navy is prepared to risk its men and vessels in a live firing of an anti-ship missile.

History tends to repeat itself, and modern navies are in the same position as they were at the beginning of this century. Then the only previous experience was the Battle of Lissa in 1866, which led everyone to believe in ramming tactics; today we rely on flimsy evidence from the two Arab-Israeli wars and Vietnam to predict the future.

# Missiles

▶ This view of a Sea Dart missile launcher being lowered into position on board HMS *Southampton* gives some idea of the complexity of a typical twin-arm SAM launcher. Though lighter than a gun mounting, it has to rotate and elevate and is exposed to salt water. With its associated loading and hoist mechanisms it is another piece of complex machinery to be maintained, and opinion is turning against this type of launcher. Thrust-vector control will soon make it possible to launch missiles from vertical stowage and then angle them onto the correct bearing, thus cutting out the need for mechanical handling altogether.

▼ A trial shot from HMS *Sheffield*'s Sea Dart launcher bathes the bridge front in a lurid glow. Apart from peeling off large quantities of paintwork, the blast of all missiles causes problems. SAMs, which require a substantial boost to accelerate them to maximum speed as quickly as possible, are particularly demanding in this respect. Not only is it necessary to provide some form of flash deflectors if possible, but flash protection has to be provided for the hatches to the hoists. As SAM launchers are designed to train through wide arcs, it is not possible to provide complete blast deflection.

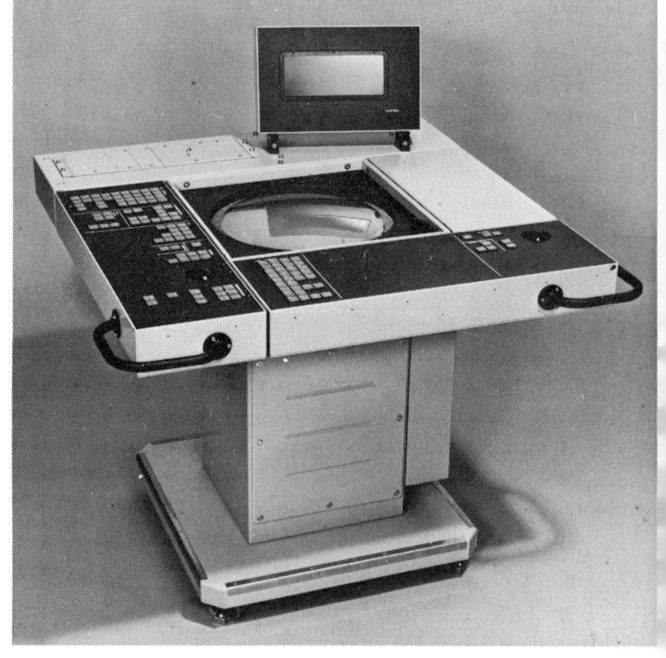

# Fire control

▶ A typical horizontal display for tactical control, in this case the console for use with the Swedish Philips 9LV200 Mk 2 fire-control system fitted to Swedish fast strike craft. The push-buttons enable various functions to be plotted and data displayed alphanumerically, and the two operators can use the tracker balls at each lower corner to "hook" specific targets on the central plan-position indicator. Tracking and display are then automatic, freeing the operators to check other information and to give the commanding officer concise information about the nature of the threat.

# Missiles

◀ The six-cell launcher for the British Seawolf close-range missile defence system. Above-decks stowage was chosen to allow quick reaction, though this meant that weatherproof containers had to be provided, as solid-fuel missiles are vulnerable to the effects of salt spray and extremes of temperature. Assuming that two missiles are needed for each target, after three engagements the launcher must be hand loaded. The new Lightweight Seawolf system will use a twin launcher reloaded through deck hatches. The mounting trains and elevates by remote control, following the movements of the director in the same way as a gun mounting.

▶ The Type 910 tracker for Seawolf has two smaller antennas transmitting commands to the missile itself, as well as a TV tracker for use in heavy jamming. Seawolf uses command-to-line-of-sight guidance, with the radar tracking both missile and target and then sending microwave signals to bring the missile onto the right course. Because the missile itself carries no homing head it can be kept small, though this has not prevented Seawolf from tracking and destroying 4.5in shells in flight. The only anti-missile missile afloat, Seawolf offers a much-needed counter to the sea-skimmer.

◀ A Standard SM-2 SAM fired during tests aboard the USS *Wainwright*. This missile is derived from the earlier Tartar; the Medium-Range (MR) version will replace Tartar and the Extended-Range (ER) will supplant Terrier. The SM-2 has inertial guidance and requires illumination by a radar only during the launch and terminal phases of its flight. The MR and ER versions can be used from older launchers and from the new Mk 26, and Standard is part of the Aegis fleet defence system. Test firings of the SM-2 began in December 1976 from the trials ship *Norton Sound*. Standard will gradually replace older missiles.

► Twin SA-N-1 Goa SAMs on board a Soviet Kashin-class destroyer, with a saluting gun in the foreground and the fire control for her 76mm guns to the right. The Goa is assumed to be a simple adaptation of the land-based missile given the original Nato code name, though its associated equipment is different. The missiles load through deck hatches and on to the front of the launch arms. Western sources claim a slant range of about 15km and a ceiling of about 12,000m. Although superseded by the SA-N-3 Goblet, the Goa is still mounted aboard the Kotlin, Kanin, Kashin, Kynda and Kresta I classes.

◄ Twin MM.38 Exocet launchers aboard the modernised French destroyer *Duperré*, with their blast-deflectors visible in the foreground. The Exocet was still in the development stage when in 1967 the sinking of the Israeli destroyer *Eilat* focused attention on the Western navies' lack of a surface-to-surface missile. The French Government, encouraged by the interest shown by the British, immediately granted more money for the project, with the result that the first live firings took place in 1972. Exocet is a "fire and forget" missile, which makes it easy to mount in smaller warships such as FPBs.

► An eight-cell launcher for Nato Sea Sparrow missiles on the hangar roof of the Italian frigate *Lupo*. To meet the crucial need for a point-defence system (i.e. one ship defending herself against air attack), the US Navy started in 1964 to adapt the Sparrow III air-to-air missile to the Asroc A/S launcher. This became the Basic Point Defence Missile System (BPDMS) and led to Sea Sparrow. To make the system available to Nato a third variant, Nato Sea Sparrow, was developed, with components sub-contracted to various Nato countries. The Italian Oto-Melara company, for example, makes the launchers.

◀ The Type 909 Sea Dart missile tracker is usually hidden beneath a fibreglass dome to protect it from the weather, but here it is seen in full view aboard HMS *Sheffield*. The big Cassegrain-type antenna is 2.44m in diameter and has two small unidentified domes (probably IFF aerials) on top. The 909 radar provides illumination of the target, on the principle of a searchlight, as against the beam-riding guidance provided by such radars as the Type 901 in the "County"-class DLGs. This enables a number of targets to be engaged simultaneously, using the computer to determine priorities.

▶ The Italian Navy's hydrofoil *Sparviero* firing an Otomat surface-to-surface missile off the Sardinian Salta di Quirra range in June 1974. Otomat was originally a Franco-Italian combined venture (Engins Matra providing the engine and Oto-Melara the guidance and missile body); Oto-Melara has broken its connection with the French company and the project is now wholly Italian. A feature of Otomat is its long range, conferred by its turbojet engine. The problems of mid-course guidance have only recently begun to be solved, however, and Otomat took some time to realise its potential.

▼ Diagram of a typical surface-to-surface missile system, in this case the Sistel Mariner. **1** I-band radar **2** transceiver units for processing the various signals **3** operator's console **4** guidance computer **5** command transmitter **6** command antenna **7** pilot display **8** optical tracker with joystick control **9** missile launcher. Once launched, the missile drops its booster while flying on a ballistic course; it is then "gathered" under positive guidance and enters its cruise phase. Towards the end of the flight it comes down to sea-skimming height and homes on the target.

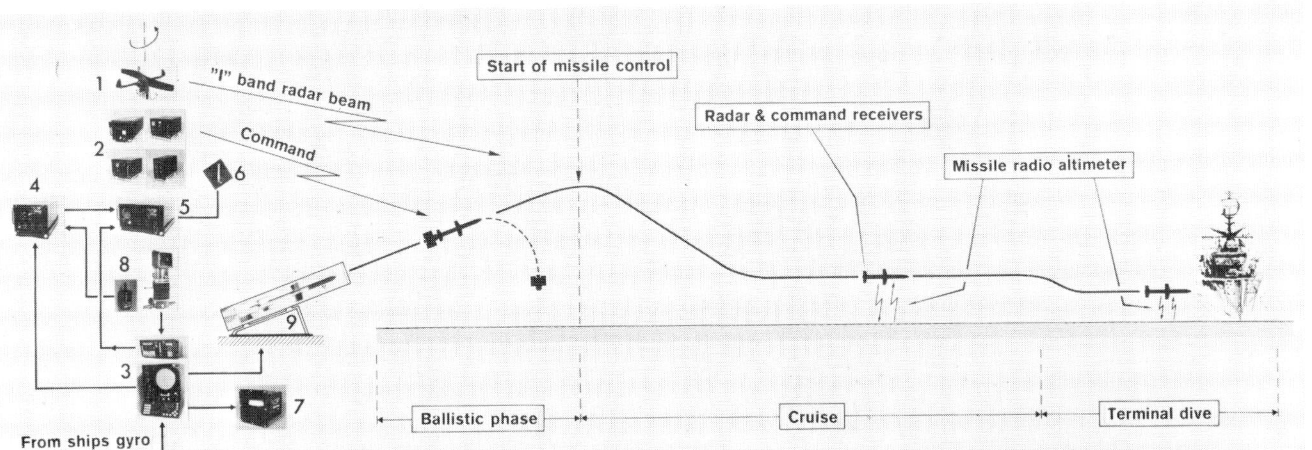

# Aircraft

► The Kaman SH-2F Seasprite has been serving as the US Navy's Interim Lamps helicopter, pending arrival of the Sikorsky Sea Hawk. The use of light shipboard helicopters for anti-submarine work was pioneered by the Royal Navy, which used Westland Wasps from frigates; the Royal Canadian Navy went a step further by adapting the Sea King for use aboard frigates. Despite its massive resources the US Navy lagged behind, having made a very expensive error with the Dash drone. Having at last been convinced of the utility of helicopters, the US Navy has gone ahead with the Sea Hawk.

◄ A Harrier V/Stol aircraft flies over HMS *Hermes* during trials carried out in 1977. After rejecting the idea of a single-seat Harrier for naval use, the RN withdrew its objections when the introduction of improved avionics made it clear that the pilot's workload could be significantly reduced. This equipment took the form of improved computer-aided navigation and attack systems. Other improvements were incorporated and the Sea Harrier was finally ordered. The first Sea Harrier flew in 1978 and the first squadrons are forming in 1980 for service in the *Hermes* and the new *Invincible*-class carriers.

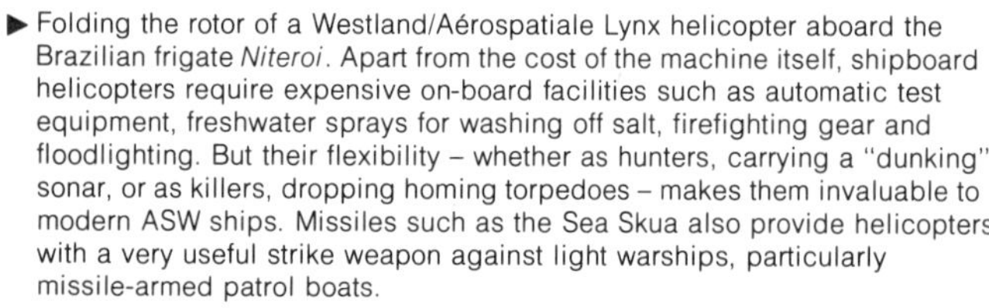
► Folding the rotor of a Westland/Aérospatiale Lynx helicopter aboard the Brazilian frigate *Niteroi*. Apart from the cost of the machine itself, shipboard helicopters require expensive on-board facilities such as automatic test equipment, freshwater sprays for washing off salt, firefighting gear and floodlighting. But their flexibility – whether as hunters, carrying a "dunking" sonar, or as killers, dropping homing torpedoes – makes them invaluable to modern ASW ships. Missiles such as the Sea Skua also provide helicopters with a very useful strike weapon against light warships, particularly missile-armed patrol boats.

## Guns

► The Royal Navy devoted much time and money to developing the Mk 26 twin 6in gun mounting from 1945 onwards. It was inspired by a similar US Navy weapon and was intended to provide heavy anti-aircraft fire as well as surface fire. A rate of fire of 20 rounds per minute was achieved, which required water cooling for the barrels, and the guns could elevate to 80°. Its introduction in the *Tiger* class was the high-water mark for British naval guns, but the complexity of the mounting meant that it was never repeated. Today only two mountings remain in service and even they will soon be scrapped.

◄ The Oerlikon-Bührle GAM-BO1 20mm gun is the successor to the wartime shipboard gun fitted in its thousands to British and American warships. A simple, lightweight gun with belt feed, it is aimed in elevation and traverse by means of the shoulder rest, which is statically balanced so that the gunner bears no weight. The value of such guns continues to lie in their simplicity and the fact that they can be installed in small craft. Even larger warships find it necessary to mount one or two lights guns purely for "junk-bashing," such are the cost and destructive power of modern major weapons.

▼ The Oerlikon-Bührle company produces the GCM-AO1 30mm twin mounting for shipboard use, bridging the gap between the 40mm and 20mm calibres. The mounting was actually designed in England at the BMARC subsidiary of the Swiss parent firm, and it is now widely used in patrol craft or as a secondary weapon in frigates. Offering a high rate of fire and power training and elevating, the GCM-AO1 has a number of applications and has even been tested against missile targets. The manufacturer claims that, using existing fire-control equipment, it could destroy 50 per cent of missile targets.

▼ Two *Ruissalo*-class large patrol craft of the Finnish Navy in line-ahead, with gunners firing the 40mm gun to port. The Bofors gun and its derivatives is still one of the most widely used naval weapons, principally because it fires an impressive number of shells and yet is simple to operate. Similar guns are in use in the RN, German, French, Italian and other navies. The Italians have been particularly successful in boosting the rate of fire, and the 40mm L/70 Compact produced by Breda Meccanica fires pre-fragmented, proximity-fuzed shells against sea-skimming missiles.

▶ The 20mm Vulcan Phalanx Close-In Weapon System (CIWS) has been developed from the revolving Gatling gun to put up a "wall of lead" in the path of an incoming aircraft or missile. The on-mount radar set tracks the target and the stream of 20mm projectiles to ensure maximum hits, and the ammunition is made of depleted uranium to assist in penetration of missile bodies and aircraft fuselages. Depleted uranium is much denser than lead and has greater penetrating power than steel, and a rate of fire of some 3,000 rounds per minute means that a short burst is very destructive.

◀ Rear view of a 4.5in Mk 8 gun mounting on board the Brazilian frigate *Niteroi*. Typical of modern medium-calibre ship guns, the Mk 8 is much more modest in its parameters than previous guns, with a claimed rate of fire of only 25 rounds per minute. Against this, the designers claim a much greater reliability (on test a prototype fired 4,000 rounds without a stoppage) and the ability to open fire instantly and without a gun crew closed up. The modern emphasis on small crews makes this a valuable quality, and the experience with fast-firing guns in the past 30 years tends to confirm the need for more reliability.

▶ The missile cruiser *Andrea Doria* firing her starboard 76mm guns during an exercise. This mounting was introduced in 1961 and is a forerunner, incorporating the same barrel, of the current 76mm/62-cal Compact made under licence in the United States and Japan. The Italians chose to develop the 76mm calibre because Nato specified it as the smallest AA gun which could take a proximity or variable-time (VT) fuze. Although this belief has now been proved wrong, large stocks of 76mm ammunition exist in the United States and elsewhere for the older 3in/50-cal.

# Torpedoes

Triple A/S torpedo tubes on board the *Niteroi* (with a lightweight Seacat SAM launcher overhead). The US Navy developed the Mk 32 triple launcher for the 12.75in (324mm) Mk 44 and Mk 46 torpedoes. These are short-range acoustic homing torpedoes which run on a pre-set pattern until the noise of a cavitating propeller is picked up; the torpedo then homes on the source of the noise. In the 1970s the British developed the system further into the Ship's Torpedo Weapon System (STWS) by providing an integrated fire-control system, although the torpedoes used are still the basic Mk 44 and 46.

◀ The German *Hamburg*-class destroyers have a unique method of loading their A/S torpedo tubes. The tubes are built into the stern, firing aft through the transom, and lift up for reloading from the quarterdeck. The torpedoes are wire-guided, which has the advantage of keeping the weapon under positive control all the way to the target. The wire is very light and falls to the seabed or lies at neutral buoyancy in the water, ensuring that it is never submitted to any undue stretching. The command signals are passed down the wire from the fire-control equipment aboard the ship.

▸ The latest solution to the problem of locating torpedo tubes in ships is to keep them under cover. This prevents deterioration as a result of salt-water corrosion and makes routine maintenance of both torpedoes and launchers much simpler. The first ships in the US Navy to adopt this method are the *Spruance* class, which house the standard Mk 32 triple launcher behind a door in the superstructure. The racks to the left hold spare torpedoes, and the torpedoes are moved mechanically to the tubes; the Mk 44 and 46 are however light enough to be manhandled if necessary.

# Radar

► A Sperry GWS-22 director, used for controlling the Seacat SAMs in a Royal Navy "County"-class DLG. This was developed in 1962 from the MRS3, itself an Anglicised version of the US Navy's Mk 56 destroyer fire-control system. Several variants of this equipment exist; this one has a "pram hood" at the rear of the director and a TV camera (wrapped in polythene) over the tracker dish. The Royal Navy uses MRS3 directors to control 3in, 4.5in and 6in guns in the *Tiger*, "County," *Rothesay*, "Tribal" and *Leander* classes, supplementing the GWS-22 variants in these ships.

◄ The top of the wheelhouse of the French *aviso d'Estienne d'Orves*, showing her DRBC-32E fire-control radar in the foreground and the DRBV-51 surveillance radar at the masthead. The DRBC group is a family of X-band radars adapted to suit different fire-control directors, and so they appear in ships of widely varying size and complexity. The DRBV-51, on the other hand, is a new lightweight surveillance radar which replaces earlier L-band systems. It is designed to track air and surface targets rather than to designate individual targets for the ship's 100mm gun.

## Sonar

► This giant honeycomb structure is the SQS-53 sonar mounted in the bulbous bow of a *Spruance*-class destroyer. The transducer (combined transmitter/receiver) is only a small part of a sonar system, which requires as much processing and display as a missile system. For this reason modern ASW ships like the American *Spruance* and the British *Broadsword* classes tend to be very big. Positioning the sonar in the forefoot offers several advantages – in particular, hull noise is minimised – though in rough weather the dome tends to lift out of the water and slam down.

## Anti-submarine missiles

◄ A Subroc UUM-44A missile being lowered through the hatch of a US nuclear submarine. This missile is launched underwater and follows a short trajectory before emerging from the water. The main motor then ignites and sends the warhead on a ballistic path; when it reaches the target area explosive bolts fire to release a nuclear depth charge. Development began in 1958 but operational deployment did not start until 1965. Nuclear boats carry four or six Subrocs for use against other submarines. Introduction of the Mk 48 torpedo means that Subroc will soon be phased out to make room for Sub-Harpoon or Tomahawk missiles.

## Countermeasures

▶ A Bofors 375mm anti-submarine rocket is fired from the twin launcher aboard the *Niteroi*. Although considered dated by the leading ASW navies, these rocket launchers are very popular with smaller forces, and Bofors has produced a range of improved versions with longer range. There are three different launchers: the original four-barrelled type, a six-barrelled type made by Creusot-Loire in France, and a lighter two-barrelled version capable of mechanical reloading. The original M/50 rocket had a range of only 830m, but the Erika version can reach 1,600m and the latest, the Nelli, is credited with 3,600m.

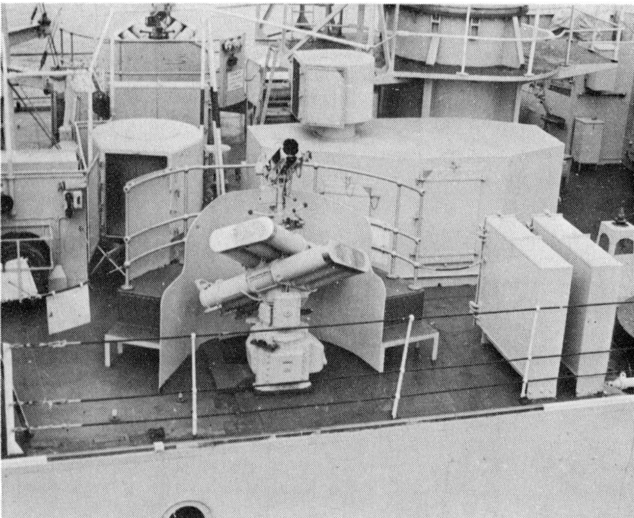

◀ The British were first off the mark with a counter following the sinking of the *Eilat* by Styx missiles in 1967. It took the form of 3in rockets dispensing metallic chaff (like the wartime "Window") in the air. The chaff produces a confusing echo on enemy radar screens and, because it is very light, does not disperse too quickly. This persuades a missile's seeker to "see" and home on an echo corresponding to a large target. This is the prototype, the six-barrelled Mk 1, code-named Corvus; a later variant has eight barrels to allow a bigger spread.

▶ Another method of dispensing chaff is to use small grenades. This is the MEL Protean grenade launcher, which is similar to the Swedish Philax system. The grenade blows the chaff out in packets, whereas the Corvus rocket fires a piston to push the chaff out more gently and evenly. Both methods are popular: grenades are faster but rockets do not damage the chaff as much. Whatever the arguments for and against these methods, chaff systems are a vital part of the defences of a modern warship against missile attack, and were a major factor in an Israeli victory over Syrian missile boats in 1973.

# Abbreviations and Acronyms

**AA** Anti-aircraft
**AAW** Anti-aircraft warfare
**AIO** Action information organisation
**ASW** Anti-submarine warfare
**ASM** Anti-ship missile or anti-submarine missile
**bhp** Brake horsepower (diesel engines)
**BPDMS** Basic Point Defence Missile System
**BB** Battleship (US Navy)
**CAH** Helicopter carrier
**CIC** Combat information centre
**CG/CGN** Guided-missile cruiser (nuclear)
**CIWS** Close-In Weapon System
**CV/CVN** Aircraft carrier (nuclear)
**CVA/CVAN** Attack carrier (nuclear)
**Dash** Drone Anti-Submarine Helicopter
**DCAN** Direction des Constructions Armées Navales
**DD/DDG** Destroyer/Guided-missile destroyer
**DE** Destroyer escort
**DLG/DLGN** Guided-missile destroyer leader/Frigate (nuclear)
**DP** Dual-purpose
**DTCN** Direction Techniques des Constructions Navales
**ECM** Electronic countermeasures
**ECCM** Electronic counter-countermeasures
**E-Boat** Incorrect British term for S-Boat
**ESM** Electronic support measures
**FF/FFG** Frigate/Guided-missile frigate
**FGN** Federal German Navy
**FPB** Fast patrol boat
**FRAM** Fleet Rehabilitation and Modernisation programme
**FY** Fiscal year
**GUPPY** Greater Underwater Propulsive Power programme
**HMS** Her Majesty's Ship
**HSA** Hollandse Signaalapparaten
**LAMPS** Light Airborne Multi-purpose System (United States Navy anti-submarine and anti-missile system)
**LPH** Amphibious assault ship
**MAS** Originally: Motobarca Armata SVAN Later: Motobarca Anti-Sommergibili/Motobarca Armata Silurante/Motoscafo Anti-Sommergibili
**MGB** Motor gunboat
**MTB** Motor torpedo boat
**PT-Boat** Patrol torpedo boat (American term for MTB)
**PUFFS** Passive Underwater Fire-Control System
**RN** Royal Navy
**SAM** Surface-to-air missile
**S-Boat** *Schnellboot* (German term for MTB)
**SSBN** Nuclear ballistic missile submarine
**shp** Shaft horsepower (turbines only)
**SS** Hunter-killer submersible (conventional)
**SSN** Nuclear submarine
**SSM** Surface-to-surface missile
**STOVL** Short take-off and vertical landing (Harrier/AV-8A)
**V/STOL** Vertical or short take-off and landing (general term)
**VTOL** Vertical take-off and landing (Yak-36)
**U-Boat** *Unterseeboot* (German term for submarine)
**USN** United States Navy
**USS** United States Ship
**VT** Variable-time (proximity) fuze

# Glossary

**Action information organisation (AIO)** British term equivalent to American **CIC**. Centralised handling of data from the sensors to facilitate command and fighting the ship.
**Acoustic influence** Weapon actuation by sound, normally from the cavitating effect of propellers but also from hull noise. First used in mines by the British in 1918 and experimentally in torpedo warheads by the Germans at about the same time, and employed on a large scale in mines and torpedoes in the Second World War. Still used in torpedo warheads, though in mines an acoustic device is normally linked with magnetic and pressure systems.
**Active homing** Used in both torpedoes and missiles, this guidance method relies on signals emitted by the homing head. ECM active jamming operates in a similar way, sending a signal out to the target. See also **Sonar**.
**Area defence** Defence of a group of ships. Normally applied to surface-to-air missiles.
**Attack** In the US Navy and others the word has replaced the word "fleet". For example, an attack carrier has a major strike capability and an attack submarine is intended to sink enemy shipping and submarines.
**Battleship** Formerly the major surface warship, battleships now remain only with the US Navy. Although their main function of long-range gun action against other ships was taken over by the bombs and torpedoes of carrier aircraft, they proved capable of providing long-range bombardment. The *New Jersey* was reactivated during the Vietnam War for this purpose.
**Combat information centre (CIC)** Developed by the USN during the last years of the Second World War as a means of collating information from lookouts, radar, aircraft and other ships, so that the captain could reach a quick decision in action. The complexity of modern weapons has since made CIC indispensable. See also **AIO**.
**Diesel** Compression-ignition engine of German origin widely used in all sizes of warships, partly because of its economy but also because its fuel presents a low fire risk.
**Electronics** The sensors, computer hardware and software, and communications gear in warships.
**Fire control** The guidance equipment in a weapon system. Typically includes a director above decks and computer hardware and software below decks, but may comprise as little as an optical sight.
**Fin** British equivalent of the American submarine "sail," the modern term for conning tower.
**Gas turbine** Marine development of the original turbojet engine, used both for generating auxiliary power and for main drive. Most marine gas turbines are "aero-derived," having been developed from aircraft engines, but some are based on industrial turbines.
**Guided weapon system** A missile and its launchers, control equipment and associated radars.
**Gun** Any ballistic weapon larger than rifle calibre and not relying on rocket propulsion. The largest guns are now all but obsolete except for shore bombardment, though during the Vietnam War cruisers fired Rocket-Assisted Projectiles (RAPs) to very long ranges.
**Gunboat** Wide classification covering minor warships armed with guns rather than missiles.
**Influence mine** Any mine detonated not by direct contact with a ship's hull but by acoustic, magnetic or pressure methods. All three are normally part of a mine's firing system. Torpedoes are also fitted with influence firing devices in order to give a wider lethal radius.
**Launcher** Any mechanism designed to support a weapon before it leaves the ship. Particularly applied to guided missile rocket systems.
**Mine** Underwater explosive device, laid offensively in enemy waters or defensively in home waters. The most sophisticated mines are the influence type but the simpler contact types are still used because they can be mass-produced cheaply. Moored mines can be used in deep water as their depth can be adjusted automatically; ground mines lie on the seabed and so are usually restricted to shallower waters. An exception is the Captor mine, which is laid on the seabed in deeper waters to catch submarines; it responds to hostile submarines by releasing homing torpedoes.
**Minehunting** Slow and laborious method of clearing a path through a minefield, but the only certain way of dealing with the latest influence mines. High-definition sonar is used to pinpoint individual mines, which are then demolished, either by a clearance diver or a remotely controlled vehicle.
**Minesweeping** Traditional method of dealing with mines, either by cutting mooring wires or detonating influence mines with towed equipment creating noise or a magnetic field.
**Nuclear power** The use of fissionable material, normally enriched uranium, to provide steam through a heat-exchanger. This steam is then supplied to a conventional steam turbine. Nuclear power was first adapted for marine purposes in an effort to extend the underwater endurance of submarines by eliminating the need to surface to recharge batteries. In surface ships it permits very high performance without the need for frequent refuelling.
**Passive homing** Used in torpedoes, particularly the anti-submarine type, which respond to acoustic signals from the target. It can also be applied to missiles, though purely passive guided weapons are unusual.
**Point defence** American term for the self-defence of individual ships.
**Proximity fuze** More usually known as a variable-time (VT) fuze, this device explodes a shell within a lethal radius of the target. Modern anti-aircraft and anti-missile gun systems rely on pre-fragmented, proximity-fuzed ammunition which spreads a "wall of steel" in the path of the incoming target.
**Sea control ship** US Navy term for a small carrier intended to escort task forces or convoys. The concept of sea control is regarded as the opposite of "sea denial," the raiding or interdicting of the enemy's communications while trying to avoid a full-scale trial of strength with his main forces.
**Signature** The influence – magnetic, acoustic and pressure – generated by a ship in the surrounding water. The

magnetic signature derives from the latent magnetism of a steel hull; the acoustic signature is generated by machinery and propellers; and the pressure signature is caused by the displacement of water as the ship moves through it.
**Ski-jump** Upward-curved ramp designed to facilitate short take-off from a flight deck. Particularly advantageous to V/Stol aircraft, which rely on both engine and wing lift. In the case of the Sea Harrier a 6½° Ski-jump permits the aircraft to take off with 1,500lb more payload.
**Sensors** Radars, sonars, passive infra-red and radar detectors, and optical sights.
**Sonar** Modern term for what used to be known as Asdic. Can be used in two modes, active and passive. Sonar systems either transmit a signal or listen for a sound made by the target, though underwater sound propagation is such that a sonar's range is much greater in the passive mode. Sonars can also be deployed in a variety of different ways: hull-mounted, bow-mounted, variable-depth, "dunked" by helicopters, towed astern and in sonobuoys. Much research is going on into new sonar technology and the latest ships are fitted with arrays towed up to 2,000 yards astern, where the sonar can "listen" well clear of hull and propeller noise.
**Strategic** Term describing nuclear weapons deployed against the Soviet heartland, and including Polaris, Poseidon and the new Tomahawk cruise missile. Thus Polaris submarines are regarded as strategic forces, whereas other naval forces are purely tactical even if equipped with nuclear weapons.
**Submersible** Modern term for a diesel-electric "conventional" submarine, as against the nuclear-powered "true" submarine.
**Steam turbine** Standard form of warship propulsion, particularly for major ships. The steam is generated by boilers or, in the case of nuclear ships, a heat-exchanger. Modern boilers can burn a standard distillate fuel which produces less pollution and is usable in diesel engines.
**Through-deck cruiser** Cumbersome term concocted by the Royal Navy to obtain political and Treasury approval for a ship designed to operate helicopters and V/Stol aircraft. The "through deck" was a euphemism for a full-length flight deck, but the name was subsequently changed, first to Command Cruiser, then to ASW Cruiser and now to Carrier (CAH).
**Torpedo** Underwater weapon used either by submarines to attack other ships or by aircraft and ships to attack submarines. The long-range torpedoes used by submarines are known as heavyweight types, while helicopters and ships use lightweight types. Many forms of guidance are used, both active and passive, but most submarines use wire guidance, in which both submarine and torpedo pay out a thin wire down which command signals are sent from the submarine's fire-control system or back from the homing head in the torpedo. Wire guidance has the advantage of being free from interference, while the submarine has the torpedo under positive control all the time. Some navies have abandoned the concept of surface attack with torpedoes, but Sweden and West Germany, for example, rely on small strike craft armed with long-range wire-guided torpedoes as well as missiles. The theory is that the myriad islands in the Baltic favour hit-and-run tactics, for which the torpedo has as good a chance as a missile.

# Class Index



# General Index